THE SALZBURGERS

AND

THEIR DESCENDANTS

JERUSALEM CHURCH, EBENEZER, GA. Erected 1767.

THE SALZBURGERS AND Their Descendants

by P. A. Strobel

WITH FOREWORD, APPENDIX, AND INDEX
BY EDWARD D. WELLS, SR.

Southern Historical Press, Inc.
Greenville, South Carolina

This volume was reproduced from
An personal Copy located in the
Publisher's private Library

All rights reserved. No part of this publication may be reproduced,
stored in a retrieval system, transmitted in any form, posted
on to the web in any form or by any means without
the prior written permission of the publisher.

Please direct all correspondence and orders to:

www.southernhistoricalpress.com
or
**SOUTHERN HISTORICAL PRESS, Inc.
PO Box 1267
375 West Broad Street
Greenville, SC   29601**
southernhistoricalpress@gmail.com

Originally published: Baltimore, MD. 1855
ISBN #0-89308-771-8
All rights Reserved.
Printed in the United States of America

Foreword

In sponsoring the reprinting of Strobel's *The Salzburgers and Their Descendants* I am mindful of his great contribution to the history of Georgia and of the pride he engendered in the hearts of the descendants through his exposition of the fine characters of the settlers. The well-ordered lives of these pioneers has had a beneficial influence on the successive generations of Salzburger descendants. Their leadership in the educational and cultural life of the state is evidenced by the fact that the first schools in the colony (Bethany and Ebenezer) and the first orphanage (Ebenezer) were established and operating before there was a school in Savannah and before Bethesda Orphanage was established by the Reverend George Whitefield. Also, an accepted task of these pious people seems to have been the building of churches; there were Jerusalem, Zion, Goshen, Bethany, and perhaps one called Salem. In addition to the religious and cultural heritage left us by the Salzburgers there are material heritages—one of these being the Austrian pine, sometimes called black pine, the seeds of which are said to have been inadvertently brought to St. Matthew's Parish in the baggage of the settlers.

The Salzburgers of St. Matthew's Parish had before 1800 enjoyed contact and visitations as well as aid and encouragement from the outstanding men of the period. General James Oglethorpe, General Anthony Wayne, and the Reverends John and Charles Wesley and George Whitefield all paid homage to them. The great American botanist William Bartram of Philadelphia visited the Parish in 1773 and mentioned it in *The Travels of William Bartram,* wherein he noted the finding of the Fiery Azalea.

FOREWORD

There is a certain attraction or romance about the name Salzburger, probably due to the heroic struggle these people made for freedom of speech, thought, and conscience—a freedom so precious that they dared the rigors and hardships of life in the New World. In the early part of the 18th century, the people of Salzburg exhibited a fervor and determination to achieve the right to think for themselves, and on the second of December 1733 the first party embarked at Rotterdam to begin the voyage in search of peace and mercy.

Furthermore, the word Salzburg suggests an appreciation of the finer things of life: religion, music, art, and science. Joseph Schaitberger, the author of the Protestants' Confession of Faith and the inspirer of the emigrating groups, was born within a few miles of Salzburg and lived his eventful life there (1658-1733). He died while the first group of Protestants were on the high seas enroute to Georgia. Wolfgang Amadeus Mozart (1756-1791), the musical genius, was born there. Salzburg Festivals have been to the musical world what Oberammergau is to the religious world. Salzburg is an ancient city, for history tells us that Attila, a king of the Huns who styled himself "the Scourge of God," destroyed it in the fifth century, A.D., but like a phoenix it rose again from its ashes, and by 1700 was the only military fortress in North Austria.

All of the Salzburgers who emigrated to Georgia did not settle at Ebenezer or in St. Matthew's Parish; some of them went to Frederica, Abercorn, and Vernonburg (White Bluff), but none of these three locations was a permanent Salzburger settlement. Some of those who settled at Ebenezer or in St. Matthew's Parish came in from Savannah and Purisburg (Purysburg) after the original settlement at Ebenezer. The story is adequately told in Strobel's history.

FOREWORD

The Salzburgers in Georgia seem to have been rooted a little better than other groups of Europeans who came to the New World. These Salzburgers and their descendants seem to have remained largely in the community of settlement. There are at present (1953) about 9,000 people in Effingham County and 150,000 in Chatham. Of this number it is estimated that around 25,000 are of Salzburger descent. It has now been 219 years since the first group landed. Within this period seven generations have been born, and each generation, like its predecessor, has contributed to the American ideal of citizenship—abiding by the laws of the land, attending to religious duties, and proving by their demeanor that they value their heritage.

Edward Descombe Wells, Sr.

Savannah, Georgia

THE SALZBURGERS

AND

𝕿𝖍𝖊𝖎𝖗 𝕯𝖊𝖘𝖈𝖊𝖓𝖉𝖆𝖓𝖙𝖘:

BEING THE HISTORY OF

A COLONY OF GERMAN (LUTHERAN) PROTESTANTS, WHO
EMIGRATED TO GEORGIA IN 1734, AND SETTLED AT
EBENEZER, TWENTY-FIVE MILES ABOVE
THE CITY OF SAVANNAH.

BY

REV. P. A. STROBEL,

OF THE SOUTH CAROLINA SYNOD, AND PRINCIPAL OF THE FEMALE INSTITUTE,
AMERICUS, GEORGIA.

"Alii multa perficiunt; nos nonnulla conamur; Illi possunt; nos volumus."

"Others accomplish many things—we endeavour to effect something; *they* have the power, *we* have the will."

BALTIMORE:
PUBLISHED BY T. NEWTON KURTZ,
No. 151 WEST PRATT STREET.
1855.

Entered according to Act of Congress, in the year 1855, by
P. A. STROBEL,
in the Clerk's Office of the District Court of the United States for the District of Georgia.

STEREOTYPED BY L. JOHNSON & CO.
PHILADELPHIA.

Dedication.

To my brethren in the Lutheran ministry, this volume is most affectionately and respectfully inscribed; with the fervent prayer, that by carefully studying the history of the Salzburgers, and especially the unfeigned devotion and ardent zeal of the first preachers of the American Lutheran Church, we may all be stimulated to aim at a more elevated standard of piety, and consecrate ourselves afresh to His service, who hath redeemed us with his blood, and honoured us by appointing us his ambassadors, to reconcile the world unto himself.

THE AUTHOR.

Preface.

THIS little volume is submitted to the public with an unfeigned diffidence, and with many apprehensions that it may not meet the expectations, even of those who have most warmly urged its publication. The means of information which the author possessed, were too limited, to justify the belief that the book could possibly be regarded as a complete and satisfactory history of the Salzburgers. It is, however, to be hoped, that notwithstanding its many defects, a sufficient number of interesting facts have been presented, to render the work acceptable to those who read for instruction, and not to indulge a spirit of captious criticism. The author is sensible of his incompetency to do justice to the subject, and he would cheerfully have committed the undertaking to abler hands. If he shall accomplish no more than to rescue the Salzburgers from the obscurity into which they have been permitted to lapse, he will not have laboured in vain. The hope is cherished that, under the blessing of God, this work may be the means of kindling in the heart of every one who may peruse it, a sincere desire to emulate the lofty piety and Christian heroism of those, who in the maintenance of their religious principles cheerfully suffered "the loss of all things," and have furnished an example of patient endurance, under every form of persecution, and of ardent zeal in the cause of Christ, which furnishes one of the brightest pages in the history of the church since the days of the apostles.

P. A. STROBEL.

AMERICUS, Georgia, *March*, 1855.

Recommendation from the Synod of South Carolina.

"THE Committee appointed by Synod to examine the manuscript 'History of the Salzburgers and their Descendants at Ebenezer,' by the Rev. P. A. Strobel, beg leave to submit the following report:

"They have carefully examined the manuscript, and cheerfully express their gratification at the judicious selection of the materials from various sources difficult of attainment, by which a historical sketch has been given of the cruel persecutions, the Christian firmness, and devoted piety of the ancient Salzburgers.

"In recommending the work to the patronage of the Christian public, and especially the members of our own communion, they feel assured that the readers will be amply rewarded in the elevated standard of Christianity which this volume holds out for their imitation."

JOHN BACHMAN, D.D.
L. EICHELBERGER, D.D.
A. J. KARN.

November 13, 1854.

Contents.

CHAPTER I.

The causes which led to the Colonization of America—French Colony in Florida—Colony of Massachusetts Bay—The Puritans—Intolerance of the Church of England—The Salzburgers—Contrast between them and the Puritans—Injustice done to the former—The Origin of the Salzburgers—Their persecutions by the dukes of Savoy—They embrace the Doctrines of the Reformation—Cruelty toward their pastor—The Valleys of Teffereck—Their Retreats discovered—Miximilian Gudolph—Salzburgers before the Bishop's Court at Hallein—Renewed persecutions—Sympathy of Protestant States—Elector of Brandenburg—Corpus Evangelicum—Return of the Teffereckers—Duplicity and Treachery of the Catholic Authorities—Penalties imposed on the Salzburgers—Banishment and Confiscation of their Estates—Severe Sufferings of the Exiles—Joseph Schaitberger—Remarkable conversion of his daughter—Schaitberger as an author—The Confession of Faith—The Salzburg Emigrant's Song—Persecutions under Leopold—Archbishopric of Salzburg—The City of Salzburg—Thirty thousand Protestants exiled—Their reception by Protestant States...................*Page* 19

CHAPTER II.

Charter granted by Charles II. to the Trustees for establishing the Colony of Georgia—The design of the colony—General Oglethorpe—English settlers arrive at Savannah—

"Society for the Propagation of Christian Knowledge"—Interest on behalf of the Salzburgers—Arrangements to remove the Salzburgers to Georgia—Fifty families engaged for the first transportation—Provision made by the "Society"—Liberality of the "Trustees"—First company of emigrants—Love of country—Departure from their homes—Incidents of their journey—The city of Augsburg—Hospitalities extended to the Salzburgers—Recommence their travels—Rev. S. Urlsperger—Effects of the sojourn of the Salzburgers at Augsburg—Revival of religion—Further Incidents—Arrival in the city of Frankfort—Conduct of the Burgers—Procession—Entrance into the city—Hospitality of the inhabitants—Departure from Frankfort—The Maine and Rhine—Arrival at Rotterdam—Rev. Messrs. Bolzius and Gronau—Departure from Rotterdam—Arrival at Dover, in England—Impressions made by the emigrants on their English benefactors—Preparations for leaving England—Departure of the Purisburg, first ship with German emigrants...*Page* 44

CHAPTER III.

The Salzburgers at sea—Conduct during the voyage—Arrival at Charleston, S. C.—General Oglethorpe—Departure from Charleston—Arrival at Savannah—Sentiments of the emigrants—Their reception at Savannah—Notes of Mr. Bolzius—Baron Von Reck—Conduct of the Indians—Disembarkation of the Salzburgers—Liberality of General Oglethorpe—Expedition into the country—Description of the country—Devout conduct of the Salzburgers—Ebenezer—Foundation of the colony—Location of their settlement—Uchee Indians—St. Matthew's Parish—Lord Effingham—Town laid out—Salzburgers remove to their new home—Impressions in relation to the nature of the country—Baron Von Reck's enthusiastic description—Real character of the country—Assignment of lots—Hardships incident to colonization—Scarcity of mechanics and materials for building—Other trials—Sickness and death among the colonists

CONTENTS.

—Extracts from Mr. Bolzius's journal—Influence of affliction—Arrival of a second company of Salzburgers—Improvement in the condition of the colony—Progress of the town, &c...Page 57

CHAPTER IV.

General Oglethorpe visits England—Favourable condition of the colony—Trustees determine to send out reinforcements—Aid from British Parliament—Character of the colonists engaged—Highlanders and Salzburgers—Liberal terms proposed by the Trustees—Captain Hermsdorff and Baron Von Reck—The Trustees charter the "London Merchant" and the "Symond"—The "great embarkation"—English and German emigrants—Moravians under Bishop Nitschman—John and Charles Wesley—Departure from England—Storm at sea—Effect of the conduct of the Germans upon Mr. Wesley—Testimony of Dr. Jackson, President of British Conference—Mr. Wesley's spiritual condition—Conference with Mr. Spangenburg—Influence of the Moravians—Rev. Peter Bochler—Salzburgers confounded with the Moravians—Mistake of Mr. Bancroft—Removal of Moravians to Pennsylvania—Mr. Wesley's religious experience—Extract from his journal—Subsequent visit to England—His conversion—Luther's preface to the Epistle to the Romans—Mr. Wesley's preaching after his conversion—Forms "Societies," the basis of Wesleyan Methodism—The Methodist Church a fruit of the Lutheran Reformation—Arrival of the "embarkation" at Savannah—Settlement of Salzburgers on St. Simon's Island—Views of the Germans in relation to war—Reinforcement at Ebenezer—Lutheran settlement at Frederica—Rev. U. Dreisler—Revs. Bolzius and Gronau visit Savannah—Conference with General Oglethorpe—Salzburgers dissatisfied with their location, and desire a change—General Oglethorpe visits Ebenezer—Reasons of the Salzburgers for desiring to remove—General Oglethorpe's advice and kindness to the Salzburgers—Change of location determined upon...... 73

CONTENTS.

CHAPTER V.

New Ebenezer—Its location, and the plan upon which is was laid out—The environs of the town—Its rapid growth—Municipal and other regulations—Rules originally adopted for the government of the congregation—The duties of pastors set forth—Elders and wardens—Parochial schools—Church members, &c.—Dr. H. M. Muhlenberg—Salaries of the pastors—Their responsibilities—Relation to the church in Germany—Sale of rum prohibited, and the introduction of Negro slaves—Effects of these regulations on the colony at Ebenezer—Mr. Bolzius, Rev. George Whitfield, and Baron Von Reck on slavery—Position of Mr. Bolzius—Views of Hon. James Habersham and Rev. S. Urlsperger—Controversy settled, and slavery allowed—The Salzburgers and the Lutheran Church in Germany—Liberality of the latter—Education—"Bethany" church—Favourable condition of the settlement—Religious character of the inhabitants—Their industry, frugality, &c.—Letter of Mr. Bolzius—Rev. George Whitfield at Ebenezer—His testimony in favour of the Salzburgers—He visits the Orphan House—Letter of Thomas Jones—Principal settlers at Ebenezer up to 1741—The invasion of Georgia by Spaniards—Another letter of Mr. Bolzius—Extracts from his journal—Statement of Mr. Benjamin Martyn—New arrivals—Emigrants bind themselves as servants—Frederick Helfenstein—Lutheran church in Savannah founded—Rev. U. Driesler—His death—Rev. Mr. Zublii—The town of Frederica—Dr. H. M. Muhlenberg visits Ebenezer—Mr. Gronau—"Jerusalem" church at Ebenezer—"Zion's" church—Extracts from Mr. Bolzius's journal—Death of Mr. Gronau...*Page* 90

CHAPTER VI.

State of feeling at Ebenezer consequent on the death of Mr. Gronau—Mr. Bolzius writes to Germany for an assistant—

His humility and devotion—The church in Germany send over another pastor—Rev. H. H. Lembke arrives at Ebenezer—His reception—Marries the widow of Mr. Gronau—Mr. Bolzius retains his position—Mr. Bolzius, as trustee, erects mills—Silk culture introduced at Ebenezer—Mr. Amatis of Piedmont—Mulberry-trees planted at Ebenezer—Success of the Salzburgers in raising silk—Bridge and causeway over Ebenezer Creek—New church and school-house erected—Pastoral labours—Extent of the field to be cultivated—Goshen church—Abercorn—Extension of the settlements around Ebenezer—Demand for more ministerial labour—Rev. C. Rabenhorst arrives at Ebenezer—Mr. Bolzius's letter on his arrival—Change of views—Provision for the support of the new pastor—Condition of the colony—Mr. Bolzius assigns his trusteeship to Mr. Lembke—Copy of the deed of trust—The "Trust" to be transferred—Subsequent change—Erection of another mill—Mr. Bolzius begins to decline in health—The symbolical books—Proper views in relation to the "Fathers"—Confessions and catechisms—Deep-toned piety of the first pastors at Ebenezer—Mr. Bolzius's labours—His letters—Rev. S. Urlsperger and Dr. Zeigenhagen—Close of his ministerial duties—His illness and death—Mr. Bolzius's family...*Page* 125

CHAPTER VII.

State of affairs at Ebenezer consequent upon the death of Mr. Bolzius—Increase of population and of ministerial labour—Transfer of trust to Mr. Rabenhorst—Harmony between the two pastors—Jerusalem church built at Ebenezer—Description of the edifice—The Swan, Luther's coat of arms—Death of Mr. Lembke—His character as a preacher—Gottlieb Snider—Rev. C. F. Triebner sent over as successor to Mr. Lembke—His character—Marries a daughter of Mr. Lembke—Injudicious selection—Division in the church—Controversy between Messrs. Rabenhorst and Triebner—Dr. H. M. Muhlenberg arrives at Ebenezer—Object of his mission—His prudent and judicious conduct—The grounds of dispute stated—Elders prefer charges against Mr. Triebner—Origin of the difficulty—Dr. Muhlenberg's efforts to reconcile the parties—His views of the case—Opinion of Mr. Triebner—Plan of settlement proposed—Reconciliation—Dr. Muhlenberg's reflections—His opinion of Mr. Rabenhorst—Exculpates him from all censure—His estimation of Mr. Rabenhorst as a man and as a preacher—Dr. Muhlenberg's labours among the Salzburgers—Saves the church property from alienation........*Page* 148

CHAPTER VIII.

Dr. Muhlenberg still at Ebenezer—Church discipline—Views and practices of the founders of American Lutheran Church—Evils arising from want of discipline—False views on the subject—The discipline adopted at Ebenezer in 1774, and duties of pastors, officers, and church members defined—List of church members who signed the discipline, as certified by Dr. Muhlenberg—Settlements at Abercorn and Goshen—Mr. Knox buys the lands at Abercorn—Moravian missionaries brought over to preach to the Negroes—Labours of the Moravians at Goshen—Fears of Dr. Muhlenberg—Moravians not successful—Advice to them by one of the Salzburgers—Fears of Dr. Muhlenberg not realized—Moravians leave the settlement—Dr. Muhlenberg's successful labours at Ebenezer—He leaves Georgia for Philadelphia—Condition of the congregation at Philadelphia—Reflections.. 164

CHAPTER IX.

Affairs at Ebenezer after Dr. Muhlenburg's departure—Rabenhorst and Triebner—Pastors cease to be Trustees, and the *trust* transferred to the church officers—Mr. Rabenhorst created *first* pastor—State of feeling between the two pastors—Inventory of church property—Its estimated value—Church funds—Views of the propriety of creating them—A case of necessity with the Salzburgers—General state of the colony—Prosperity of Ebenezer—A fancy sketch—Commercial relations of Ebenezer—Gradual extension of the settlements—New settlers come in—Commencement of the Revolution—Stamp Act and tax on tea—State of the public mind in the Province of Georgia—Position of the Salzburgers—Provincial Congress in Savannah—Salzburgers in that Congress—Majority of them side with the Colonists—Protest of a portion of the Salzburgers—Adherents to the Crown in St. Matthew's Parish—Patriotic and noble sentiments of the Salzburgers—Mr. Triebner sides with the Crown—Judicious course of Mr. Rabenhorst—His long and successful labours, and death............*Page* 188

CHAPTER X.

Descent of the British upon Georgia—General Provost takes Savannah—British posts along the river—Mr. Triebner takes the oath of allegiance to the crown, and conducts troops to Ebenezer—A garrison established under Major Maitland—Proclamation issued by Major Maitland—Some of the Salzburgers take "protections"—Majority of the Salzburgers Whigs—Governor Treutlen—Holsendorf—John and Samuel Stirk—John Schnider—Strohaker—Jonathan and Gottlieb Schnider—Jonathan Rahn—Ernest Zittrauer—Joshua and Jacob Helfenstein—Sufferings of the Salzburgers during the war—Tories—Eichel and Martin Dasher—Marauding parties—Frederick Helfenstein and his two sons—General Wayne—The Salzburgers forced to abandon their homes—Sufferings at Ebenezer—Prisoners—Sergeants Jasper and Newton—Sacrilegious act of the British toward the church at Ebenezer—Other acts of cruelty—Mistaken policy of the British—Sad influence of the licentiousness of the British troops upon the morals of Ebenezer—Pastor Triebner—His removal to England and death—General character of the pastors at Ebenezer—Triebner an exception—Dispensations of Providence—General Wayne attempts the reduction of Savannah—British troops withdrawn from Ebenezer—General Wayne makes his head-quarters there—British evacuate Savannah—Salzburgers return to Ebenezer—Scene of desolation—Condition of the church—Congregation without a pastor—Petition sent to Germany—Dr. Muhlenburg's concern for the Salzburgers—A minister visits Ebenezer—Dr. Muhlenburg's letter—Vindication of Mr. Triebner—Pastor to be sent in the spring—Despondency among the Salzburgers—Darkness begins to disappear—New pastor about to be sent.....*Page* 201

CHAPTER XI.

The arrival of a pastor anticipated—Solicitude on the subject—The Rev. John Earnest Bergman arrives at Ebenezer—His early history—His qualifications for the ministry—State of affairs at Ebenezer and Savannah—Mr. Bergman's defects—Parochial schools—Mr. Bernhardt—Mr. Probst—Mr. Ernst—Increase of pastoral labours—Church in Savannah—Letter from Mr. Scheuber—Correct views of the sacraments—Usages of the Lutheran Church—Mr. Bergman's marriage—His family—Mr. Bergman as a scholar—His correspondence—Parsonage at Ebenezer—Bishop Francis Asbury—His letter to Mr. Bergman—Improvement in temporal affairs—Bad habits among the Salzburgers—Want of church discipline—Disaffection toward the church—Members withdraw—Ebenezer Bridge—Ebenezer becomes the county site—Effects of this measure—County site changed to Springfield—The mills—Demand for English preaching—Letter from Bishop Asbury—Mistaken policy—Methodists in Savannah—Obligations of the Methodists to the Lutheran Church—Rev. Hope Hull—Jonathan Jackson—Josiah Randle—John Garvin—Rev. S. Dunwoody—First Methodist Society in Savannah—Mr. Bergman relinquishes the church in Savannah—Letter to Rev. H. Holcombe—Savannah church without a pastor—Rev. S. A. Mealy—Salzburgers in other churches—Jesse Lee visits Ebenezer—Mr. Bergman curtails his labours—"Bethel" church erected—Personal difficulty—Letter of Rev. J. McVean—Efforts to proselyte—Lax state of morals—

Want of discipline—Mr. Bergman's grief at the condition of the colony—External prosperity—Spiritual declension—Death of Mrs. Neidlinger—Mr. Bergman's health declines—His death...*Page* 218

CHAPTER XII.

Gloomy prospects at Ebenezer—Rev. C. F. Bergman—His early religious sentiments—Calvinistic tendency—Attends the Georgia Presbytery—Letter to Rev. M. Rauch—Conflicting views—Becomes a member of Presbytery—Receives a call to St. Matthew's Lutheran Church—Dr. J. Bachman visits Savannah and Ebenezer—Interview and correspondence with Mr. Bergman—Mr. Bergman changes his views, joins South Carolina Synod, and becomes pastor at Ebenezer—His piety and qualification for the work—State of the congregation—Methodist and Baptist churches organized—Methodist church at Goshen—Rev. J. O. Andrew — Delusion — A false Messiah — Strange scene at Goshen—Sad results—Rev. L. Myers locates at Goshen—His character, labours, and death —Temperance movement at Ebenezer—Mr. Bergman introduces English preaching—His marriage—His children—Temporal and spiritual prosperity—Emigration of Salzburgers to other counties—Church in Savannah—Rev. S. A. Mealy—Rev. N. Aldrich—New church in Savannah—Rev. A. J. Karn—German congregation—Rev. W. Epping—Disaffection at Ebenezer—Other churches built up by Salzburgers—Mr. Bergman as a scholar—Trials—Indifference to education—Mr. Bergman's sickness and death—Rev. J. D. Schenck—Rev. E. A. Bolles—Difficulties at Ebenezer—Rev. P. A. Strobel—Death of Mrs. Bergman—Rev. E. Kieffer—Rev. G. Haltiwanger—Rev. J. Austin—Present condition of the church —"Father Snider.".. 249

CHAPTER XIII.

The town of Ebenezer—Its present appearance—The results of this experiment at colonization—The colonies in New

England, Virginia, and the Carolinas—Royal Historical Society of Austria—Inquiries as to the fate of the Salzburgers answered—Religious and social influence of the Salzburgers upon the other colonists—Religious sentiments of the first pastors—Dr. Hazelius's testimony—Present condition and pursuits of their descendants—Effingham county—General reflections—Conclusion............................*Page* 278

THE
Salzburgers and their Descendants.

CHAPTER I.

The causes which led to the Colonization of America—French Colony in Florida—Colony of Massachusetts Bay—The Puritans—Intolerance of the Church of England—The Salzburgers—Contrast between them and the Puritans—Injustice done to the former—The Origin of the Salzburgers—Their Persecutions by the Dukes of Savoy—They embrace the Doctrines of the Reformation—Cruelty toward their Pastors—The Valleys of Teffereck—Their Retreats discovered—Miximilian Gudolph—Salzburgers before the Bishop's Court at Hallein—Renewed Persecutions—Sympathy of Protestant States—Elector of Brandenburg—Corpus Evangelicum—Return of the Tefferockers—Duplicity and Treachery of the Catholic Authorities—Penalties imposed on the Salzburgers—Banishment and Confiscation of their Estates—Severe Sufferings of the Exiles—Joseph Schaitberger—Remarkable Conversion of his Daughter—Schaitberger as an Author—The Confession of Faith—The Salzburg Emigrant's Song—Persecution under Leopold—Archbishopric of Salzburg—The City of Salzburg—Thirty Thousand Protestants Exiled—Their Reception by Protestant States.

THE colonial history of our country derives much of its interest from the fact, that many of the early settlers were those who had been expatriated for conscience' sake and were brought hither by their high veneration for the gospel. Forsaking their country and their homes—severing all those ties which bind man so strongly to the place of his nativity—abandoning the comforts and endearments of civilized life, they came to the wilderness of America, that they might enjoy without restraint that great birthright of the immortal mind—"freedom to worship God" at "a faith's pure shrine."

From the middle of the sixteenth to the latter part of the eighteenth century, companies of emigrants reached our shores from Great Britain and different parts of continental Europe, who were driven hither by the relentless persecutions of their religious adversaries. It is well known that those who came from England were outlawed by the bigotry and intolerance of the Established Church. By the act of Uniformity, passed in the reign of Edward VI., the Church of England attempted to conform the opinions of all British subjects, as well as their modes of worship, to her Canons and Liturgy. As might have been expected, these efforts to enslave the human mind and shackle the conscience were boldly resisted, and hundreds and thousands preferred imprisonment, exile, and even death, rather than endanger their spiritual interests by embracing error, or submitting their wills to "the commandments and ordinances of men." Those who came from the continent of Europe, were Protestants, who had embraced the doctrines of the Reformation, as taught by Luther or Calvin, as distinguished from the doctrines of the Church of Rome, and who were consequently driven into exile, by the proscriptive and relentless spirit, which has always characterized that church.

As early as the year 1564, a colony of Huguenots, or French Protestants, was planted in Florida by John Ribault, under the patronage of the noble and philanthropic Admiral Coligny. The cruel sufferings endured by these devoted Christians during the reign of the imbecile Charles IX. and his perfidious mother, Catherine de Medicis, compelled them to forsake the vine-clad hills and the beautiful vales of France, to seek in the wilderness of the West, a retreat from the sword and fagot of the persecutor. Of the unhappy fate of this colony it is not necessary to speak, further than to remark, that it was entirely destroyed in 1565 by Pedro Melendez, the inhuman agent of the bigoted Philip II. of Spain, who murdered all the colonists, and completely devastated their settlement.

On the 22d of December, 1620, the colony of Massachusetts was commenced by the landing of the Pilgrim Fathers at Plymouth Rock. These venerable men, as is well known, were from England, where, by their rigid virtues and their resistance to the spiritual domination of the Established Church, they had acquired the name of *Puritans*, then a term of reproach, but now synonymous with unostentatious piety, sterling integrity, and uncompromising opposition to every species of despotism; and which shall be forever identified with the great principles of civil and religious freedom. By asserting the rights of conscience, and by refusing their assent to the unjust and unreasonable pretensions set up by the Church of England under the sanction of the British parliament, they became obnoxious to the displeasure of their civil and religious rulers. Arraigned before the Court of High Commission, the Puritans boldly asserted the principles of religious toleration, and claimed the free exercise of their judgment in all matters of faith. But in the liberal views that they entertained, they were too far in advance of the age in which they lived. They were consequently condemned. Hundreds of their ministers were deposed and deprived of their livings, and with their flocks, sentenced to imprisonment and the loss of country, and even of life.

It was for these causes and under these circumstances that the Pilgrims quitted the shores of England, and sought, among the savages of the New World, the free exercise of those privileges which they had been denied in the Old. Nor were they disappointed. Infusing their principles into all their institutions, civil, political, and religious, they prepared the way for the establishment of that great fabric of American freedom, which is now the pride of their posterity and the admiration of the civilized world. And by the influence which they exerted in shaping the destines of this republic, they have erected for themselves a monument which shall be coequal with our national existence.

Without stopping to notice other colonies of less importance, we pass on to the one which is more especially the subject of this little volume. We allude to the colony of Salzburgers, which was planted in Georgia in 1733. It has often been a matter of surprise, that so little notice has been taken of this colony in the various histories of our country which have been published from time to time. Like the Pilgrim Fathers, the Salzburgers were the victims of religious persecution: like them they were driven from their country and their homes on account of their unwavering attachment to the principles of the gospel; and there is a striking parellel in their characters and their early history. If the Puritans could boast of the venerable Robinson, as their pastor, the Salzburgers could point to their Bolzius and Gronau. If the Puritans were proud of Brewster and Carver, of Bradford, and Winslow, and Standish, the Salzburgers had their Von Reck, and Vatt, and Hermsdorf, and Dreisler, all men of mark, and who, in point of energy, firmness of principle, powers of endurance, and upright and consistent character, would compare favourably with any of the fathers of New England. But while the story of the Pilgrims has been a fruitful theme for the historian and the poet, the Salzburgers have either been entirely overlooked, or their history has been sketched very hastily and unsatisfactorily. This may be owing, in a measure, to the comparatively secluded spot which they selected for their settlement, together with the quietness and unobtrusiveness of their character. Beside which, the prevalence of the German language among them, the little intercourse which they cultivated with their English neighbours, and the preservation of their records in their native language, have no doubt all tended to obscure them, and deprive them of that position in the annals of our country to which their sufferings, their virtues, and their influence so justly entitle them.

The most satisfactory accounts of this interesting people which have been published in this country, are to be found in the collections of the Georgia Historical Society, Bancroft's History of the United States, Dr. Hazelius' History of the American Lutheran Church, and Dr. Steven's History of Georgia. But while these authors have done much to rescue the Salzburgers from the obscurity into which they had been permitted to pass, it was not to have been expected, from the very character of these publications, that ample justice could have been done to the subject.

In attempting a particular history of the *Salzburgers*, it must be admitted that the work is attended with difficulty. Many of their records have been lost or destroyed, and those which have been preserved are so voluminous, and at the same time comprise so much matter that is of very little historical importance, that it would require months, if not years, of patient research to investigate them thoroughly. All that we shall aim at, therefore, will be, to notice briefly the origin of the Salzburgers, and the immediate causes which led to the planting of the colony in Georgia, with an account of their settlement at Ebenezer, and so much of their subsequent history as may be deemed of general interest.

The Salzburgers were descended from the Vallenses, a name derived from the Alpine valleys of Piedmont, and which was applied to all who had emigrated into that region, especially from the East. The Vallenses had, for several centuries prior to the Reformation, opposed the corruptions of the Church of Rome, and had consequently exposed themselves to severe persecutions, especially at the hands of the Dukes of Savoy, who waged against them a war of extermination. We may properly enumerate in their history ten bloody persecutions, from the establishment of their church in the commencement of the fifteenth century, until their exodus, which occurred toward the middle of the eighteenth century. To escape the dangers to which they were exposed, and to enjoy the free exercise of their religion, they were compelled to secrete themselves in the most inaccessible mountains of Dauphine in France, and the Alps of Switzerland and the Tyrol. Here, in their mountain retreats, secluded from the enjoyments of more civilized life, amid the wild majesty and grandeur of nature, they worshipped God in the true simplicity of the gospel, holding communion with Him, "who prefers above all temples the upright heart and pure;" and acquiring continually, by a faithful improvement of their advantages, a fitness for that kingdom where the foot of the oppressor shall never enter, and the conflicts of the faithful shall end in everlasting peace and glory.

Nor were they content in seeking their own improvement: embarrassing as their circumstances no doubt were, they felt that it was their duty to embrace every opportunity to impart to others those religious truths which they had derived from the sacred Scriptures. Hence, as far as their situation would permit, they were constantly engaged in efforts to disseminate the doctrines of Christianity among the untutored inhabitants of those mountainous regions. And their labour of love was not in vain; for through their instructions, and more especially by the purity of their lives, hundreds were won to the cause of truth.

But this favourable state of things, which had continued for many years, was interrupted in the commencement of the seventeenth century. The doctrines of the Reformation, as taught by Luther and Calvin, having been proclaimed throughout Europe, found their way to the retreats of these devoted Christians; and panting, as they no doubt did, for clearer views of religious truth, they readily embraced the doctrines of the reformed faith, and identified themselves with the friends of evangelical religion. When, therefore, the Church of Rome determined to stop the progress of the Reformation, by persecuting and if need be, by exterminating all who favoured it, these devoted people again became the subjects of Popish superstition and rage. They were hunted like wild beasts by the emissaries of Rome, and made to suffer every cruelty and indignity which the malice of man could possibly devise. One of their ministers, Anthony Brassus, was decapitated, and, as if to add insult to injury, his head was nailed to his pulpit; others were scourged with such severity that they expired at the whipping-post; and every pastor who fell into the hands of the priests was put to death under the most revolting circumstances. Nor were the lay members of these churches more fortunate than their spiritual shepherds. Some were blown up with gunpowder, others were driven into barns and houses, and suffocated, or made to perish amid the flames of their own dwellings. Neither age nor sex procured exemption from the cruelties of these inhuman monsters; and nothing but the providential escape of a small number, saved this entire people from extermination.

Those who survived this persecution retreated into the secluded valleys of Teffereck. Here they remained undisturbed, maintaining their religious principles amid great poverty and distress, but still with unshaken confidence in God, though they knew not how soon they would be exposed to new forms of cruelty and death. At the expiration of about seventy years, (during which time Protestantism was supposed to be extinct in the Archbishopric of Salzburg,) a whole congregation of Christians was discoved to exist, and it was ascertained that it had maintained its organization and regular worship for more than half a century. Teffereck is a valley of Salzburg, on the borders of the Tyrol, in the district called Windisch-

Matrey; and in its solitudes and in the depths and darkness of its ravines, true faith seemed long to have found a safe retreat. The people had no minister or public instructor of any kind, but met together by night, in thick forests, or in the mines for mutual edification, by singing and prayer; reading of the Scriptures, Luther's and Spangenberg's sermons, the Augsburg Confession, the Shorter Catechism, and other good books. These were carefully perused in the families of such as could read, and the doctrines which they inculcated were communicated to their children and more intimate associates. In public, they occasionally attended the services of the Romish Church and partook of the Sacrament, but they were still regarded with suspicion by the public authorities, and were stigmatized by the priests as "Secret Lutherans." Still they continued for a long time to enjoy something like peace. But as their numbers increased, they began to be watched more carefully, and the appointment for that suffragan of a priest who had been educated by the Jesuits, finally brought matters to a crisis. This man was exceedingly haughty and violent, and frequently denounced the pure doctrines of the gospel, which he suspected that these people had embraced. Hence their attendance at church became less and less frequent, and some of them, when there, arose and left the house when they heard what they regarded as the most essential truths of Christianity misrepresented and blasphemed. The reigning bishop, Maximilian Gaudolph was speedily informed of the state of things, and he immediately cited two of their number before his court at Hallein. Upon appearing in his presence, he asked where their Lutheran books were, and demanded to know why they did not attend confession and mass? Upon honestly confessing their sentiments, they were thrown into prison and put into chains. During three days' confinement they were treated with the utmost severity, after which they were conveyed to Salzburg, to be examined before a higher court. Here they were again asked whether they were Lutherans or Papists; and upon their answering that they believed the Lutheran doctrines to be clearly founded upon the gospel, they were again imprisoned for fifty days. While in prison two old Capuchin monks were sent to convert them, but these priestly confessors could not shake their faith, being themselves discomfited by the apt quotations that these humble Christians made from the sacred Scriptures. Reason, or rather sophistry, failing to make any impression, resort was had to torture and the most terrible threatenings; but these witnesses for the truth remained firm. At length, they were required to furnish the archbishop with a written confession of their faith. With this demand they cheerfully complied, and accompanied their confession with a very humble petition, that they might either be tolerated in their native land, or allowed to depart from it with their wives and children. This confession was drawn up by Joseph Schaitberger, a poor miner, who had enjoyed no opportunities of education out of his own family, but it is in all respects a remarkable document. It commences thus:—" Most noble Prince, our most gracious Lord: Those are truly strong and terrible words, which our Lord Jesus Christ himself has spoken to hypocritical Christians, who deny their faith before the world, when he says: 'He that is ashamed of me and denies me before men, of him will I be ashamed, and will deny him before my Father and the holy angels.' Luke ix. and Matt. x. These words, may it please your princely grace, move us not to deny our faith before men, lest we should prove to be hypocrites in the sight of God and of men, which may God prevent." They then proceed to say, that his highness must be aware, that they had always conducted themselves as dutiful subjects, but that as regarded things spiritual, they felt themselves bound to obey God, rather than man; and while "rendering unto Cæsar the things that are Cæsar's, to render unto God the things that are God's." In reference, therefore, to the two points on which they were specifically interrogated, viz. the worship of saints and the Lord's Supper, they would express themselves as simply as they could, in explanation of what they believed to be in accordance with the plain teachings of the word of God. In doing this, they very clearly announced their faith in the great doctrines of Christianity, especially the doctrine of justification by faith alone; and occasionally refer to the Augsburg Confession and declare their agreement with its teachings. In reference to the Lord's Supper, they thus expressed themselves: "As it regards the Holy Supper and Testament of our Lord Jesus Christ, it rests most heavily upon our hearts and consciences, in view of our soul's salvation, as one of our highest duties. But that we have not hitherto drank, according to Christ's command, the blood of Christ in the cup, this we and our forefathers have ever lamented, for it is indeed written, 'Drink ye all of it,' that is not only priests, but *all men.* Matt. xxvi."

The result of this confession was a universal persecution of all, who were even suspected of having embraced these "heretical" views. They were refused employment, and their property was all taken from them. Their books were seized whenever found, and either torn or burnt. They were put to hard labour upon bread and water for fourteen days, and then required to recant. Some few were subdued by these cruelties, and such were required to renounce Lutheranism, as a new and damnable heresy, and profess their faith in all the doctrines of the papacy, such as the mass, the intercession of the Virgin Mary and other saints, the sufficiency of the sacraments under one form, purgatory, &c. Others endeavoured to flee, with their wives and children in the dead of winter, and left all their earthly possessions behind. But not even this privilege was accorded to them by their relentless persecutors. Their children were taken from them, under the pretence of giving them religious instruction. From one thousand parents who were driven from their country during the years 1684 to 1686, not less than six hundred children are said to have been taken. The accounts given by the fugitives of the indignities and cruelties to which they had been subjected, finally excited the sympathy of those Protestant princes in whose territories they had sought for refuge. About the commencement of the year 1685, Fredrick William, Elector of Brandenburg, addressed a letter to the Archbishop of Salzburg, in which he mildly remonstrated against these proceedings, and expressed the hope that they were unauthorized by his grace, especially as they were in direct violation of the peace of Westphalia. He also intimated, that in the absence of every other consideration, *prudence* alone would dictate another course, as Protestant states might become so incensed by such conduct as to retaliate upon their Roman Catholic subjects. In June of the same year, the evangelical representatives, (Corpus Evangelicum,) assembled at Regensburg, also addressed a remonstrance to the archbishop, who replied, that these people were neither Lutheran nor Reformed, and consequently could not claim the benefits of the treaty of Westphalia. But the evangelical body reiterating their demands early in the following year, and claiming these exiles as their brethren in a common faith, the episcopal government had no longer any pretext for their violent and illegal conduct, and the Catholic authorities agreed to restore to the Protestants their children and their rights of property. Filled with joy and holy gratitude, a number of the Teffereckers hastened to their once happy valley, provided with every thing which was regarded as necessary to establish their rights as parents and citizens. Great, however, was their surprise, when the Salzburg magistrate, Wolff Adam, to whom they reported themselves, without giving them an audience, thus addressed them: "What are you doing here, you Lutheran dogs? Where are your passports?" These being produced, he continued his revilings while he sent for a priest to assist in their examination. Upon his arrival their packs were searched, and all their books taken from them, with this remark, "When we have our baking done, we will use these books to heat the oven." That night these devoted Christians were kept in prison under a guard of twenty soldiers, and the next morning they were ordered to pay a fine of *thirty-four florins*. Upon their demurring to do so, they were threatened with additional cruelties, until one of their number gave an order for the amount, to be raised from his property in the valley, upon which a guard conducted them over the frontier, and warned them never again to attempt to enter the country. Representations were duly made to the archbishop in relation to the conduct of his subordinates and an examination was *professedly* made, but the accused party escaped with a light reprimand. Finally, the archbishop endeavoured to extricate himself from all censure, by alleging that the valley of Teffereck was not under his jurisdiction, but a part of the Tyrol, and so subject to the Emperor of Austria. All representations made to the Imperial court were equally unavailing; and thus these poor people were stripped of all their earthly possessions. Nor was this all. Their wives and children were wrested from them, except when they succeeded in penetrating the country, and, despite the vigilance of the guards, carried off sometimes a wife, sometimes a child, or perhaps in a few cases, their whole family. During all this time, their sufferings were indescribable. Driven from their homes, they had no place of shelter. Deprived of all employment, they were destitute of the means of providing the necessaries of life. Going forth in the dead of winter, they suffered incredibly from cold and hunger, so that many, after reaching some Protestant state, perished from exhaustion. Still more melancholy was the fate of those from whom their children were torn, and given into the hands of their bitterest enemies, to be trained up under the most dangerous and ruinous errors.

One of the most remarkable of these sufferers was *Joseph Schaitberger*, to whom reference has already been made as the author of the Confession of Faith, which was presented to the archbishop. He was born on the 18th of March, 1658, at Dŭrenburg, in the district of Hallein, about two German miles from the city of Salzburg. His parents were both pious and decidedly attached to the evangelical faith, in which he was carefully educated. Being early taught to read by his brother, (who was a schoolmaster,) he soon manifested the deepest love for the sacred Scriptures, so that, like the Psalmist, he "meditated in them by day and by night," and consequently became intimately acquainted with them. He was condemned by the archbishop's court as a heretic, and his two daughters taken from him. He returned twice to recover them, but never succeeded. One of them, however, was finally restored to him in a most remarkable manner. Educated as a most zealous and bigoted Catholic, she had been taught to regard her father as a heretic, for whom there was no hope of salvation. When she had grown up, and was married, she became so interested in his eternal welfare as to make a journey to Nuremberg, where he was then residing, for the purpose of attempting his conversion. Her filial piety was rewarded; for the conversations with her father were so blessed to her, that she became a convert to the true faith, and after vainly attempting to induce her husband to follow her example, she spent the rest of her life, a voluntary exile, in Nuremburg, knowing that she would not be allowed to exercise her religion in Salzburg.

After his banishment, Schaitberger at first supported himself by cutting wood and other severe manual labour in the city in which he had taken refuge. But his zeal for religion knew no abatement, and he devoted himself to the spiritual interests of his countrymen, especially those whom he had left behind in Salzburg.

Besides visiting them on various occasions, he wrote letters and religious tracts for their instruction and edification, and poured forth his devout feelings in hymns admirably adapted to their circumstances. The influence of these simple productions, though for a long time circulated in manuscript, appears to have been very extraordinary. It is not known at what time they were first printed, but it was certainly some years after their good effects became manifest. They were, however, at length collected into a small volume, which was eagerly sought by the vast body of Protestants, who seemed suddenly to spring up from the soil out of which, it was supposed, that every germ of evangelical truth had been eradicated. As that immense body of martyrs wended their way to Prussia and other parts of Protestant Germany, and even to Holland and America, they were everywhere heard singing his simple hymns, especially that which was called "The Exile's Hymn," a translation of which is here appended. We are indebted for this translation, as well as much of the information in regard to Schaitberger, to Dr. Reynolds, President of Capitol University, Columbus, (Ohio.) Schaitberger lived to see this great work of revival in Salzburg, as he died at Nuremburg, toward the close of 1733. His last years were rendered comfortable by the provision made for him by the magistrate of the city, to whom he had so strongly recommended himself by his unblemished life.

THE SALZBURG EMIGRANT'S SONG.

I.

I AM a wretched exile here—
    Thus must my name be given—
From native land and all's that dear,
    For God's word, I am driven.

II.

Full well I know, Lord Jesus Christ,
    Thy treatment was no better:
Thy follower I now will be;
    To do thy will I'm debtor.

III.

Henceforth, a pilgrim I must be,
    In foreign climes must wander;
O Lord! my prayer ascends to thee,
    That thou my path will ponder.

IV.

O faithful God! be thou my stay;
    I give me to thy keeping;
Forsake me not in this my day,
    Nor when in death I'm sleeping.

V.

Thy faith I freely have confessed:
    Dare I deny it? Never!
Not though they call me "heretic,"
    And soul and body sever.

VI.

My ornament, the galling chain;
    For Jesus' sake I wear it,
And scarcely feel its weight or pain,
    While in his faith I bear it.

VII.

Though Satan and the world conspire
  To seize each earthly treasure,
If in my heart true faith but dwell,
  I'm rich beyond all measure.

VIII.

Thy will, O God! be done! May I
  Still cheerfully obey thee!
And may thy arm of power and love
  Encompass still, and stay me!

IX.

Though I go forth to poverty,
  For Christ's sake, I am going,
And see in heaven, reserved for me,
  A crown with glory glowing.

X.

Forth from my home I now must go:
  My children! Must I leave them?
O God! my tears in anguish flow—
  Shall I no more receive them?

XI.

My God conduct me to a place,
  Though in some distant nation,
Where I may have thy glorious word,
  And learn thy great salvation.

XII.

And though in this dark vale of tears
  I yet awhile must tarry,
I know that thou to heaven, at length,
  My ransomed soul will carry!

We come now to speak of the persecution which brought those emigrants to America who are more especially the subjects of this narrative. For forty years the persecuted Protestants who resided in the glens and fastnesses of the Alps had been permitted to enjoy their religion in comparative quiet. But, as we have intimated, their doctrines were spreading with too much rapidity, and it was therefore deemed necessary, to interpose the strong arm of civil power to arrest their further progress. This persecution, which was the most cruel and extensive of any that preceded it, was begun at the instance and under the direction of Leopold, Count of Firmain and Archbishop of Salzburg, who, having discovered that many of his subjects had renounced the religion of Rome, determined either to reduce them to submission or to extirpate them from his dominions.

The Archbishopric of Salzburg comprised at this time, the Suffragans of Friessingen, Ratisbon, Passau, Chiemré, Seckau, Lavant, Briscen, Gurk, and Neustadt, and contained, according to some authorities, a population of not less than 150,000 souls. We cannot ascertain exactly what was the proportion of Protestants within its jurisdiction, but it must have been considerable, if we may judge from the large numbers who were compelled to seek a place of safety in other countries. This archbishopric was then the most eastern district of Bavaria, but now forms a detached province in Upper Austria. It is called Salzburg, from the broad valley of the Salza, which is made by the approximating of the Norric and Rhetian Alps. All who resided in this region were consequently denominated Salzburgers.

Salzburg is the principal city in this district, and as a matter of history it may not be inappropriate to remark, that it is a place of great antiquity. It was destroyed by Attila in the year 448, but was afterward rebuilt by the Bavarian dukes, at the request of St. Rupert. It was the birthplace of the famous Paracelsus, and here his ashes repose. It contains the remains of the ancient Roman baths, from which many valuable antiquities have been obtained. The population is estimated at 15,000. It is the only fortress in Upper Austria.

Returning from this short digression, we remark that the persecution under Leopold commenced in 1729, and continued with unabated violence until 1732. The objects of his rage were sought out and pursued by the priests and soldiery of Rome, and experienced every species of outrage which an unbridled fanaticism could suggest. Resort was had to whipping and imprisonment, and when these failed the unhappy victims were murdered or banished, and their property confiscated. All the natural and sacred ties of life were disregarded. Husbands and wives were separated. Children were torn from the embraces of their parents, and forced into monasteries for education in the Romish faith. During this persecution upward of THIRTY THOUSAND Protestants were exiled, and compelled to seek for safety and peace among their Protestant brethren. Nor were the hearts of those brethren closed against them. Twenty thousand were received in the Prussian dominions, and many of them took up their abode in Wurtemburg, Baden, the city of Augsburg, and other free cities of Swabia. Some also emigrated to Holland and England, where they were received with kindness and Christian sympathy, and every effort made to relieve their wants and mitigate their sufferings. Though persecuted, they were not forsaken. Though they were forced to wander about as outcasts from the land of their nativity, yet God was with them, and in the course of his providence was preparing the way, for their permanent escape from spiritual despotism, and was about to transplant some of them at least, to a better country; where, freed from the fear of man, they could worship Him without molestation, and under circumstances far more favourable, than any in which they had been placed in their much-loved fatherland.

CHAPTER II.

Charter granted by Charles II. to the Trustees for establishing the colony of Georgia—The design of the colony—General Oglethorpe—English settlers arrive at Savannah—"Society for the Propagation of Christian Knowledge"—Interest on behalf of the Salzburgers—Arrangements to remove the Salzburgers to Georgia—Fifty families engaged for the first transportation—Provision made by the "Society"—Liberality of the "Trustees"—First company of emigrants—Love of country—Departure from their homes—Incidents of their journey—The city of Augsburg—Hospitalities extended to the Salzburgers—Recommence their travels—Rev. S. Urlsperger—Effects of the sojourn of the Salzburgers at Augsburg—Revival of religion—Further incidents—Arrival at the city of Frankfort—Conduct of the Burgers—Procession—Entrance into the city—Hospitality of the inhabitants—Departure from Frankfort—The Maine and Rhine—Arrival at Rotterdam—Rev. Messrs. Bolzius and Gronau—Departure from Rotterdam—Arrival at Dover, in England—Impressions made by the emigrants on their English benefactors—Preparations for leaving England—Departure of the Purisburg, first ship with German emigrants.

WHILE the scenes recorded in the latter part of the previous chapter were transpiring, events were occurring in England, which in the providence of God, were destined to result in lasting benefits to the Salzburgers. In 1732, a charter was granted by Charles II. to twenty-one noblemen and gentlemen in England, constituting them a body corporate, by the name of, "The Trustees for establishing the Colony of Georgia, in America." The design of this enterprise, as stated by the trustees themselves, was not only to provide a home and the means of subsistence for the indigent inhabitants of Great Britain, but also to furnish "a refuge for the distressed Salzburgers and other Protestants." This colony was planted by General James Oglethorpe, who arrived in Georgia, with the first company of English settlers, on the 20th of January, 1733, and laid the foundation of the city of Savannah.

No sooner was this corporation organized and its objects made known, than the "Society for the Propagation of Christian Knowledge" began to interest itself for the removal of some of the Salzburgers to Georgia; and as early as the 12th of October, 1732, they made application to the "Trustees" to aid them in their benevolent designs. The "Trustees" did not feel authorized at this time, to do more for the Salzburgers than to offer them grants of land in their new colony; all the funds which they controlled having been raised for a different purpose. Steps were however immediately taken, to ascertain whether any of the German Protestants were willing to remove to Georgia, and become British subjects; submitting themselves to such rules as the "Trustees" might prescribe. "The Society for the Propagation of Christian Knowledge" opened a correspondence with several prominent Protestant ministers in different parts of Germany, in order to ascertain if the Salzburgers were disposed to avail themselves of their kind offices, and remove to the asylum which it was proposed to provide for them in America.

From their correspondents the "Society" learned, that there were hundreds of the persecuted Protestants who were not only willing, but anxious to emigrate. This fact was communicated to the "Trustees," who, warranted by a special fund, recently raised for the purpose, sent in December, 1732, an invitation to fifty families of the Salzburgers to remove to Georgia.

At the same time, the venerable "Society" proposed to pay their expenses from Germany to Rotterdam, and to furnish the means to support among them a pastor and a catechist. Various causes prevented the immediate execution of these plans. In the mean time, a liberal grant of money was made by the British Parliament to aid the colony, which, together with three or four thousand pounds from private benefactions, enabled the "Trustees" to carry out more fully the benevolent intentions of the Society. They consequently wrote again to Germany and requested that a portion of the Salzburgers might be sent over to England, to prepare for their transportation to America; and, in the mean time, money and articles of clothing were forwarded to the continent, to supply their wants and relieve their distresses during the journey.

One cannot but admire the liberality which the trustees displayed, in the terms upon which they proposed to transplant these poor, persecuted Germans to their new colony. To such as were deemed worthy of their patronage, they advanced the funds necessary to pay their passage and furnish sea-stores. On arriving in Georgia, each Salzburger was to receive *three* lots. "One for a house and yard within the town, and one for a garden near the town, and one for tillage at a short distance from the town, (the whole embracing fifty acres,) said lands to be a free-hold to them and to their heirs forever." In addition to this, the trustees engaged to furnish them with provisions until their lands could be made available for their own support. In consideration of these very liberal grants, the Salzburgers were to obligate themselves to obey the trustees' orders, and become citizens of Georgia, with all the rights and privileges of Englishmen.

The necessary arrangements having all been completed, the first company of emigrants began to prepare for their journey. These were from the town of Berchtolsgaden and its vicinity. One may readily imagine the varied sensations of these devoted Christians, as the time drew near which was to witness their departure from their homes and their country. True, they had there endured severe persecutions and trials; but they were men whose natural affections had been refined by the mild influences of Christianity, and, with all its faults, they loved their country still. There, too, were the scenes of their childhood, endeared by all the fond recollections of early life, and hallowed by those religious associations so peculiarly grateful to the pious heart. Yet, how dear soever were their native hills and vales, and painfully pleasing as were many of the reminiscences of the past, they could not have failed to realize that they were the objects of a cruel hate, and that they held their property and their lives at the disposal of a merciless foe. Beside, their religious principles, which they esteemed more precious than life, had been denounced as heresy, and the right to worship God in accordance with their views and feelings had been denied them. Thus circumstanced, how peculiarly grateful must have been the prospects which unfolded themselves to their vision, as they contemplated their removal from what might, with propriety, be styled the land of their captivity and cruel oppression, to a country where, freed from the restrictions now imposed upon them, and placed beyond the reach of their spiritual enemies, they could worship the God of their fathers without hindrance, and secure to themselves and their posterity a heritage of freedom.

At length the day for their departure arrived. Behold now these pious pilgrims about to leave forever their country and their homes. "They were indeed a noble army of martyrs going forth in the strength of God, and triumphing in the faith of the gospel, under the severest hardships and the most rigorous persecutions. They were marshalled under no banners, save that of the cross, and were preceded by no leaders, save their spiritual teachers and the great Captain of their salvation."* They carried with them no weapons, save their hymn-books and their Bibles, and as they journeyed they made the air vocal with their praises to Him who, though he had permitted them to be persecuted and even exiled, had not left them without protection and friends, nor given them up into the hands of their oppressors.

Setting out on foot, the direction of their journey required them to pass through Bavaria, and at almost every step they were exposed to insult. Whenever it suited the Catholic authorities, these wanderers were turned aside from their course, and every effort was made to embarrass them and render their situation unpleasant. But no hindrances could check their

---

* Bancroft.

zeal, no promises or threats could change their determination. Onward they march, through the midst of foes, until at last they pass the territory of Bavaria, and arrive before the gates of the free city of Augsburg, in Swabia. But the gates of that renowned city were closed against them.*

This was indeed a severe trial. In this very place, two hundred years previously, Melancthon and Luther had presented to the Emperor Charles V. and the assembled princes of Germany, that venerable symbol of the reformed faith which from this city received the name of the *Augsburg Confession*.† It was for embracing this confession, and for their consistent and unwavering maintenance of its doctrines, that they had endured so much persecution, and were now wandering in exile, seeking for a home in a distant and unknown clime. However, though at first repulsed, the officers of the city, overawed by the Protestant inhabitants, reluctantly admitted the emigrants, and their Lutheran brethren immediately made provision for their entertainment and the supply of their wants. Here for a season they rested, enjoying the kind hospitality of their Christian friends, and gathering from their sympathy and their offices of love, fresh courage and encouragement for the

---

* Stevens. † Ibid.

further prosecution of their long and tedious journey.

The news of the arrival of the Salzburgers at Augsburg, soon spread through the neighbouring countries, and now it would seem that the sympathies of evangelical Christians were generally aroused on their behalf. Not only did the Lutheran pastors and their flocks manifest a deep interest in their welfare, but princes, professors, and students in the universities and colleges vied with each other in doing honour to those who, in obeying the dictates of their consciences and yielding to a sense of religious obligation, had preferred banishment, rather than renounce their attachment to the gospel.*

On the 21st day of October, 1733, the Salzburgers recommenced their pilgrimage, after a discourse and prayer, and a benediction. This company of emigrants consisted of forty-two men, with their families, numbering in all *seventy-eight persons*. The arrangements for their transportation to Georgia had been previously made with the "Trustees," by the venerable Samuel Urlsperger, then pastor of the Lutheran church of St. Ann in the city of Augsburg, who bestowed special attention upon them during their sojourn, and ever afterward watched over their welfare with the solicitude of an affectionate

---

* Stevens.

father. On leaving the city, the Salzburgers, were furnished by their friends, with three rude carts, in one of which they placed their baggage, while the others conveyed their feeble women and helpless children; the rest travelled on foot. It was under such circumstances that they began their weary march, as pilgrims seeking a better country.

The sojourn of the Salzburgers in Augsburg was not without its practical effects upon the inhabitants of the city. The power of the gospel was so strikingly exemplified in the patience and fortitude which they displayed amid all their sufferings, and they evinced a spirit of such deep and fervent piety in their general deportment, that by their example many were awakened, and the churches were blessed with a very gracious revival of religion. Thus, while they were flying from persecution, God was employing their instrumentality in multiplying the triumphs of evangelical truth.

After leaving Augsburg, the incidents connected with their journey varied according to the religious character of the country through which they passed. At one time they are encouraged by the hospitality and sympathy of friends; at other times, exposed to the scoffs and maltreatment of their enemies. To-day they receive every assistance which Christian kindness can suggest; to-morrow they are threatened by their adversaries, and turned aside from their way by their intolerant enemies. But amid the most trying circumstances they were cheerful and happy, always looking up to the throne of God with joyful hope, and sustained by the promise, "I will never leave you nor forsake you."

Pursuing their weary pilgrimage, they arrived at length at the Protestant city of Frankfort, in Nassau. The burghers of the city, hearing of their approach, went out to meet and welcome them, and extend to them a hospitable reception. We can easily imagine with what warm enthusiasm these Christian men greeted the toil-worn exiles, and how affecting was the scene, as they embraced each other as the disciples of the same Saviour, and as the professors of a common faith. Their salutations being over, and the first gust of feeling having subsided, a procession was formed, headed by the pious burghers, and they marched into the city two by two. And how solemn and imposing their entrance! No clangour of trumpets, no notes of martial music herald their approach. They pass into the city, not amid the shouts of the noisy multitude, but singing one of those beautiful psalms in which they had been wont, in their native land, to pour forth the pious aspirations of their souls to their Saviour and their God. This little incident speaks volumes in testimony of the truly devotional spirit which characterized these people, and shows, too, that their strength lay in the simplicity of their faith.

At Frankfort, as at Augsburg, the Salzburgers experienced every attention which Christian affection could suggest and an ample charity provide. After remaining here for a few days to refresh themselves, and to partake of the bounty of their brethren, they embarked upon the Maine, and soon found themselves floating upon the waters of the beautiful Rhine. "As they passed between the castled crags, the vineyards, and the white-walled towns that adorn its banks, their conversation, amid hymns and psalms, is of justification and sanctification."* Thus employed, the hours glided away, not only pleasantly but profitably, and they realize every day more fully the joys and consolations of that religion for the enjoyment of which they had suffered the loss of all things.

On the 27th of November they reached the city of Rotterdam. Here they were joined by their chosen teachers, the Rev. John Martin Bolzius, and Rev. Israel Christian Gronau. The former had been superintendent of the Latin Orphan House at Halle, and the latter a tutor in the same institution. These pious men, in the exercise of a truly missionary spirit, had

---
* Bancroft.

consented to relinquish the lucrative and honourable positions which they held in the institution at Halle, that they might accompany the Salzburgers to Georgia, and minister to their spiritual wants. Subsequent events showed, that this important trust was confided to those who were in every respect worthy of it. Very little is known of the early history of Messrs. Bolzius and Gronau. All that has been ascertained in reference to Mr. Bolzius is, that he was born on the 15th of December, 1703, and ordained to the gospel ministry on the 11th of November, 1733.

After staying for a week at Rotterdam, the emigrants, in company with their pastors, embarked on board of one of the Trustees' ships on the 2d of December. Their passage down the English Channel was a long and tedious one, the weather having been boisterous and the winds adverse.

On the 21st day of December they arrived safely at Dover, in England. Here they were visited by the "Trustees," who bestowed on them every attention which their circumstances seemed to require. Nor did they fail to engage the sympathies of their English friends. Their piety and humility, their exemplary conduct under all circumstances, together with the sufferings and privations which they had endured in the cause of Christian truth, commended them to the confidence and the kind regards of all who were capable of appreciating their virtues or pitying their wrongs.

The arrangements for their voyage to America were made with all reasonable despatch, and the 28th day of December was fixed upon as the time for their departure for their new homes. The Trustees administered to each Salzburger an "oath of strict piety, loyalty, and fidelity," after which they spent several hours in devotional exercises.* Their pastor preached to them an appropriate sermon from the words, (Isa. xlix. 10,) "He that hath mercy on them will lead them." In this address he endeavoured, by reviewing the mercies which they had experienced under the most trying circumstances, to inspire them with fresh confidence in the goodness of God. He encouraged them to believe, that He who had hitherto been their protector, and had defended them against all the machinations of their enemies, would watch over them amidst the dangers of the trackless ocean, as well as those to which they might be exposed in the strange land whither they were going. After singing a hymn and uniting in prayer, the Purisburg, (the first ship conveying German emigrants,) unfolded her sails, and the first company of Salzburgers who were to aid in the colonization of Georgia, departed for their distant home.

---

* Stevens.

CHAPTER III.

The Salzburgers at sea—Conduct during the voyage—Arrival at Charleston, S. C.—General Oglethorpe—Departure from Charleston—Arrival at Savannah—Sentiments of the emigrants—Their reception at Savannah—Notes of Mr. Bolzius—Baron Von Reck—Conduct of the Indians—Disembarkation of the Salzburgers—Liberality of General Oglethorpe—Expedition into the country—Description of the country—Devout conduct of the Salzburgers—Ebenezer—Foundation of the colony—Location of their settlement—Uchee Indians—St. Matthew's Parish—Lord Effingham—Town laid out—Salzburgers remove to their new home—Impressions in relation to the nature of the country—Baron Von Reck's enthusiastic description—Real character of the country—Assignment of lots—Hardships incident to colonization—Scarcity of mechanics and materials for building—Other trials—Sickness and death among the colonists—Extracts from Mr. Bolzius' journal—Influence of affliction—Arrival of a second company of Salzburgers—Improvement in the condition of the colony—Progress of the town, &c.

To one who has always resided at a distance from the sea-board, few objects appear more awfully grand than the mighty ocean, with its seemingly boundless space of waters. Nowhere will man be more fully impressed with a sense of his dependence than when he is isolated from the rest of the world, and left to the mercy of the winds and waves. If at any time the soul is disposed for holy contemplation, it must be when man is removed far away from human succour and in the consciousness of his own helplessness is forced to meditate upon the power and goodness of his Creator.

Such was now the situation of the Salzburgers. Coming from the interior of Europe, they knew nothing of the ocean, except what they had heard; and to them the perils of a voyage at sea no doubt assumed a fearful character. Launched upon its bosom, every thing was new to them, and they knew not which to admire most, its strangeness or its sublimity. But though its wonders inspired them with awe and humility, their hearts, sustained by a holy fortitude, experienced no fear; and no sooner did the shores of England vanish from their vision, than they broke forth in psalms of praise to Him " who measures the waters in the hollow of His hands." Every day furnished them with new subjects of contemplation. The ocean hushed into repose, or lashed by the winds into furious commotion; the dark and lowering storm howling through their vessel; the gentle breezes wafting them gayly on their course, all supply them with themes of thanksgiving, and awaken in their souls new emotions of gratitude.

Nor did they, in the exciting scenes which surrounded them, neglect their spiritual improvement. Blessed with the presence of two pious teachers, much of their time was spent in religious conversation. Daily worship was observed; and when the Sabbath arrived, their ship became their Bethel, where they were favored with the faithful preaching of the gospel, and enjoyed, as far as their situation would permit, all the privileges of the sanctuary.

After a perilous passage of one hundred and four days, they reached Charleston, S. C., early in March, 1734. Here they providentially met General Oglethorpe, who had gone thither for the purpose of making a voyage to England, with a view to procure reinforcements for the colony. As soon, however, as he heard of the arrival of the Salzburgers, with his usual benevolence of heart he relinquished his intended journey, and returned to Georgia to aid these exiles in making an advantageous settlement.

Remaining in Charleston a few days, the Salzburgers re-embarked on the 9th day of March. On the 11th they entered the Savannah River. This, according to the Lutheran Calendar, was "Reminiscere Sunday." Here was indeed a striking coincidence, and the occasion suggested a train of very pleasing reflections. No doubt they recalled the memories of other days, when they endured so much affliction for conscience sake; and in dwelling upon the scenes of trial through which they had passed, the kindness with which God had safely conducted them through every danger, and the favourable prospects which now opened to them, their hearts were oppressed by a sense of gratitude too great for utterance. But amid the associations of this hallowed day their minds were calm. The promises of peace and mercy tranquillized their spirits, and no anxious cares for the future disturbed their repose. One of their number, in a letter to a friend in Germany, speaks thus of this occasion: "While we lay off the banks of our dear Georgia, in a very lovely calm, and heard the birds singing sweetly, all was cheerful on board. It was really edifying to us, that we came to the borders of the promised land this day, when, as we are taught by its lessons from the gospel, Jesus came to the sea-coast after he had endured persecution and rejection by his countrymen."* To commemorate this day, it was resolved to celebrate it as an annual festival of thanksgiving to God; and this practice was observed for a very long period.

On the 12th of March the Salzburgers reached Savannah, and here a truly cordial reception was given them. They were greeted with the acclamations of the colonists, and entertained with every mark of hospitality. General Oglethorpe himself went down to the river to meet and welcome them to their new homes, and with his accustomed liberality offered to give them any of the un-

---
* Stevens.

appropriated lands upon which they might prefer to settle, and to furnish them with every facility that he could command. Such were the favourable circumstances under which these pilgrims reached the land of their adoption.

Mr. Bolzius, in his journal, under date of March 11, 1734, says, "At the place of our landing almost all the inhabitants of Savannah were gathered together. They fired off some cannon, and cried huzza! which was answered by our sailors, and other English people in our ship, in the same manner. A good dinner was prepared for us. We, the commissary, and Dr. Twiffler, our physician were lodged in the house of the Rev. Mr. Quincy, the English missionary."

Baron Von Reck thus records the same event: "The citizens returned our salute of five guns with three; and all the magistrates, the citizens, and the Indians came to the river side. The two divines, (Messrs. Bolzius and Gronau,) Mr. Dunbar, some others, and myself went ashore in a boat. We were received with all possible demonstrations of joy, friendship, and civility. The Indians reached their hands to me, as a testimony of their joy also for our arrival. The Salzburgers came on shore after us, and we immediately pitched a tent for them in the square of the town."

The Salzburgers having all safely disembarked, the next object of interest was to select a location for their settlement. General Oglethorpe informed Baron Von Reck (who conducted this expedition) that his people might exercise their own choice in this particular. This fact being communicated to them, they expressed a desire to be removed to some distance from the sea, where the scenery was diversified with hill and dale, and they might be supplied with springs of water. This wish, no doubt, originated in the associations connected with home, such having been the nature of the country in which they had been reared. To carry out their views, General Oglethorpe, in company with Paul Jenys, Esq., Speaker of the South Carolina House of Assembly, Baron Von Reck, Mr. Gronau, Dr. Twiffler, their physician, and one of the Lutheran elders, together with some Indians, made a tour of observation into the adjoining country, while the great body of the Germans remained in the city to rest themselves from the effects of their long and tedious voyage.

The "corps of observation," in the accomplishment of their mission, penetrated nearly thirty miles into the interior, where they discovered a location which, it was supposed, would meet the wishes of the emigrants. The place was described as being on "the banks of a river of clear water, the sides high, the country of the neighbourhood hilly, with valleys of rich cane-land, intermixed with little brooks and springs of water." The Salzburgers who were of this company expressed themselves as highly gratified with the situation and the general appearance of the country. But as they had been wont to sanctify every act by thanksgiving and prayer, and as the events of this day would probably exert an important influence upon their future prosperity, they meekly bowed beside the water, and invoked the divine protection and blessing. They finished their journey, as they commenced it, with fervent praise to God for his great goodness as displayed in their past history, but especially in bringing them to so goodly a land. After singing a psalm, they set up a rock, which they found upon the spot, and, in the spirit of the pious Samuel, named the place Ebenezer, (the stone of help,) for they could truly say, "Hitherto the Lord hath helped us." Thus, with devout gratitude to God, and humble reliance upon his goodness, the foundation was laid for the COLONY OF THE SALZBURGERS.

It may be well here to remark that the lands alloted to the Salzburgers bordered on the possessions of the Uchee Indians, from whom General Oglethorpe obtained them some time previously. It is worthy of note that though these Indians were near neighbours to the Germans, they never manifested any hostile disposition. On the contrary, there is reason to believe that the most friendly relations always subsisted between them. It may be proper to state here that the place selected was about twenty-five miles from the city of Savannah, in a district of country afterward known as St. Matthew's Parish, and subsequently erected into a county, which was called Effingham, after an English nobleman—Lord Effingham—who defended, in the British Parliament, in 1775, the resistance of the American Colonies to the usurpations of the mother country, and resigned his commission in the British army when he ascertained that his regiment was about to be ordered to America, to aid in enforcing the unjust exactions of the crown. The county still bears that title.

The site for a settlement having been agreed upon, General Oglethorpe marked out the town, and sent up workmen to assist the colonists in clearing lands and erecting temporary dwellings, which consisted of tents and sheds constructed of rough planks. In a few weeks, the preparations for the accommodation of the settlers being in a suitable state of forwardness, the whole body of Germans, in company with their pastors, went up to their new homes at Ebenezer. Here in the wilderness of Georgia, far distant from the land of their birth and the graves of their fathers, these exiles ended their wanderings, and found at last a resting-place, where, freed from the censorship of man, and unawed by fears of violence, they could enjoy repose and worship God, "under their own vine and fig-tree." Hitherto they had been driven from place to place, and nowhere had they found "A sheltering home of sympathy and love." But now their conflicts were measurably ended. The providence of God had placed them beyond the reach of persecution, and they could erect their spiritual temples, enjoy the teachings of their faithful pastors, rear their offspring to virtue and to usefulness under the benign influences of the gospel; and living in the grateful use of the bounties of a kind Providence, and the faithful improvement of the means of grace, pass their days in contentment and peace, and acquire continually a fitness for that still more glorious heritage prepared for them in heaven.

We may learn from the journal of Baron Von Reck how the Salzburgers esteemed their new residence. He states that "the lands are enclosed between two rivers which fall into the Savannah. The town is to be built near the largest, which is called Ebenezer, in remembrance that God has brought them hither. It is navigable, being twelve feet deep. A little rivulet, whose water is clear as crystal, glides by the town. Another runs through it and both fall into the Ebenezer. The woods here are not so thick as in other places. The sweet zephyrs preserve a delicious coolness, notwithstanding the scorching beams of the sun. There are very fine meadows, in which a great quantity of hay might be made with very little trouble. The hillocks are also very fit for vines. The cedar, walnut, pine, cypress, and oak make the greatest part of the woods. There are likewise a great quantity of myrtle-trees, out of which they extract, by boiling the berries, a green wax very proper to make candles with. There is much sassafras, and a great quantity of those plants of which indigo is made, and an abundance of China-root. The earth is so fertile, that it will bring forth any thing that can be sown or planted in it, whether fruits, herbs, or trees. There are wild vines, which run up to the tops of the tallest trees, and the country is so good that any one may ride in full gallop twenty or thirty miles. As to game, here are eagles, wild turkeys, roe-bucks, wild goats, stags, wild cows, horses, hares, partridges, and buffaloes."

To one living at this distant period, and who is at all acquainted with the locality of old Ebenezer, and the general character of the surrounding country, the above description by the enthusiastic baron appears to partake somewhat of the marvellous. We must either make considerable allowances for the warmth of his imagination, or conclude that the country has undergone a very great change. The site of their town was about four miles below Springfield, the present seat of justice for Effingham county, in a region which is composed of hills and plains that are very sterile, and upon which no one, having a correct knowledge of the character of the soil, would ever think of settling a farm. But circumstanced as the Salzburgers were, exiled from their country and worn out by the fatigue of travelling both by sea and by land, they no doubt were inclined to regard with favour any spot, which promised them rest from their toils and a period to their cruel sufferings.

Upon the arrival of the Salzburgers at Ebenezer, it was deemed proper to assign a lot of land to each family, according to the design of the Trustees. This having been done, arrangements were made for the erection of more permament and comfortable dwellings, and a plan was adopted for a house of worship. But now these devoted people were to experience many of the difficulties and hardships which are always incident upon a new settlement. In building their houses, they were very much hindered by the scarcity of materials. It is true, the Trustees had furnished a supply of plank and other timber, but not in sufficient quantities to meet the demand of the settlers. Besides, there were among them very few mechanics; and not being able to erect either saw or grist mills, their situation became very trying. In a newly-settled country, too, the means of transportation were necessarily very limited; and having no boats or wagons of their own, they were entirely dependant on the government for the conveyance of their supplies; and such were the straits to which they were at times reduced, that they were compelled to carry their provisions upon their backs from Savannah, a distance of twenty-five miles. To add to their sufferings, much sickness prevailed among them, superinduced no doubt, by exposure and excessive fatigue in a warm climate. The mortality which ensued was very distressing; but we learn from the journal of Pastor Bolzius, that those who became victims to disease and death endured their afflictions with Christian resignation, and closed their earthly pilgrimage with joy and triumph.

Among those of whom special mention is made, was a Mrs. Goshwandel. Speaking of her, Mr. Bolzius remarks: "It had pleased Almighty God to lead her through tedious and painful hours previous to her death. She improved the Passion Week to derive spiritual strength and comfort from contemplating the sufferings of her Saviour, and would have been rejoiced had the Lord called her home on the anniversary of his death. No complaints escaped her lips; and when visitors noticed her distress, she would say: 'Our Lord is kind to me, and he can restore me, if it is his will, and resignation to that will is all I desire.' God granted her great comfort during the last moments of her life."

Speaking of a visit to another about the same time, Mr. Bolzius remarks: "Our sick friend expressed his dissatisfaction with himself on account of his negligence and carelessness toward all that was most valuable to man; he observed that the zeal he had felt during the persecutions in Salzburg had left him, which grieved him very much. He remembered perfectly well, he said, how the most ignorant people in Salzburg had frequently assembled in mountains and among the cliffs of rocks for the purpose of singing, praying, and the reading of the Scriptures, being full of hunger and thirst after the word; and how they had experienced the goodness and mercy of God in these meetings. In this frame he expired." In recording the death of another person, this faithful pastor says: "To-day our friend departed this life. In the midst of great pain, her trust and confidence were in the will of the Lord, and she was anxious to be with him."

Having visited a sick-man by the name of Schofpach, the pastor states: "I found him very low-spirited, and spoke to him about our dear Saviour, setting forth to him how we might both live and die happily in communion with Christ. He assented to all that I had said, and stated that he was now experiencing that man, in himself, was nothing at all; that sin was the greatest of all evils; and that it was necessary to treasure up much of the grace of God and the hopes of the gospel for the contest of the last hour. Having prayed with him, I left him in hopes that the Lord would bless that visit. A few days after, this man expired with a joyful confidence in the atonement of Christ."

Thus it will be seen that death was making inroads upon the infant town, and filling many a family with sorrow and mourning. But these seemingly adverse circumstances were not without their salutary effect, in checking every thing like worldly-mindedness and indifference to religious duty, and in endearing to the hearts of this people that religion, which could not only cheer and support them under every trial of life, but was capable of imparting serenity and triumph in the hour of death. Amid all these scenes of suffering and distress, the emigrants laboured patiently, though they were exposed to sickness and hunger, and even death, hoping for better and happier days.

Such was the state of things at Ebenezer, when a second party of emigrants arrived. These were likewise Salzburgers, who had been sent over by the Trustees in the ship "Prince of Wales," which vessel left England in November, 1734, and arrived in Georgia the early part of the next year. This expedition, which consisted of fifty-seven persons, was conducted by Mr. Vatt. On reaching Savannah, they immediately set out to join their brethren at their new town. They were kindly received, and provision made for them as far as the means of the colonists would warrant. It was with difficulty, however, that they could be furnished with lodgings, and the stock of food in the colony was not very abundant. Nevertheless, by this accession to their numbers, the colonists were greatly benefited, for among the new comers were many mechanics, whose labours were of essential service. By their aid, planks were soon sawed, timber hewed, boards and shingles split, and the good people went cheerfully to work to improve their dwellings. As to their church, they were compelled as yet to worship in a large wooden tent, which during a part of the time had been the residence of their ministers. By degrees, many of their houses were finished; and here in the wilderness of Georgia, upon the very borders of an Indian tribe, sprung up a thrifty little town, with its humble cottages; and here, far away from the abodes of civilization, a Christian community was established, in which the pure doctrines of the gospel were taught, and God was worshipped in the simplicity and sincerity which characterized the first ages of the church. Would to God that this state of things had always continued! That it did not, was not attributable to any want of fidelity on the part of their religious teachers, or to any heterodoxy in doctrine or laxity of discipline. But it will not do to anticipate the future.

CHAPTER IV.

General Oglethorpe visits England—Favourable condition of the colony—Trustees determine to send out reinforcements—Aid from British Parliament—Character of the colonists engaged—Highlanders and Salzburgers—Liberal terms proposed by the Trustees—Captain Hermsdorff and Baron Von Reck—The Trustees charter the "London Merchant" and the "Symond"—The "great embarkation"—English and German emigrants—Moravians under Bishop Nitschman—John and Charles Wesley—Departure from England—Storm at sea—Effect of the conduct of the Germans upon Mr. Wesley—Testimony of Dr. Jackson, President of British Conference—Mr. Wesley's spiritual condition—Conference with Mr. Spangenburg—Influence of the Moravians—Rev. Peter Boehler—Salzburgers confounded with the Moravians—Mistake of Mr. Bancroft—Removal of Moravians to Pennsylvania—Mr. Wesley's religious experience—Extract from his journal—Subsequent visit to England—His conversion—Luther's preface to the Epistle to the Romans—Mr. Wesley's preaching after his conversion—Forms "Societies," the basis of Wesleyan Methodism—The Methodist Church a fruit of the Lutheran Reformation—Arrival of the "embarkation" at Savannah—Settlement of Salzburgers on St. Simon's Island—Views of the Germans in relation to war—Reinforcement at Ebenezer—Lutheran settlement at Frederica—Rev. U. Dreisler—Revs. Bolzius and Gronau visit Savannah—Conference with General Oglethorpe—Salzburgers dissatisfied with their location, and desire a change—General Oglethorpe visits Ebenezer—Reasons of the Salzburgers for desiring to remove—General Oglethorpe's advice and kindness to the Salzburgers—Change of location determined upon.

THE affairs of the colonists, both at Savannah and at Ebenezer, being considered in a favourable condition, General Oglethorpe determined to visit his friends in England. Taking with him a number of Indians and other persons, he departed from Savannah in the winter of 1734, and arrived in England early the following spring. His representations to the Trustees of the flattering prospects of their colony, induced that honourable body to resolve upon strengthening it by sending out new settlers, and by taking the necessary steps to provide for its greater security.

In July, 1735, publication was made, that the Trustees would provide for the transportation of a given number of such persons as might be approved by them. The terms proposed were so liberal, and the success of the colony being no longer a matter of doubt, upward of twelve hundred persons made application to be sent over to Georgia. Though the funds of the Trustees had been greatly increased by the very liberal grant from the British Parliament of £26,000, yet they did not feel warranted in giving encouragement to any but worthy persons, and such as would be likely to prove of advantage to the colony. It was therefore resolved that this embarkation should consist chiefly of the Highlanders from Scotland and the persecuted Salzburgers from Germany.

In accordance with this determination, the Trustees invited one hundred Germans from the city of Ratisbon to remove to Georgia, and settle under their patronage. They engaged to give them a free passage, with an ample supply of sea-stores, and a freehold of fifty acres of land to every settler, together with such an outfit of clothes, tools, and farming utensils, as might be deemed necessary. To these proposals the Salzburgers consented, and about eighty of them, under the conduct of Captain Hermsdorf and Baron Von Reck, repaired to England to avail themselves of the liberality of the Trustees.

A sufficient number of emigrants having been secured, the Trustees chartered for their transportation two ships, the *Symond*, of two hundred tons, Captain Joseph Cornish, and the *London Merchant*, of the same burden, Captain John Thomas. The whole number consisted of *two hundred and twenty-seven persons*. This was called the *great embarkation*. Besides the Salzburgers and a number from England, there were twenty-seven Moravians, under the care of one of their bishops, the Rev. David Nitschman. General Oglethorpe accompanied this expedition, and took with him several English gentlemen of distinction. Among the passengers were Messrs. John and Charles Wesley, the former of whom was going to Georgia, by invitation of General Oglethorpe, to preach the gospel to the Indians, and to improve, as far as might be practicable, the moral and religious condition of the colony.

The Symond and the London Merchant sailed from Gravesend on the 20th of October, 1735, under convoy of His Majesty's sloop-of-war Hawk, Captain Gascoine. It was not, however, until the 10th of December that they passed the Needles, and lost sight of the English coast. This voyage was a long and tempestuous one. There were frequent and violent storms, and on several occasions the vessels were in imminent danger of being shipwrecked. During one of these terrible gales, an incident occurred, the results of which will in all probability be felt until the end of time.

It has been noticed that among the passengers were Messrs. John and Charles Wesley. The former had received orders in the Church of England, and was now on his voyage to engage in the duties of his high vocation. The German passengers, by their humble piety, had attracted Mr. Wesley's attention, and awakened in his mind special interest on their behalf; and God, in his providence, seems to have designed that they were to exercise an important influence upon his religious character and his future history. On a Sabbath, about noon, while the Salzburgers and other Germans were engaged in public worship, a storm suddenly arose, which seems to have surpassed in violence every other that occurred during the voyage. Amid the commotion of the elements nearly every heart quaked, and some almost died with fear. Mr. Wesley himself was seriously alarmed at the imminent peril in which he and his fellow-passengers were placed. Notwithstanding his Christian profession, and his relation to the church as one of her accredited ministers, there was something wanting in his spiritual experience to fortify his mind against the fear of death. But far otherwise were the feelings of the pious Salzburgers and Moravians. While the tempest raged and the swelling billows threatened to engulf them, they calmly sang the praises of God, and manifested the most perfect self-composure and exemption from all fear, under the most appalling circumstances.

When the tempest had subsided, Mr. Wesley inquired of one of the Germans, "Were you not afraid?" He mildly replied, "I thank God, no!" "But were not your women and children afraid?" He answered, "No! our women and children are not afraid to die!" Dr. Jackson, President of the British Conference, speaking of this occurrence in his Centenary of Methodism, remarks: "In these strangers the English Methodists beheld Christianity in a light more gentle, attractive, and consoling than that in which they had ever before seen it.

"In storms and hurricanes, when others were

ready to die with fear, they calmly sang the praises of God, expressing a cheerful confidence and resignation in the prospect of immediately perishing in the great deep. With the tempers of these people the Wesleys were, at this time, personally unacquainted. Neither of them was delivered from the fear of death, and they had no just conception of the holy cheerfulness which is produced by an application of the blood of Christ to the conscience, and the abiding witness and operations of the heavenly Comforter. Theirs was a religion of fear and mortification, rather than of holy peace and joy."

It was under these circumstances that Mr. Wesley's attention was for the first time arrested to his spiritual condition; and now he realized what he had never done before, the groundlessness of his religious hopes, and his destitution of that religious faith which is necessary to justify the sinner and impart perfect peace to the mind.

The impressions made upon Mr. Wesley by the conduct of these Germans during the voyage were strengthened upon his arrival at Savannah. Here he was introduced to Mr. Spangenburg, one of the Moravian pastors, who had reached that place some time previously. Mr. Wesley immediately applied to this devoted man for advice in reference to his future course. Mr. Spangenburg, in complying with Mr. Wesley's wishes, questioned him very closely concerning his religious experience. This conversation, while it revealed more fully to Mr. Wesley his ignorance of experimental religion, also explained the cause of those fears which he had experienced during the storm at sea. "His heart was not yet right in the sight of God."

It will not be denied that Mr. Wesley received more instruction from the Moravians than from the Salzburgers; and he himself declares that he had derived more light from the Rev. Peter Boehler than from any other man with whom he had ever conversed. But still it will be manifest to every impartial mind that is familiar with all the facts, that Mr. Wesley beheld in the persons of the Germans who were his fellow-passengers, and by far the great majority of whom were Salzburgers, the first practical illustration of the happy influence of genuine piety upon the disposition, affections, and general deportment of those who have experienced it. Whatever benefit Mr. Wesley may have subsequently received from the Moravians, and especially from Mr. Boehler, it is clear, that it was through his intercourse with the Salzburgers and other Germans at sea, under the circumstances already mentioned, that he obtained views of the true state of his own soul which he had never before experienced, and realized for the first time his want of that acceptance with God which is necessary to tranquillize the heart, and give serenity to the conscience, under all the varied circumstances of life.

The question might be asked, why does Mr. Wesley make such particular mention of the "Moravians," and the instructions which he had received from their pastors, while he says nothing of the Salzburgers, who were Lutherans? The answer to this question is, that Mr. Wesley seems not to have distinguished the former from the latter, their characters being so very similar; and hence he speaks of them all as "Germans."

A similar error has been committed by Mr. Bancroft in his history of the United States. In every instance in which he speaks of the German colonists at Ebenezer, he calls them "Moravians." It is time that these false impressions had been removed.

The Moravians never made any permanent settlement in Georgia. When the Spanish war broke out, they removed, almost to a man, to the State of Pennsylvania, because it was contrary to their religious faith to take up arms in any cause. Hence, they never left the impress of their peculiar tenets and usages upon any portion of the colony.

Beside this, the pastors of the Moravians were with them, and it was very natural that Mr. Wesley should look to them for instruction;

but the Salzburgers were unaccompanied by any spiritual teacher, their pastors having been settled at Ebenezer for nearly two years. Now, whatever may have been the causes operating upon Mr. Wesley afterward, and by what means soever he was more fully indoctrinated in the essential principles of Christianity, it must still remain true, that it was at sea, while sailing with the German emigrants, that the practical influence of evangelical religion was first realized by him; and it may not be assuming too much to express the opinion that, but for his intercourse with the *Salzburgers* and other Germans, connected with the peculiar incidents of this voyage, he might have long remained unconscious of his spiritual condition, and he might possibly never have realized it. For, as he himself remarks, "I was ignorant of the nature of saving faith, apprehending it to mean no more than a firm assent to all the propositions contained in the Old and New Testament."

Two years after his first visit to Georgia, Mr. Wesley returned to England, and shortly after his arrival he made the following note in his journal: "It is now two years and nearly four months since I went to America to teach the Georgia Indians the nature of Christianity; but what have I learned of myself in the mean time? why (what of all I least expected) that I, who went to America to convert others, was never myself converted to God." It is a matter of history, that subsequently Mr. Wesley was converted at a prayer-meeting, which he attended among the Moravians in Aldersgate street, London, while one was reading Luther's preface to Paul's Epistle to the Romans, in which the great Reformer has given such a clear elucidation of the doctrine of *justification by faith.*

No sooner was Mr. Wesley converted, than he commenced to preach the great doctrines of repentance and faith, and the necessity of a radical change of heart and life to all who would secure their salvation. The proclamation of these doctrines in England, where religion in the Established Church had degenerated into a lifeless formality, together with the earnest and convincing manner in which he enforced them, aroused against him so strong a prejudice, that he was, as if by common consent, excluded from the churches of the Establishment, and was compelled to preach in the open air. One measure naturally led to another, and soon Mr. Wesley found it necessary to form those "Societies" which afterward became the basis of that ecclesiastical organization known as "Wesleyan Methodism;" a system, whose beneficial effects upon the spiritual condition of the world, have been seen and felt in almost every part of the globe, and will no doubt continue to exert a wider and still wider influence until the end of time.

It is, therefore, not assuming too much, to say that Mr. Wesley's conversion and the establishment of the Methodist Church may be regarded as the legitimate fruits of the Lutheran Reformation. And it is an easy matter, in this view of the subject, to account for the striking similarity which exists between the doctrines of the Lutheran and Methodist churches.

In contemplating these occurrences, we are constrained to admire the mysterious combination of circumstances by which God accomplishes some of his most gracious purposes. We see in the German exiles, who were fellow-passengers with Mr. Wesley, a band of faithful disciples, flying from religious intolerance in the land of their nativity, and seeking for freedom of conscience in a distant country. Going forth upon their pilgrimage, they are, in the providence of God, brought in contact with a personage of great genius and learning, upon whose heart their exemplary deportment and calm and heavenly temperament make a lasting impression; and he subsequently becomes, through the transforming power of the gospel, a chosen instrument, by which is put in motion the greatest moral revolution that has occurred since the Reformation by Luther. Thus, while the Christian pilgrim wanders to and fro in the earth, an outcast from his country, and exposed to privation and danger, he is made to sow, broad-cast as it were, the seed of divine truth; and the fruit of that sowing is seen increasing from generation to generation, and extending even to the latest period of time. Thus strangely, yet wisely, does God execute his merciful designs. "Oh the depth of riches, both of the wisdom and knowledge of God! How unsearchable are his judgments, and his ways past finding out!"

But we must resume the thread of our narrative. The whole embarkation reached Georgia in safety, early in the month of February, 1736. General Oglethorpe proceeded immediately to arrange the colonists, and to send them to their respective places of destination. It would appear that it was originally designed that a great portion of the Salzburgers who came over at this time were to go to the southward, and aid in establishing the town of Frederica, on St. Simon's Island, where it was proposed also to erect a fort and plant a garrison, to protect the frontier settlements. As, however, the Salzburgers manifested an unwillingness to go to the south, General Oglethorpe did not insist upon it. The reasons assigned by these pious men for this course were, that from the rumours which they had heard of the threatened invasion of Georgia by the Spaniards, their position at Frederica might render it necessary for them to take up arms, and as "fighting was against their religion," they preferred not to place themselves in a situation where they would be compelled to do violence to their consciences. Besides, at the new settlement there would be no church, at least not for some time, and they therefore preferred to go to Ebenezer, where a congregation of their own people was already organized, and they could enjoy the instructions of the two pious ministers who resided there. However, although this was the feeling of the great mass of Germans, Captain Hermsdorf succeeded in raising a small company of volunteers, and they offered their services to General Oglethorpe, who requested that they might be put upon any service that might be deemed necessary. This company was accordingly ordered to Frederica, to aid in the defence of that place. It became the nucleus for a Lutheran church, which was organized in 1735, under the pastoral care of the Rev. Ulrich Driesler, a German missionary, sent over by the Trustees, and supported from their funds.

From the conduct of the Salzburgers on this occasion, we may learn something of the spirit which governed all their actions. Their religion taught them that war is inconsistent with the genius of Christianity, and is therefore to be avoided. As their spiritual improvement was of more importance than any worldly advantages which they might enjoy in other portions of the colony, they chose to relinquish these advantages, rather than forego the enjoyment of the preached word and the ordinances of the sanctuary. For these reasons the great majority of the Germans were allowed to go to Ebenezer, which they did without delay. Their arrival was hailed with much joy, and many were the kind greetings which these brethren exchanged upon being brought together under such favourable auspices. Thus, from the 12th of March, 1734, to the 8th of February, 1736, the day on which this last company arrived, about two hundred Salzburgers were settled at Ebenezer.

About this time Messrs. Bolzius and Gronau visited Savannah, to confer with General Oglethorpe in reference to the propriety of changing the location of the town. These gentlemen stated that there was very great dissatisfaction among their people; and they represented the colony at Ebenezer as being in such an unfavourable condition, that the general deemed it advisable for him to visit that place immediately. For this purpose he set out on the 10th of February, in company with the two ministers.

On reaching Ebenezer, where he was received with every mark of consideration due to his station, he patiently inquired into the causes of discontent among the people. These were various.

They had been disappointed in the character of the soil, and their lands had not yielded them any thing like an adequate support. The climate had proved very unhealty, and many of their numbers had fallen victims to disease. Besides, the impracticability of navigating to any advantage the stream upon which their town was located, rendered their situation peculiarly distressing.

These reasons were not without weight, especially the latter. Here it may not be improper to inform the reader of the character of the watercourse upon which the Salzburgers originally settled. It is not properly a *river*, but a *creek*, which at times is swollen to a considerable size; and there is in Georgia hardly another stream so serpentine in its course, and so difficult to traverse. Some idea may be formed on this subject, when it is stated that although the distance from old Ebenezer to the Savannah river by land does not exceed *six miles*, the distance by the course of the creek is not less than *twenty-five*. Farms situated on its banks within two and three miles of each other, cannot be reached by water without travelling five to eight miles. It will thus be seen, that the difficulty of navigating this creek, which was the only outlet to the Savannah river, did furnish reasonable cause for dissatisfaction. The other grounds of complaint were equally worthy of consideration. There had been considerable mortality among the settlers, and the products of their farms had been so inadequate to their wants, that, but for the occasional supplies furnished by the Trustees from the public stores, their situation would have been very deplorable.

General Oglethorpe listened patiently to all the statements of the Salzburgers, and then counselled them with the kindness and frankness of an affectionate parent. He admitted that their dissatisfaction was not groundless, and that there were many embarrassments connected with their situation; but still their situation was not without its advantages. They had cleared their lands, erected dwellings, and made considerable progress with their town. If now they should remove, such a measure would be attended with great trouble and privation. The labour which they had expended would be all lost, and their circumstances, now sufficiently embarrassing, would be rendered still more so by the inconveniences and hardships of making a new settlement. He was also satisfied, from his acquaintance with the situation of the country to which they desired to remove, that as soon as the forests should be cleared, and the lands brought under cultivation, they would again be subject to the diseases peculiar to the climate, and would be forced to leave the neighbourhood. Still, if they persisted in their wishes, he would not oppose them, but would assist them, as far as practicable, in carrying out their designs. Subsequent events proved too painfully, the foresight and correct judgment of General Oglethorpe, and what was then merely an *opinion*, is now a matter of *history*. The general, having discharged his duty, in giving the Salzburgers such advice as was called for by the occasion, returned to Savannah, and left them to adopt such measures as they might deem most likely to promote their comfort and their interest.

Immediately upon the departure of General Oglethorpe, the Salzburgers held a consultation in reference to the expediency of seeking a new settlement. After giving the subject a serious and prayerful consideration, it was decided that it was not only desirable, but absolutely indispensable to the prosperity of the colony, to seek a more favourable locality. Thus, after remaining at old Ebenezer for only two years, it was found necessary to abandon it.

CHAPTER V.

New Ebenezer—Its location, and the plan upon which it was laid out—The environs of the town—Its rapid growth—Municipal and other regulations—Rules originally adopted for the government of the congregation—The duties of pastors set forth—Elders and wardens—Parochial schools—Church members, &c.—Dr. H. M. Muhlenberg—Salaries of the pastors—Their responsibilities—Relation to the church in Germany—Sale of rum prohibited, and the introduction of Negro slaves—Effects of these regulations on the colony at Ebenezer—Mr. Bolzius, Rev. George Whitfield, and Baron Von Reck on slavery—Position of Mr. Bolzius—Views of Hon. James Habersham and Rev. S. Urlsperger—Controversy settled, and slavery allowed—The Salzburgers and the Lutheran Church in Germany—Liberality of the latter—Education—"Bethany" church—Favourable condition of the settlement—Religious character of the inhabitants—Their industry, frugality, &c.—Letter of Mr. Bolzius—Rev. George Whitefield at Ebenezer—His testimony in favour of the Salzburgers—He visits the Orphan House—Letter of Thomas Jones—Principal settlers at Ebenezer, up to 1741—The invasion of Georgia by Spaniards—Another letter of Mr. Bolzius—Extracts from his journal—Statement of Mr. Benjamin Martyn—New arrivals—Emigrants bind themselves as servants—Frederick Helfenstein—Lutheran church in Savannah founded—Rev. U. Driesler—His death—Rev. Mr. Zublii—The town of Frederica—Dr. H. M. Muhlenberg visits Ebenezer—Mr. Gronau—"Jerusalem" church at Ebenezer—"Zion's" church—Extracts from Mr. Bolzius' journal—Death of Mr. Gronau.

THE site selected for a new town was on a high ridge within a short distance of the river, and which, from the peculiar colour of the soil on the margin of the water, was called "Red Bluff." The spot was quite a romantic one. On the east, lay the Savannah with its broad, smooth surface, and its ever-varying and beautiful scenery. On the south was a small stream, then called Little Creek, but now known as Lockner's Creek, and a large lake called "Neidlinger's Sea." While to the north, not very distant from the town, was to be seen their old acquaintance, Ebenezer Creek, sluggishly winding its way to mingle with the waters of the Savannah. The surrounding country was gently undulating, and covered with a fine growth of forest-trees, while the jessamine, the woodbine, and the beautiful azalia, with its variety of gaudy colours, added a peculiar richness to the picturesque scene. But unfortunately for the permament prosperity of the town, it was surrounded on three sides by low swamps, which were subject to periodical inundation, and consequently generated a poisonous miasma prejudicial to the health of the inhabitants.

The new town was laid off after the plan of the city of Savannah, and covered an area of a quarter of a mile square. This space was divided into small squares, each containing ten building lots, and the latter numbered one hundred and sixty. Three wide streets passed through the town from east to west, which were intersected at right angles by four others running from north to south; beside which there were a number of narrow lanes, but these extended in only one direction—north and south. Four squares were appropriated to the sale of produce, and called "market-places," and four were reserved as public parks or promenade grounds. Two-thirds of a square were appropriated to the church, parsonage, and academy, and an equal quantity to the orphan asylum and the public storehouse respectively. On the east, a short distance from the town, was the cemetery. On the north and east was a large pasture for cattle, and on the south was one for sheep and goats. On the north and south, garden-lots were laid out, and still farther south, beyond Little Creek and Mill Creek, and upon their waters, the farms were located, each farm consisting of fifty acres. The country to the north, beyond Ebenezer Creek, was occupied by the Uchee Indians, that section not having been included in any of the grants made by them to the Trustees. The whole plan of the town, with its environs, was well conceived, and one can but admire the great judgment displayed in the whole arrangement.

In the course of a few years, Ebenezer began to give evidences of its future growth and prosperity. Houses were again erected. Gardens and farms were enclosed and brought under cultivation, and the community assumed an air of great activity and industry. Whether it was owing to the want of means, or materials, or both, there was no church erected here for several years; as, however, funds had been received from Germany for the establishment of an orphan asylum, and as that building was among the first that was erected, it was temporarily used as a place of worship.

Having now described the location of "Ebenezer" and its environs, it may be proper here to notice the government under which the colony was placed. As a religious community, the Salzburgers may be properly viewed as a missionary station, under the fostering care of the English Society for the Propagation of Christian Knowledge, and the Evangelical Lutheran Church in Germany. It was required of the pastors and each member of the congregation to subscribe to the "Augsburg Confession" and the "Symbolical Books," and to submit to a code of regulations drawn up by the Rev. Samuel Urlsperger of Augsburg, Rev. Frederick M. Zeigenhagen of London, and Rev. Gotthelf Augustus Francké of Halle. These regulations were prepared in 1733, and continued in force, with some few alterations, (which were made principally by Dr. Muhlenburg, in 1774,) until 1843. It is not asserting too much to say, that no better church-discipline is needed than that laid down in these regulations.

We insert here a copy of the original rules, with a view to show the character of the discipline which our pious forefathers adopted for the government of the churches. It is worthy of preservation, both on account of its antiquity and its intrinsic excellence. It reads thus:

"In the name of God:—The fundamental constitution, articles, and rules upon which a German Evangelical Lutheran congregation was formally established, upon the basis of the Holy Bible, our Augsburg Confession, (and the other Symbolical Books,) since the year 1733, in and about Ebenezer, in His Great Britannic Majesty's province of Georgia; and which were unanimously approved, confirmed, and unalterably determined upon, under hand and seal, by the reverened founders, viz. Messrs. Samuel Urlsperger, Frederick Michael Zeigenhagen, Gotthelf Augustus Francké, most worthy members of the venerable society in England, instituted for the promotion of the knowledge of Christ; together with the first ministers, elders, deacons, and regular church-members, His Great Britannic Protestant Majesty's faithful subjects. (Vide Preface to the first article of the Americanische Ackerwerck Gottes, p. 3.)

CHAPTER I.

"That no congregation can preserve its establishment and regulations, and maintain good order for the furtherance of its true interests, unless there be elected as deacons men who are members of the congregation, and who have both the qualifications and authority to provide for the maintenance of good regulation and wholesome discipline of the whole congregation, is taught by sound reason, the Holy Scriptures, and experience. Therefore, as we are taught in the important admonition contained in the last verse of the fourteenth chapter of 1 Cor.: 'Let all things be done decently and orderly,' (or in accordance with good regulations and decorum.) And that we may be the more encouraged to obey this injunction, the holy apostle declares, in the twenty-eighth verse of the twelfth chapter, preceding, 'that God, being a God of order in his churches purchased with a precious price, appointed not only apostles, prophets, and ministers,' but also adjutors and rulers: that is, men highly gifted and favoured, who have, both by word and in deed, contributed, as the wants and ordinances of the churches required, every thing that was possible for the good regulation and the maintainment of the churches. It is also a fact, clearly taught by the word of God, that such men were appointed in the church of God, even in the Old Testament dispensation, from the time of Moses, for the purpose of maintaining good order. Accordingly, it is in perfect keeping with the will of God and the example, not only of the primitive, but also of the succeeding Christian churches, that such church elders, or adjutors and rulers, have been jointly elected by the whole congregation; also among us, whose duty it is to promote the best interests of this our parish, as is directed by the English ecclesiastical canon. As, however, our congregation does not properly belong to the English Church, and consequently cannot, in all points, exist under its ecclesiastical canon, but must enact its own regulations for the worship of God and for edification, it becomes necessary for the members of our congregation to invest the proposed church-elders, as is the practice of the Evangelical Lutheran Church in London, (and others which need not be mentioned,) with special authority to support our congregation; and intrust to them also their establishments and regulations. For all this, if made incumbent upon the ministers alone, is a burden far too onerous and insupportable.

"If, now, men thus chosen and empowered are to promote by word and in deed, both the existence and the welfare of the congregation, so that it may endure and be maintained by its establishments and regulations; and as such well-being of the congregation cannot be promoted without means, it follows quite naturally, that the requisite means must be placed in their hands by the members of the congregation, as is done by the Evangelical Lutheran Congregation in London, before alluded to, and also by all other Christian congregations.

"Hence, inasmuch as the government, or the English ecclesiastical constitution, provides nothing for this purpose, and as, in consequence of the troublesome and warlike times in our German fatherland, we cannot, with certainty, expect as much aid as was received in former years from our beloved benefactors in Germany, toward the maintainment of our church and school establishments, and also toward the alleviation of the wants of the poor and sick, it becomes a stern demand of necessity, that is, the honour of God and our spiritual welfare require, that the members of the congregation bind themselves, in love, mutually to contribute from year to year as much money as is and will continue to be requisite to the support of the school-teachers, and the preservation of the church and school edifices and the parsonage. Those persons, therefore, who are members of the congregation, and who are desirous of participating in its spiritual benefit and privileges, will, it is hoped, also be disposed to lend their assistance in bearing the expenses of the congregation, by contributing cheerfully their share toward the sustainment of the said proposed regulations and establishments. Those, however, who are unwilling to take upon themselves any of the labours, and who will not perform what is their covenant duty with feelings of gratitude, notwithstanding their ability to do so, debar themselves and their families, by these very means from the congregation and its spiritual benefits; which will not surely tend to their advantage: 'God loveth a cheerful giver.' 'He that soweth bountifully, shall reap also bountifully." 2 Cor. ix. 6, 7, 8; (ix. 10.) Such as are members of this our evangelical congregation, and are willing to contribute as much as may, from time to time be found requisite, according to the amount which the appointed church-deacons may compute and deem proper, toward the support of the school-teachers, the parsonage, the church, and school edifices, and also the supplying of any other necessities, will please subscribe their names to this writing, and annex the sum that they will give. And as, through the gracious providence of God, our beloved inhabitants have, in this respect, a great advantage in point of privilege and ease from cares over many other Christian congregations, because they are not required to compensate their pastors, nor minister to their temporal support, it is expected that they will be the more prompt in contributing their quota toward the sustainment of the above regulations and establishments, which are designed for the support of the congregation and the upholding of the worship of God. They should even rejoice that the opportunity is afforded them to manifest the activity of their faith, through the love of God, to his word, the church, and the schools; but when there is no active love, there is no true faith. 'Show me thy faith by thy works.' James ii. 18.

"Finally, touching the office and duties of the church-elders, in regard to the ministers in the churches, the teachers in the schools, the whole congregation, and the money intrusted to them, it shall, in conclusion, be indicated in the words of the printed London German Church Discipline, given to us, altered, however, in several instances, to accord with our peculiar circumstances, as follows:—

"1st. They shall employ the utmost diligence in providing that the word of God be declared unto the Christians of our congregation, in its purity and without admixture, by pious teachers and ministers; that the holy sacraments enjoined and instituted by our Lord Jesus Christ be administered, and that the pure doctrines be preserved and transmitted to our posterity. And in order that this object may be attained, some of them, at least, in case all cannot, shall always be present when the word is preached.

"2d. It shall be their duty to see that the school-teachers receive duly their stipulated salary semi-anuually: likewise, that every thing else which may concern the congregation be fully performed. For this purpose they shall also collect, half-yearly, the contributions of the congregation, and enter the receipts regularly into the church register. They shall also, semi-annually, receive from the parents whose children receive instruction in the schools, a certain amount of payment for tuition, proportionate to their means; so that the contribution of the whole congregation for the defrayment of the congregational expenses, may be somewhat diminished.

"3d. The church-deacons shall make it their duty, in conjunction with the ministers, to see that all sins, disgraceful conduct, and scandal be avoided; or, otherwise, duly punished and corrected.

"4th. They shall keep a particular account of all expenditures made on behalf of the congregation, and also of every thing which any one may have voluntarily vowed or promised to give toward the support of the churches. And, after the expiration of his office, each one shall submit his account to all the other church-deacons collectively.

"5th. They shall, at the end of the year, and when leaving their office and service, render an account to the contributing portion of the congregation, of all the money which they received during their official year for the use of the church; so that each one may know how the funds of the congregation are applied and expended, and thus be the more willing to contribute again.

"6th. They shall submit the church register to the inspection of any one of the contributors who may desire to see how the money has been employed.

"7th. Those church-deacons who have served their term of office shall be in duty bound to assist on all occasions, by word or deed, at the meetings of the deacons and of the congregation, if desired; and when cited to do so, they shall appear without refusal.

"8th. The church-deacons newly inducted, and at all times those coming into office successively, shall also be held responsible for the performance and fulfilment of all measures which may have been resolved and agreed upon by their predecessors, conducive to the tranquillity, peace, prosperity, and advantage of the congregation.

"9th. On those Sabbaths when the Lord's Supper is administered, they shall also stand at the doors of the church with suitable vessels (dishes or bowls) to receive and collect from the congregation while leaving the church, gifts and contributions for the benefit of the church and the poor. It is also reasonably expected that not only residents should contribute something for the administration of the rite of baptism, the performance of the marriage ceremony, and for the celebration of the Lord's Supper, but strangers should also be held to the performance of this duty. For if the congregation is not sustained by its institutions, these can also not enjoy the privileges mentioned.

"These above-mentioned deacons, of whom not less than seven shall be elected annually from among the members of our Evangelical Lutheran congregation, conscientiously and according to the best of their knowledge, have the power to apply the money intrusted to them to this purpose; yet, in very important matters, as when a church is to be built, or an important repair is to be undertaken, &c., the acquiesence and approval of the whole congregation convened in mass must be obtained. To these establishments may God, who is a God of order, add his heavenly grace, for the sake of Jesus Christ! Amen."

It has been stated that this was the original discipline, subsequently amended by Dr. Muhlenburg in 1774. It is impossible to state to what extent it was altered, but that Dr. Muhlenburg made some additions to it, and changed several of the articles, cannot be questioned. In another place it will be necessary to refer again to the subject of church discipline, when a synopsis will be given of the one signed by the pastors, elders, and deacons, and all the male members of church, in 1774 and 1775.

It will be seen, from this extract, that the principal objects for which collections were made in the congregation, were the proper support of schools, the relief of widows, orphans, and the superannuated, and the maintenance of the church edifice, whenever erected. It is worthy of remark that the salaries for the support of the pastors at Ebenezer were for many years contributed by the patrons of the church in Germany. At first, the amount allowed was about forty pounds for the senior pastor, and thirty pounds for his assistant. This allowance continued until 1770, when Rev. Mr. Urlsperger decided that the salaries should not be less than sixty pounds and fifty pounds, respectively, and that the deficiency should be made up from the revenues arising from those institutions which had been founded by European benefactions.

The civil and military affairs of the entire colony, including the settlements at Ebenezer, Savannah, Frederica, &c., were under the control of the Trustees, who, through their agent, General Oglethorpe, assigned lands to the colonists, planned and laid off towns, built fortifications, and so regulated the whole industrial economy as in his judgment was best calculated to promote the welfare of the settlers and carry out the designs of the Trustees.

The immediate superintendence of the settlement at Ebenezer was assigned to the Rev. John Martin Bolzius and his colleague, Mr. Gronau; and we doubt very much if the affairs of the colony could have been more judiciously managed than they were by these eminently pious and prudent men. Their duties were at times not only arduous, but distressingly embarrassing; but they performed them with a conscientious faithfulness worthy of all praise, and with a degree of success that is truly surprising. Sustaining an indirect relation to the Trustees in England, and a direct connection with the society above mentioned, (from whom they derived part of their support,) as well as with the Lutheran Church in Germany, and having to superintend and manage the civil, as well as the ecclesiastical interests of the colony, it required no small degree of judgment and discretion to meet the wishes of their benefactors in England and their Christian friends and advisers in Germany. But we believe they fulfilled their trust to the satisfaction of all parties.

Among the municipal regulations adopted by the "Trustees," was one forbidding the introduction and sale of rum, and another inhibiting the importation of Negro slaves. The enforcement of these measures was attended with very serious difficulty in all parts of the colony, except at Ebenezer. The first measure was one, the propriety of which the Salzburgers never questioned. Temperance societies were then unknown; but no such agency was necessary to teach our pious ancestors that the use of alcoholic drinks is attended with incalculable evils, and that the most specific remedy for these evils, is not to pass license laws *to regulate* the sale of spirits, but to remove entirely the *cause* that produced them. It is mentioned as a striking fact in the subsequent history of Ebenezer, that the exclusion of ardent spirits had contributed materially to promote the health of the inhabitants, while sickness prevailed in all those places where the sale was permitted. We wish that this wholesome regulation had always been enforced, not only at Ebenezer, but throughout our country; and especially that the descendants of the Salzburgers had always imitated, in this respect, the example of their pious forefathers.

It is difficult to ascertain fully the grounds upon which the Salzburgers opposed so strenuously, and for so many years, the introduction of Negro slaves. Whether their own history, with its many scenes of wrong and oppression, had predisposed them against every species of servitude, or whether they judged that the existence of slaves among them would render the colonists indolent, and perhaps weaken and embarrass their community by exposing it to the evils of a servile war, are questions which it would not be easy to answer satisfactorily. We may, however, gather some instruction from a remark of Baron Von Reck. He says, in one of his letters, "The purchase of Negroes is forbidden, on account of the vicinity of the Spaniards. The colony also is an asylum for the distressed, and slaves starve the poor labourer."

It is a matter of history, however, which need not to be disguised, that the Salzburgers, including their pastors, did very warmly oppose the importation of slaves; and if the question had been left for them to decide, without any influences from abroad being employed to bias their minds, slavery would not have existed in the colony. Mr. Bolzius was, perhaps, among the very last to yield his opposition. He even reproved Mr. Whitefield very sharply, for his vacillation, in changing his opinions, after having in the first instance expressed his disapprobation of this measure, and then subsequently favouring it. Mr. Whitefield denied having any participation in the matter, and said that he believed, with Pope, "Whatever is, is best;" that God had some wise ends to accomplish in reference to African slavery; and that he had no doubt it would terminate in advantage to the Africans.

When Pastor Bolzius yielded his objections to this measure, the ground which he assumed, as far as we can learn from his letters, was as follows:—He admitted that there was wrong, in the abstract, to place our fellow-men in a state of bondage; yet if, by removing the African from the heathenism of his native land to a country where his mind would be enlightened by the gospel, and provision made for the salvation of his soul, the evils of slavery might be endured in consideration of the moral and spiritual advantages which it bestows upon its unfortunate victims. By this mode of reasoning, and by means of an essay from the pen of James Habersham, Esq., the Salzburgers, including their pastors, after considerable hesitation, consented to have slaves brought into the colony. They did not do so, however, until after they had freely conferred with their Christian friends in Germany. The Rev. S. Urlsperger, in advising them upon this subject, says: "If you take slaves in faith, and with the intent of conducting them to Christ, the action will not be a sin, but may prove a 'benediction.'" This advice determined their future course in reference to this important question. The discussion of this subject had, however, produced great excitement in the colony. In the language of another, "The whole province dwelt, as it were, on the brink of a volcano, whose intestine fires raged higher and higher, threatening at no distant period a desolating eruption." It was under these circumstances, and when the community seemed to be on the brink of a civil war, that Mr. Bolzius wrote to the Trustees, withdrawing, on behalf of himself and the Salzburgers, their objection to the repeal of the law.

We have already intimated that the Lutheran congregation at Ebenezer was connected with the church in Germany, and it was accordingly required that the pastors should keep up a regular correspondence, especially with the authorities at Augsburg and Halle, which were then the two principal Protestant cities on the continent. This correspondence contained a minute detail of all the occurrences at Ebenezer, and the most important part of it was published in the Nachrichten of Rev. S. Urlsperger, of Augsburg, and much of it is still extant.

But while the church in Germany kept up its ecclesiastical connection with the church at Ebenezer, and sought to direct its spiritual affairs, it was not backward in raising means for its maintenance. Even prior to the emigration of the Salzburgers, collections had been taken up in various parts of Germany, and after their settlement at Ebenezer they continued to receive donations from their transatlantic brethren;

and such was the liberality displayed toward them, that a church fund was raised amounting to twelve thousand guilders, for the support of the pastors, and other benevolent purposes.

It ought to be mentioned that, in the establishment of the colony, the cause of education was not overlooked, and in every instance in which a pastor was sent over, a schoolmaster accompanied him, unless one was already provided. A fund, too, was subsequently created for his support; for our pious forefathers judged, and very correctly too, that no country can prosper in which provision is not made for the mental culture and improvement of the rising generation. Thus we find that there was a regular school kept up during the lifetime of Mr. Bolzius and many years afterward, at Ebenezer, and one at Zion's Church, four miles below Ebenezer. Subsequently, when the church called "Bethany" was built on the bluff above Ebenezer, a schoolhouse was also erected, and a fund established for the support of the teacher. From this it will be seen how much importance was attached to the subject of education, and how careful the Salzburgers were to make provision for the support of their teachers. In this respect there is another striking parallel between the Salzburgers and the Puritans of New England; and if the former had been as favourably situated as the latter, there is no doubt that they would have accomplished fully as much in making provision for the proper intellectual training of their offspring. At all events, they showed most conclusively that they had enlightened and liberal views upon the subject of education, and employed every means in their power to promote it.

Such were the circumstances under which the colony at Ebenezer was commenced. The foundation was laid by the Trustees for the colonization of Georgia, aided by the Society for the Propagation of Christian Knowledge, and the liberal donations of Christian friends in Germany. Let us now take a look at this little community. In the year 1736 the place began to assume the appearance of a village, giving evidence, by its neat cottages, of the presence of civilization almost in the midst of savage tribes of Indians. Within its precincts stand the school-house for the education of the children, and the asylum for the widow and orphan, within whose walls the pastors and their flocks, as yet, meet for the worship of God. There, too, is the comfortable parsonage, in which dwell those holy men whose greatest happiness is derived from the spiritual prosperity of their people, and who labour patiently and unremittingly for the temporal and eternal welfare of those committed to their charge, pointing them, by their precept and example, to a holier and happier state above. The people, too, are obedient to the voice of their shepherds. They receive their instructions respectfully and dutifully; and yielding their hearts to the influences of Christian principles, they become "living epistles" to the power of our holy religion to change the heart and regulate the conduct.

One cannot well conceive of a community more happily constituted than this was. The civil and municipal laws were few and simple; their church-discipline scriptural and rigid. At the head of the community stand the pastors and elders of the congregation. These constitute the umpire before which all questions both civil and religious are brought; and such is the integrity of those who compose this tribunal, and such the prudence and wisdom and impartiality which characterize all their proceedings, that their decisions are always satisfactory, and no appeals are ever made from their judgment.

Under these circumstances Ebenezer, as might have been expected, was destined to enjoy, for a season at least, a good measure of prosperity. Its inhabitants were not only accustomed to hardships, but being industrious and frugal in their habits, and living always in the fear of God, they possessed within themselves all those elements necessary to the success of any enterprise. It is true, there were many difficulties to be surmounted at the outset, arising from the want of arable land and the scarcity of provisions; but as soon as their lands could be brought under cultivation, which was done in this and the following year, and a communication opened with the city of Savannah, which was effected by the purchase of a boat for that purpose, their circumstances were greatly improved.

Their easy access, too, to the river, which abounded with fish and wild-fowl, enabled them to obtain supplies of food, which tended greatly to relieve their necessities.

That the reader may form some idea of the condition of affairs at Ebenezer about this time, the following letter from Pastor Bolzius, dated the 13th of February, 1738, is inserted: "With great satisfaction we perceive that, through the grace of God, general contentment prevails among our people. The longer they are here the better they are pleased; and we are sure their utmost wishes will be gratified when they shall be able to live by their own industry.

"They are satisfied, because they are enjoying the privileges which they had long sought in vain—to have the word of God in its purity. Our heavenly Father will perhaps provide the means for building a house for worship. At present we worship in the Orphan-House, and feel that God is with us."

It was about this period that the celebrated George Whitefield visited Ebenezer. Speaking of the state of the colony, he remarks: "Their lands are surprisingly improved. They are also blessed with two such pious ministers as I have seldom seen. They have no courts of jurisdiction, but all differences are immediately settled by their pastors. They have an orphan-house, in which are seventeen children and a widow."

With the orphans' school Mr. Whitefield was very much gratified. He had it in contemplation to establish a similar institution in Georgia, for the benefit of the numerous orphans whom he found in Savannah and its vicinity. His heart had first been directed to this subject by what he had heard and read in reference to the celebrated orphan-house founded at Halle, by Dr. Franke. When he visited the Orphans' Asylum at Ebenezer, he was so much pleased, that his purposes were confirmed, and he projected his orphan-house, which he called Bethesda. This was located about eight miles from Savannah.

While on the visit above alluded to, Mr. Whitefield was so much delighted with the order and harmony at Ebenezer, that he gave part of his own "poor stores" to Mr. Bolzius, to be distributed among his orphans. Mr. Whitefield thus describes the scene: "Mr. Bolzius called all the children before him; catechized and exhorted them to give thanks to God for his good providence toward them; then prayed with them, and made them pray after him; then sung a psalm. *Afterwards the little lambs came and shook me by the hand one by one, and so we parted!"*

Mr. Whitefield never forgot this visit to the Salzburgers; and he became so deeply interested in their welfare, that a year or two afterward he interested himself to procure an English teacher for one of their schools, and offered to educate two pious young men in his orphan-house, whom the pastors at Ebenezer might select for this purpose.

In a letter written by Mr. Thomas Jones, dated Savannah, Georgia, on the 18th of September, 1740, occur the following remarks: "Thirty miles distance from this place is Ebenezer, a town on the Savannah river, inhabited by Salzburgers and other Germans, under the pastoral care of Mr. Bolzius and Mr. Gronau, who are discreet, worthy men: they consist of sixty families and upward. The town is neatly built, the situation exceedingly pleasant; the people live in the greatest harmony with their ministers and with one another, as one family. They have no drunken, idle, or profligate people among them, but are industrious, and many have grown wealthy. Their industry has been blessed with remarkable and uncommon success, to the envy of their neighbours, having great plenty of all the necessary conveniences for life (except clothing) within themselves; and supply this town (Savannah) with bread-kind, as also beef, veal, pork, poultry, &c."

For the gratification of the reader, and especially for the benefit of the descendants of the Salzburgers, we subjoin a list of the principal residents at Ebenezer in 1741:

Rev. John Martin Bolzius,
Rev. Israel Christian Gronau,
Bartholomew Reiser,
Bartholomew Zant,
Thomas Goswandel,
Gabriel Maurer,
John Maurer,
George Kogler,
Paulus Zittrauer,
Peter Reuter,
Stephen Rottenberger,
Ambrosü Zubli,
John Jacob Zubli,
Christopher Ortman,
Ruprecht Kalcher,
Leonard Rauner,
Christian Reidelsperger,
Frederick Wilhelm Müller,
Martin Hortzog,
Christian Hessler,
John Pletter,
Frank Sigismund,
John Hernberger,
George Bruckner,
Carl Sigismund Ott,
Matthias Zettler,
Ruprecht Eischberger,
John Peter Arnsdorff,
Simon Reiter,
Matthias Brandner,
Christian Leimberger,
Martin Lackner,
Luprctcht Steiner,
Veitt Lemmenhoffer,
John and Carl Floerl,
Ruprecht Zimmerman,
Simon Steiner,
George Schwaiger,
John Schmidt,
Leonard Crause,
Peter Gruber,
Jacob Schartner,
Joseph Leitner,
John Cornberger,
Andreas Grimminger,
Matthias Bergsteiner,
Veitt Landseller,
Joseph Ernst,
John Michael Reiser,
Thomas Pichler,
John Speilbiegler.

The invasion of Georgia by the Spaniards, about this time, created considerable excitement throughout the colony; and the Salzburgers not only sympathized with their English neighbours, but cheerfully contributed to the defence of the country, and bore their part of all the burdens and inconveniences incident upon such occasions. Still they never lost sight of the object of their removal to America. They seem, however, not to have been very seriously embarrassed by the war, as may be learned from a letter of Mr. Bolzius, dated the 23d of July, 1740, addressed to Dr. Franke, of Halle. He says, in that letter:

"Together with these spiritual blessings and the salutary effect of the word of God, in the conversion of many souls, we enjoy this year also, by the mercy of God, many temporal good things. The present war, and the burden of it, has not affected us much as yet, and in the great dearness the colony suffered last year we have not been in want of necessary provision. As to the present year, we have a very hopeful prospect of a good harvest, every thing in the fields and gardens growing so delightful as we have never seen before in this country. If Isaac, by the blessing of the Lord, received from what he had sowed an hundred fold, I believe I dare say, to the glory of God, our Salzburgers will receive a thousand-fold, notwithstanding the corn when it came out of the ground was entirely eaten up by worms, of which no one can form a right idea, unless he sees it with his own eyes. The land is really very fruitful, if the sins of the inhabitants, and the curse of God for such sins, does not eat it up, which was formerly the unhappy case of the blessed land of Canaan.

"And I am heartily sorry to acquaint you, that I do not find in some of the inhabitants of the colony, a due thankfulness for, and contentment with, the many blessings bestowed on them for several years together; although those who are industrious and will labour for their maintenance may, as we do, live contentedly and subsist under the blessing promised by Paul, (Heb. xiii. 5,) 'I will never leave thee nor forsake thee;' which blessing the idle and unthankful are not entitled to."

In the journal of Pastor Bolzius is found the following minute: "*10th of August*, 1741.—We have this year plenty of peaches, and as this fruit does not keep, some of the people try to make a sort of brandy of them; others give them to the swine. This is more than anybody could have promised himself or others some years ago. Even at this time when I am writing, a man brings a large dish of blue grapes to me, grown wild in the woods; they are of a sweet taste, and pretty like our European grapes, so that I am very apt to believe, the wild vines, if properly managed, would give good wine. Thanks to our gracious God, who gives us here every good thing for our support!"

"*9th of September*, 1741.—Some time ago I

wrote to an honoured friend in Europe, that the land in this country, if well managed, brings forth by the blessing of God, not only a hundred-fold, but a thousand-fold; and I was this day confirmed therein. A woman, having two years ago picked out of Indian corn no more than three grains of rye, and planting them here at Ebenezer, one of these grains produced an hundred and seventy stalks and ears, and yielded to her a bag of corn as large as a coat pocket.

"True it is, notwithstanding the fertility of the land, the first tillers of it must undergo and struggle with great difficulties; but those that come after them will reap the benefit thereof, if they go on to do their labour in the fear of God. The land is able to provide every good, and more particularly is pasturage very plenteous."

From these extracts it will be seen that the settlement at Ebenezer and its vicinity was fully as prosperous as could have been expected under the circumstances. Additions were constantly making to it by new arrivals of emigrants from the fatherland. It appears, from a statement made by Mr. Benjamin Martyn, Secretary of the Trustees, that up to 1741, over twelve hundred German Protestants had arrived in the colony. Most of these were sent over by the charity of their friends in England and Germany. There were, however, many who came in 1735, and subsequently, for whom no provision was made. So anxious, however, were they to escape persecution in their native land and find an asylum in Georgia, that they consented to bind themselves as servants to the Trustees, for five years after their arrival in Georgia, and to pay by their own labour the expense of their transportation. In fact, the indentures which they made bound not only themselves, but their children. The males who were under twenty were to serve until they were twenty-five, and the females who were above six were to serve until they arrived at the age of eighteen years.

These conditions, however, were not always rigidly enforced, for it appears, from the minutes of the Trustees, that on the 26th of July, 1742, a petition was presented to that body signed by Christian Steinharel, Theobald Keiffer, and others, stating that their term of service had expired, and praying the Trustees to grant them the freedom of their children at the expiration of the time (five years) for which the petitioners were bound. To the credit of the Trustees, it should ever be remembered, the prayer was granted.

Among the Salzburgers who were sold, and whose children were apprenticed, was one, who, from the romantic history connected with his family, deserves, perhaps, special mention.

This was Mr. Frederick Helfenstein. If the *tradition* in reference to him is correct, he was a lineal descendant of the Count of Helfenstein, who, with his wife (a daughter of the Emperor Maximilian) and their youngest child, were butchered with seventy men under his command, in the servile insurrection which occurred in the time of Luther, commonly known as "the Rebellion of the Peasantry." From that time the family were reduced to utter obscurity and the most abject poverty. Mr. Helfenstein, perhaps the last of the count's descendants, having served out an apprenticeship at the *tanner's* trade, and married a young lady to whom he became attached while learning his trade, emigrated to America, and arrived in Savannah without the means to pay his passage. Consequently he and his wife were sold as servants to defray the expenses of their passage. Having faithfully served out his time, he removed to Goshen, about twelve miles below Ebenezer, and established himself in business. In the course of time he acquired a handsome competency. But it will be necessary to speak of him hereafter.

Many of the Salzburgers remained in Savannah and its vicinity, and formed the nucleus for the organization of a church in that city. It was, however, regarded for a long time as missionary ground, and the congregation was supplied with preaching, from time to time, by the pastors at Ebenezer, and the Rev. U. Driesler, from Frederica.

This gentleman (Mr. Driesler) had been sent over in 1743, by "the Society for the Propagation of Christian Knowledge," to supply the spiritual wants of the Salzburgers, who had settled on St. Simon's Island. In 1744, he visited the brethren at Ebenezer. Mr. Bolzius thus speaks of him, under date of Febuary 24, 1744: "Mr. Driesler arrived yesterday. He labours with the blessing of God in his small congregation at Frederica, consisting of sixty-two souls. Captain Horten, the commandant of the fort at that place, gives him an honourable testimony; and we trust our friend will be an instrument to the salvation of many souls. Next Lord's day he is to preach in Savannah. This day he preaches both in Zion and Jerusalem churches."

Mr. Driesler was spared to the congregation at Frederica but a short time. The Lord called him to his rest in the early part of the year 1745. He was succeeded by the Rev. Mr. Zubli, from Switzerland, who had charge of the church for several years. He seems to have had no connection with the pastors at Ebenezer, and was probably supported by the English officers commanding the fort. Mr. Zubli continued pastor at Frederica only a few years, for as soon as the

Spanish and French war began, he removed to Orangeburg, in South Carolina.*

It has been found impracticable to gather much information in regard to the German settlement at Frederica. It must, however, have been very flourishing at one time. A gentleman who visited the island in 1743, makes particular mention "of the quiet village of the Salzburgers;" and says, "the whole town and country adjacent are quite rurally charming; and the improvements everywhere evince the greatest skill and industry, considering its late settlement." This beautiful town was, however, destined to an ephemeral existence. As early as 1749 it began to decline, and in 1751 a journalist describes it "as presenting the melancholy prospect of houses without inhabitants, barracks without soldiers, guns without carriages, and streets grown over with weeds. All appeared to me with a horrible aspect, and so different from what I once knew it, that I could scarce refrain from tears."

It was about this time that Dr. H. M. Muhlenberg first visited Ebenezer. He had, up to 1741, been pastor of Hermersdorf, in Upper Lusatia, and inspector of the orphan-house in that place, but had accepted a call to the Lutheran church in Philadelphia. The object of his journey to Ebenezer is not definitely stated, but

---
* White.

it is probable that he had been authorized by the friends and patrons of the Salzburgers in Germany to look into the condition of the colony, and report to them the result of his observations. He remained only six days, but even this short sojourn seems to have been highly gratifying to the pastors at Ebenezer, as well as their people, for Pastor Gronau makes special mention of it in his journal. He remarks: "This day (October 11, 1742) my dear colleague (Mr. Bolzius) and Mr. Muhlenberg were to start for Charleston, but evening came on before things were ready. The day had not, however, been spent in vain. The preparations for the journey having been made, my colleague took leave of us in a prayer.

"Never before have we spent so blessed and happy a season at Ebenezer. For the Lord had never before permitted us to embrace a dear friend from our native country, in whom we found a real brother in Christ." Mr. Bolzius accompanied Dr. Muhlenberg as far as Charleston, but returned in a few days to his field of labour.

It has been stated that for many years the Salzburgers were unable to build a church, and were compelled to worship in the orphan-house; but, through the assistance of their friends in Germany, they had succeeded in erecting a plain but comfortable house at Ebenezer, called "Jerusalem," and another about four miles below, called "Zion." The latter had become necessary, because the colonists were rapidly settling on the river below the town, and along the road leading from Ebenezer to Savannah. These churches were both in use in 1744.

It would be profitable, if it were deemed expedient, to make copious extracts from the journals of the pastors, to show the character of the instructions which they imparted to their people; or rather to exhibit the deep-toned piety which the pastors at Ebenezer cultivated themselves, and which they sought to impart to their people. We may safely challenge a comparison between the ministrations of these devoted men, and those of any pastors in any other churches in point of fidelity and earnestness, in inculcating not only a refined and elevated morality, but more especially a pure and transforming system of *evangelical Christianity*. Mr. Bolzius states that a little girl came to him, confessing that she had stolen a peach, and that conscience disturbed her so much on that account, that she could neither sleep nor work. I informed her, says Mr. Bolzius, that when the commission of what is generally considered a light sin disturbs our conscience, a fire begins to burn within us like the fires of hell, and then we no longer think of the distinctions between gross and trivial sins. I advised her to learn that God frequently improves the occasion of a wrong lately committed by us to bring to our mind the mass of sin that fills our hearts, so that we may repent, and ask his forgiveness for Christ's sake. Finally, I dismissed her by bringing the following text to her recollection. "If we confess our sins, God is faithful and just to forgive us our sins, and to cleanse us from all unrighteousness."*

Such a course of religious training was not without its influence in forming the characters and regulating the conduct of the colonists. In fact, they became everywhere proverbial for the correctness of their external deportment, and especially for the Christian spirit which they displayed on all occasions. The testimony of their neighbours, of the citizens of Savannah, and even that of the colonial government, furnishes evidence that the congregation at Ebenezer had acquired a very enviable reputation for their unostentatious piety. Amid their trials and privations they never lost sight of their spiritual improvement, and laboured sedulously to attain to a high standard of Christian experience and practice.

These pious people, however, were about to experience a severe loss in the death of one of their devoted and godly pastors—Rev. Israel

---

* Hazelius.

C. Gronau. This melancholy event occurred in the month of January, 1745; Pastor Bolzius, thus records the mournful event: "Last Friday, January 11th, it pleased the Lord to call my dear brother and colleague to his rest. He fell asleep full of joy in his Saviour. On a stormy and rainy day, nearly a year since, while preaching to the Germans in Savannah, he caught cold at church, so that he was hardly able to perform service here the succeeding Sabbath. From the effects of that attack he never recovered. During the last six weeks of his life he was afflicted with a continued fever. The time of his illness was a source of edification to all of us who were daily about his person. His heart continually enjoyed communion with his Redeemer. Nothing troubled him, for he had an abiding sense of reconciliation with God, and realized the joy and peace of the Holy Ghost."

When one of the Salzburg brethren took hold of his hand, which Mr. Gronau had lifted up in praise of God, he desired that the friend might support his arms in the uplifted position in which he had held them. This being done, he exclaimed, "Come, Lord Jesus! Amen, Amen!" With these words he closed his lips and eyes, and entered into the "joy of his Lord, full of peace." On the following day, his remains were interred in the cemetery connected with Jerusalem church, amid the unfeigned lamentations of his colleague and the people for whose temporal and spiritual advantage he had laboured with unremitting diligence and fidelity. As he had in all things "adorned the doctrine of God his Saviour," so he went to the grave full of hope, leaving the testimony that "God was with him."

CHAPTER VI.

State of feeling at Ebenezer consequent on the death of Mr. Gronau—Mr. Bolzius writes to Germany for an assistant—His humility and devotion—The church in Germany send over another pastor—Rev. H. H. Lembke arrives at Ebenezer—His reception—Marries the widow of Mr. Gronau—Mr. Bolzius retains his position—Mr. Bolzius, as trustee, erects mills—Silk culture introduced at Ebenezer—Mr. Amatis of Piedmont—Mulberry trees planted at Ebenezer—Success of the Salzburgers in raising silk—Bridge and causeway over Ebenezer Creek—New church and school-house erected—Pastoral labours—Extent of the field to be cultivated—Goshen church—Abercorn—Extension of the settlements around Ebenezer—Demand for more ministerial labour—Rev. C. Rabenhorst arrives at Ebenezer—Mr. Bolzius's letter on his arrival—Change of views—Provision for the support of the new pastor—Condition of the colony—Mr. Bolzius assigns his trusteeship to Mr. Lembke—Copy of the deed of trust—The "Trust" to be transferred—Subsequent change—Erection of another mill—Mr. Bolzius begins to decline in health—The symbolical books—Proper views in relation to the "Fathers"—Confessions and catechisms—Deep-toned piety of the first pastors at Ebenezer—Mr. Bolzius's labours—His letters—Rev. S. Urlsperger and Dr. Zeigenhagen—Close of his ministerial duties—His illness and death—Mr. Bolzius's family.

As was to have been expected, the death of Mr. Gronau cast quite a gloom over the settlement at Ebenezer. By his consistent Christian deportment, he had gained the confidence and esteem of the whole community. He was particularly endeared to those who had come over from Germany under his care, and for whose welfare he had made so many sacrifices. Upon no one, however, did the loss seem to fall so heavily as upon his colleague, Mr. Bolzius. They had been united by the strongest ties of friendship and Christian affection, and had laboured together for *thirteen* years under circumstances which were well calculated to unite them in indissoluble bonds. Impelled by a sense of duty to their divine Master, they had in company left their native land, to become the spiritual guides of a devoted and persecuted people. They had been fellow-sufferers in the perils of the sea, and in all the dangers and privations incident upon establishing a colony in an unbroken wilderness. For many years they had taken "sweet counsel together, and gone to the house of God in company." But all these strong and endearing relations are now broken, and Mr. Bolzius is left alone, with all the weighty responsibility of his important station. No one could feel more sensibly than he did the obligations connected with his position. Nor was he disposed to shrink from them. Nevertheless, he writes to the friends of the Salzburgers in Germany, requesting that a preacher might be sent over to supply the place of his departed friend and brother, Gronau. The following extract from his letter to Rev. S. Urlsperger, at Augsburg, is characteristic of his Christian humility: "May God send me a faithful and good man in the place of my departed friend! Will you have the goodness to select such a one for me, inasmuch as I shall not be able for any length of time to bear the burden of business that overwhelms me. I, too, feel the approach of age, and may be unexpectedly called away. Could I have my own wish, I would ask the favour of you to send a *pastor primarius* to this place, so that I might take the station of my departed brother. My mind has frequently dwelt on this subject, especially during the last illness of Mr. Gronau; and I can assure you that I would prefer by far being adjunct to the new pastor, to retaining the station I now hold, for I am too weak to stand in front of the battle. May God make an arrangement of this kind practicable!"

The request of Mr. Bolzius for the appointment of an adjunct was favourably received, and early in the spring of 1746, the Rev. Herman H. Lembke was sent over to Ebenezer to supply the vacancy occasioned by the death of the lamented Gronau. His arrival was hailed with great satisfaction by the Salzburgers, and particularly by Mr. Bolzius. Mr. Lembke entered upon his duties with great energy, and it soon became manifest that the patrons of the church in Germany had made a very judicious selection. About a year after his arrival, he married the widow of Mr. Gronau, who, it appears, was a near relative of Mr. Bolzius, and this new relation seems to have been mutually agreeable and beneficial to all parties.

Mr. Bolzius, acting under the advice of the church in Germany, continued to retain his position as principal pastor, and, as we have before seen, the management of all the affairs of the colony, both spiritual and financial, was intrusted to him. He, however, associated Mr. Lembke with him, as fully as a sense of duty would permit.

It will be proper here to state some of the responsibilities which devolved upon Mr. Bolzius. Beside the onerous ministerial duties connected with so large a field of labour, he seems to have been appointed trustee for all the funds which had been collected in Europe for the benefit of the congregation at Ebenezer. We consequently find him engaged in making investments, purchasing land, erecting rice-mills, as well as grist and saw-mills, and superintending the whole industrial economy of the colony. To carry out his plans, he procured mill-stones and other necessary materials from Germany, and enlisted the kind offices of General Oglethorpe, who cheerfully aided Mr. Bolzius in all his plans which contemplated the comfort and general improvement of the Salzburgers. During their residence at Old Ebenezer, a mill was established upon Ebenezer Creek, but this they were compelled to abandon.

Another important interest intrusted to Mr. Bolzius was the introduction among the Germans of the silk culture. As early as 1733, the "Trustees for the Settlement of Georgia," induced Mr. Nicolas Amatis, of Piedmont, to remove to Georgia, taking with him his servant, Jacques Camuse, his wife, and three sons, who were to instruct the colonists in the rearing of silk-worms and the manufacture of silk.*

In 1736, mulberry-trees were planted at Ebenezer under the direction of Mr. Bolzius, and the Salzburgers were among the first and most successful in carrying out the wishes of the Trustees in this particular. In 1742, five hundred trees were sent to Ebenezer, and a machine was erected for preparing the silk. In 1745 and 1746, specimens were sent to England, and in 1748, four hundred and sixty-four pounds were produced. In 1749, the Trustees authorized Mr. Bolzius to erect ten sheds and ten machines for reeling, and other means necessary to carry on the manufacture. In 1750, nearly all the colonists had abandoned the experiment of silk-raising, except the Salzburgers. They persevered, and every year became more skilled in the business, and in 1751, they sent over to England a *thousand pounds* of cocoons, and *seventy-four*

---
* Stevens.

pounds two ounces of raw silk, yielding the handsome sum of one hundred and ten pounds sterling, or upwards of five hundred dollars, the price being at that time thirty shillings per pound. To encourage the Germans to persevere in their efforts, which thus far had been very successful, the Trustees gave a reeling-machine to each female, who should become mistress in the art of spinning, and two pounds in money. These marks of favour were duly appreciated, and the culture of silk was carried on successfully for a number of years. Many mulberry-trees are still standing at Ebenezer, which no doubt have sprung from the original stock; and many of the descendants of the Salzburgers continue to raise silk, which they manufacture into fishing-lines, and sell very readily in Savannah.

About this time the Salzburgers, at the suggestion of Mr. Bolzius, commenced the construction of a bridge over Ebenezer Creek, and a causeway through the low grounds adjoining, thus connecting the town of Ebenezer with the settlements which had been made on the north side of that creek. These measures were of great advantage, both to the town and the adjoining neighbourhood. The population in that location, which is called even to this day "*the Bluff,*" increased so rapidly that it soon became necessary to erect a new church. For this purpose, a tract of one hundred acres of land was obtained from the Trustees, and a commodious edifice was erected, called "Bethany;" a school-house was also built, together with a residence for the teacher. This church was located about five miles north-west from Ebenezer. It continued to exist up to the year 1774, when Dr. Muhlenburg made his second visit to Ebenezer; but soon after the Revolutionary War it was allowed to decay, and was never rebuilt. The deed for this church, as we learn from Dr. Muhlenburg's journal, was originally made to H. H. Lembke, John Casper Wertseh, and John Michael, and was dated 1751. It calls for one hundred acres for Bethany church and a school-house. The object is thus defined: "In St. Matthew's *Parish* for the use of a church and school-house, and for the support and maintenance of the minister and master thereof."

Besides this church, another small one was erected at Goshen, about *ten miles* below Ebenezer, near the road leading to Savannah, for the accommodation of the Salzburgers who had settled in that neighbourhood and at Abercorn. Thus it will be seen that four Lutheran churches were now existing in the Parish of St. Matthew, besides the one in Savannah. The arrangement in reference to ministerial labour was, that the pastors should supply the church in Savannah, together with Jerusalem, Zion, Bethany, and

Goshen, dividing the labours equally among themselves, as far as might be practicable, but always under the direction of the senior pastor. It will be apparent that this was a large field to cultivate, even for two ministers. It covered an area of more than thirty miles, and besides the fatigue connected with journeying from church to church, these pious men preached every Sabbath, and catechized the youth in their congregations on the same day; and delivered weekly lectures in all the churches, besides holding their regular ministerial conference for prayer and mutual edification.

The population at Ebenezer and the surrounding settlements gradually increased, and was augmented by occasional arrivals from Germany; so that as early as 1750 numerous farms were in successful culture on both sides of the road leading from Savannah to Augusta, as well as upon the banks of the Savannah river, and Lockner's, Ebenezer, and Mill creeks. With the rapid advancement of the colony, the duties of the pastors at Ebenezer were greatly multiplied, so much so, that the patrons of the church in Germany deemed it necessary to send over an additional minister. In 1752, the Rev. Christian Rabenhorst was selected by Senior Urlsperger, at Augsburg, and with him came a colony of emigrants from Wurtemberg. Although Mr. Bolzius was very much pleased to receive these new recruits for his colony, yet he did not see any necessity, at first, for the appointment of an additional pastor. He was, however, subsequently convinced that he had been mistaken in his opinion, for in a letter addressed to Mr. Urlsperger, dated February 9, 1753, he remarks: "I have to acknowledge, with shame and humiliation, that when I first was informed of the appointment of a third minister for Ebenezer, and ever afterward when I saw him, I believed such an appointment to be superfluous; but since we have become better acquainted with him, and, through the rich grace of the Holy Spirit, felt that he was one heart and soul with us in religion, office, and brotherly conduct; and when, after my last return from Charleston, I discovered the decrease of my bodily strength, I was humbly rejoiced at the goodness of God, who has, in addition to many other precious gifts, sent us (without our wish or desire) this faithful and prudent brother, Timotheus. What gratification does it afford me, and my dear brother-in-law, Lembke, to receive the assistance, and to be supported by this cheerful, willing, and laborious man, whom we have to restrain, lest his unremitting activity may prove injurious to him before he is acclimatized. We all have work enough to do, and do all with pleasure. Mr. Rabenhorst enjoys the good-will of the people in a high degree." Thus it will be seen that

Mr. Bolzius, always ready to acknowledge the hand of God in every event of his life, and to yield submissively to the wishes of the reverend fathers in Germany, gathered fresh strength and confidence from his experience. These three pious and self-denying men continued to labour together harmoniously, and with great success for nearly twelve years; though the external affairs of the colony were at times very distressing, arising partly from the effects of the Spanish war, and partly from the occasional failure of their crops; still, amid all these untoward circumstances, the colonists were not allowed to despair. They maintained an unwavering confidence in the good providence of God, and were for the most part contented and happy.

The arrival of Mr. Rabenhorst at Ebenezer did not, however, increase the pecuniary embarrassment of the congregation, for there is evidence in the records that a capital, amounting to £649 16s. 5d., was raised in Germany and placed in his hands, from the interest of which he was to derive his support. For this money he gave his bond, obligating himself and his heirs, assigns, &c., that the fund should be used for no other purpose, and that it should be applied, after his death, for the support of his successor.

This was a wise provision, particularly at this juncture; for it was about the time of Mr.

Rabenhorst's arrival in America, that the "Trustees" surrendered their charter to the crown, and Georgia became a royal province. The Salzburgers, not being attached to the Established Church, could expect very little further aid from England, and were thrown almost entirely upon the support of their German benefactors.

In view of his increasing age and infirmity, Mr. Bolzius thought it expedient that he should transfer the *trust* which had been vested in him to the Rev. H. H. Lembke. This he did with the consent of the Lutheran pastors at London, Halle, and Augsburg. The trust was duly conveyed in a legal instrument, dated April 15, 1757. It will, perhaps, be interesting to insert here a portion of said document, inasmuch as it will serve to show the character of the property which the Salzburgers then owned, and the purpose for which it was intended. The instrument reads thus:

"In the name of Jesus: Inasmuch as it is unknown to me how soon the Lord may call me hence by death, and as it is my duty daily to set my house in order, and to explain any irregularity or misunderstanding which might possibly arise after my decease, I have deemed it necessary and expedient, as being advised by my most worthy colleague, to give information to my colleague and brother-in-law, Herman H. Lembke, as adjunct pastor and future successor in office, concerning the design of our two grist-mills, the saw-mill, and the rice stamping-mill; and to authorize him, by this instrument of writing, to take the superintendence of said mill establishment, during my life and after my death; so that the objects for which they were instituted may be gradually attained. The objects were threefold: 1. That all the mills should be firmly invested and in some respects improved. 2. That, by the profits of the same, other establishments should in the process of time be sustained in the Ebenezer congregation, such as churches and schools, and also dwellings for ministers and school-teachers, by the joint labours of the members of the congregation. Likewise, that more ample provision should be made for pastors and school-teachers. And, 3. That widows and orphans, the sick, and the superannuated should be able to derive some assistance therefrom.

"The circumstances which gave rise to the erection of said mills are these: I was solicited by the congregation for a number of years to erect a small mill, at a cost of about ten or twelve pounds sterling, to meet their most pressing wants, in grinding their Indian corn, wheat, and rye into flour. After the mill was commenced, by the assistance of the major part of the male members of the congregation, on the site where the mill now stands, the sum proposed was soon found to be totally inadequate, although I obtained gratuitously, by personal request, the mill-stones and some iron materials from General Oglethorpe. Hence it became necessary to relinquish the building of the orphan-house, and appropriate the funds placed in my hands for that purpose to the completion of the mill. For the congregation were not content to have the former without the latter, and particularly as there seemed to be no immediate demand for such an institution; they preferred to provide for the few orphans in town by taking them into their service. The money requisite to complete the mills I received partly from the Trustees, and partly from other patrons, through the exertions of our fathers in London, Augsburg, and Halle. To secure the balance of funds necessary to complete my plans, I was compelled to borrow money, trusting in God, who has hitherto led me most wonderfully, wisely, graciously, and mightily, by his paternal Providence. He has so directed, by his blessings, the operations of the mills, and the trade connected with them, and by means also of donations from Europe, that the loan was gradually refunded, and that all the debts contracted by the erection of the important saw-mill, have been duly paid. To these works the members of the congregation contributed nothing, but have cause of great thankfulness that the mills have proved such a blessing to them. Inasmuch as the boards and other lumber could not be sold for money, but were given in exchange for goods, it became necessary to establish a trading-house. For this purpose I appropriated the first fund created by the charitable donations from Europe, in the time of Mr. Mayer.

"From this statement, to the truth of which all the surviving Salzburgers can testify, (much of which is also known to Mr. Lembke,) it is very evident that the wonderful God has made use of me, unworthy as I am, as a feeble instrument for the procurement of the means and materials for the endowment of these extensive mill establishments, and the laying of the foundation of the mill-trade. There remains, therefore, no doubt, that I am authorized to confer the superintendence of the mill-establishment and the trade connected with it, upon my worthy colleague and successor Lembke alone, and none other beside or above him. This I do herewith solemnly perform, after mature reflection and deliberation, in the name of God and our reverend fathers. May God bless his exertions in behalf of these important works, by his counsel and assistance, that His great name may be glorified, and all the above objects be attained!

JOHN MARTIN BOLZIUS,
Minister in this place.

Ebenezer, in Georgia,
April 15, 1757."

This "power of attorney," as the old church record terms it, was duly signed and delivered at the time specified, and was renewed on the 19th of August, 1765, just four months before the death of Mr. Bolzius. Two years subsequently (April 30, 1767) Mr. Lembke assigned the same instrument to Mr. Rabenhorst. From this it would seem that it was originally designed that this trust should be regularly transferred by each pastor to his successor.

Subsequently, however, a change was made, by which *seven trustees* were chosen annually, on Easter Monday, from among the members, to whom the property of every kind belonging to the congregation was deeded in trust. This feature in the government of the church is maintained to the present day.

It appears, that by royal grants, and purchases made by Mr. Bolzius, nine hundred and twenty-five acres of land were connected with the mill establishments, and that the value of this property was once estimated at one thousand five hundred pounds sterling. The mills were, however, in the course of time suffered to fall to decay, and by the depreciation in the value of lands nearly the whole of this investment was lost.

Besides this mill, another was erected on a lot of *one hundred acres*, of which Messrs. Bolzius and Lembke took possession without a grant. The cost of building this mill was paid partly by contributions from Europe, and partly from the income of the other mill. But, in 1764, it was sold for fifty pounds sterling, and this amount was appropriated toward increasing the fund for the support of a third minister and a schoolmaster.

Mr. Bolzius, though declining in strength, continued to discharge his duties faithfully, and to watch over the interests of the Salzburgers with unabated concern. In fact, his solicitude seemed to increase with his advancing years; and every letter which he wrote to the friends in Germany evinced how deeply the warmest feelings of his heart were enlisted on behalf of the people of his charge, and how ardent was his zeal in promoting the glory of God.

There is one striking feature in all his letters. We allude to the deep-toned piety which pervades almost every line. It is manifest that he and all the first pastors at Ebenezer were men of a truly devotional spirit. Though, as we have seen, they were all required to give their assent to the Augsburg Confession, and the Symbolical Books, yet their religion was something more vital and soul-pervading than the cold "orthodoxy" which is too often associated with symbolism or sacramentalism. And our modern theologians, whose zeal for the Symbolical Books, and whose reverence for the "fathers," seem at times to run away with their good sense and Christian charity, would do well to study such models as Bolzius, Gronau, Lembke, and Rabenhorst. They loved and venerated our confessions and catechisms, and sought to indoctrinate their people in the principles of the Protestant faith, as taught by Luther and his noble compeers; but they had the wisdom to discriminate between those things which were *essential* and those which were *indifferent*, and made it the great object of their ministry to have the people of their charge soundly converted and made Lutherans and Christians, not by a mere outward profession, but by the cultivation and full development of a pure and holy inner life—the life of the soul renewed by grace, and united to Christ by a living, active faith.

In a letter written the early part of the year 1759, Pastor Bolzius thus speaks: "In our corner of the earth we have recently enjoyed the protection and blessing of our Heavenly Father, both in temporal and spiritual things. Though we have not been free from trials and difficulties, still they have been light, and, as we trust, have been subservient to our welfare and our furtherance in the divine life, through the kind direction of a wise providence. We acknowledge, to the praise of God, that piety and contentment still reign among us, as even strangers are willing to admit. With my dear brethren in office, Messrs. Lembke and Rabenhorst, I stand in the most friendly collegiate connection.

Every week we meet in conference and for prayer, by which meetings our mutual love is cemented through the blessing of God. The same blessing also prevents our labour among the people from being unfruitful. Among our congregation are many men and women who are truly converted to God, and who walk in the truth, are ornaments to our office, and humble assistants in the discharge of our duties. Though, on account of the war and the repeated failure of crops, every article of living is high, yet our heavenly Father gives us our daily bread in the enjoyment of peace and health among ourselves. If many, who in the first seasons of trial left us, had endured a little while longer, they would have experienced the truth of the proverb: 'After winter, spring does come.'"

This letter shows very plainly the spirit which actuated Mr. Bolzius and his colleagues in the discharge of their duties; and it should not be a matter of surprise that their faithful and self-denying labours were productive of such remarkable effects upon the moral and religious characters of their flocks. Walking themselves in the "ordinances and commandments of God blameless," they were worthy ensamples to those over whose souls they watched, and the great Head of the church set his seal of approbation to the fidelity of their ministry, in the numbers who through their instrumentality were "turned from darkness to light, and from the power of Satan unto God."

One of these devoted pastors, however, was about to be removed. About the year 1762, the faithful and undaunted *Bolzius* began to give evidence of declining health. In his letters to the patrons of the colony in Germany, he made mention of being frequently attacked with fever, which had impaired his constitution and brought on a distressing cough, which no medicine could remove. It was manifest to all who saw him that nature was yielding to the inroads of disease, and that his pilgrimage was rapidly drawing to a close. Nevertheless, he never left the post of duty, but continued to perform to the very last, as far as his strength would permit, the arduous labours of his station; being fully determined to relinquish his charge only with his life. His letters to his friends in Europe will show the state of his mind in view of his approaching end. In writing to Senior Urlsperger of Augsburg, he says: "I am hastening toward my home. He who sees his wedding-day is not concerned about trifles. It has pleased my dear Redeemer for several months to visit me with disease and infirmities, which most probably will terminate in death. I am in his hand, for he does all things well; as my own experience has taught me during my whole pilgrimage, but more especially during the *thirty-two years* of my pastoral office among my dear *Salzburgers*. Dearest heavenly Father! accept my humble thanks for all thy love and faithfulness! Expecting that my dear Redeemer will soon deliver me from every evil, and help me into his heavenly kingdom, I deem it my duty, though with a feeble hand, to write a few lines to you, to express my gratitude to you for all the spiritual and temporal acts of kindness manifested toward me, (the most unworthy of men,) toward my family, my brethren in office, and to the whole congregation for more than *thirty-two years;* and through you I wish to express my thanks once more to all the Christian benefactors of Ebenezer, who live in my beloved fatherland."

In a letter to Dr. Zeigenhagen of London, he expresses himself as follows: "This will probably be the last letter which I shall write to you, with feeble hands and weak eyes. I am so reduced with illness, that I can scarcely walk a few steps, and am unable to discharge any of the duties of my office. All that I do is, to prepare myself for a happy exit out of this world, by the word of God and prayer, through the assistance of the Holy Spirit. And God be praised, I can and may say, 'If we live, we live unto the Lord; if we die, we die unto the Lord: whether we live therefore or die, we are the Lord's.' How great is the happiness to possess this knowledge! Praised and blessed be God for the unspeakable gift of his only-begotten Son to us sinners; to me also, the chief of them; with whom he has given all we now have and enjoy in life and in death, as well as what we shall forever and ever enjoy in the house of our Father in the sweetest and most blessed communion with the Triune God! It is a faithful saying—I shall be happy forever. My eyes shall behold the source of all joy. I know in whom I have believed, and I am sure there is laid up for me a crown of righteousness."

A few months before his death there was a slight improvement in his health, and he resumed his duties as pastor. For seven successive Sabbaths he preached in Jerusalem church, nor would he spare himself, notwithstanding the entreaties of his brethren, and their offers to perform his duties for him. His general reply was, "I have soon to appear with my hearers before the judgment-seat of Christ, and I do not wish that one of them should accuse me there of having been the cause of his condemnation." His last sermon was preached on the fifteenth Sunday after Trinity, the subject of which was, "*The happiness of the true Christian.*"

From that time his disease seemed to attack him with renewed violence. The swelling in his feet increased, and he was no longer able to leave the house. His colleagues testify that he bore the severest pain with the meekness of a lamb, and with perfect resignation to the will of God.

During a visit of Pastor Lembke, he expressed the joyful state of his mind in the following terms: "I cannot describe how happy I am in my solitude, while I enjoy the presence and communion with my Saviour: happy! oh, indescribably happy. From the 7th to the 19th of November, a little gruel was all the refreshment he could take. On the 14th, he desired to unite with his Christian friends in the celebration of the Lord's Supper. Previous to the celebration of this ordinance, he remarked to Mr. Lembke: "I acknowledge our Protestant religion as a precious treasure in life and in death! In myself I discover naught but sin, but I know that God has granted me forgiveness for Christ's sake." On the 18th, Mr. Bolzius became suddenly much worse, and the family sent for Mr. Lembke. On reaching the house Mr. Lembke found him very much prostrated, but still perfectly rational. Mr. Lembke addressed him in these words: "Father, I will that they whom thou hast given me, be with me where I am, that they may see my glory, which thou hast given me." Mr. Bolzius repeated the words: "That they may see my glory;" and then continued: "Ah, how delightful it is in yonder heaven! how delightful to be with Christ!" His bodily sufferings seeming to increase, he patiently remarked, "This is a day of trial." In the evening his friends, supposing that his dissolution was approaching adjusted his pillow that he might rest the easier; but he almost immediately revived, and said, "Not yet; I have still to bear my sufferings for one night longer." The next morning, at *six o'clock*, being the 19th of *November*, 1765, this venerable servant of Christ calmly resigned his spirit into the hands of God, in the *sixty-second year* of his eventful and useful life. The day following, his remains were carried to Jerusalem church, when Mr. Lembke and Mr. Rabenhorst addressed the large assemblage, who had collected from all parts of the surrounding country, to pay a just tribute of respect to one who had been a father to them in more senses than one, and to whose wise counsels and faithful and zealous ministrations they were indebted, under God, for much of their temporal and spiritual prosperity. The scene was a truly affecting one, as many of the aged Salzburgers who had been his companions in all his travels and perils, both by sea and by land, and who had shared his sympathies and his prayers, stood and looked for the last time upon the countenance of their best earthly friend, and bedewed his corpse with their tears. He was buried in the cemetery, near Jerusalem church, where his remains still repose. It is, however, a melancholy truth, that no monument marks his resting-place, and a stranger would seek his grave in vain. Nevertheless, he sleeps none the less sweetly and hopefully, and has left in the hearts of the good and wise a monument more durable than brass. His memory will remain green as long as Lutheranism has a name in the South, or there is virtue and intelligence enough among the people of Georgia to appreciate his almost apostolic labours, and his life of long and arduous and patient toil in the cause of his divine Redeemer and the persecuted and exiled Salzburgers. Mr. Bolzius left only two children. He had lost two before his death, whose sickness and death are supposed to have been caused by opening some of the swamp-lands near Ebenezer for the cultivation of rice. At the time of his decease his only son was a student at Halle, and it is believed that he never returned to this country. When Mr. Muhlenburg visited Ebenezer, in 1774, an only maiden daughter of Mr. Bolzius (Miss Catherine) was residing in the family of her aunt, the Widow Lembke. Her subsequent history could not be ascertained. It is a melancholy thought that no one of his descendants survived to perpetuate his name in this country, and that the whole family have become extinct. Nevertheless, they live in a purer and brighter sphere, and though lost to the church on earth, they no doubt constitute a part of the church triumphant in heaven.

CHAPTER VII.

State of affairs at Ebenezer consequent upon the death of Mr. Bolzius—Increase of population and of ministerial labour—Transfer of trust to Mr. Rabenhorst—Harmony between the two pastors—Jerusalem church built at Ebenezer—Description of the edifice—The Swan, Luther's coat of arms—Death of Mr. Lembke—His character as a preacher—Gottlieb Snider—Rev. C. F. Triebner sent over as successor to Mr. Lembke—His character—Marries a daughter of Mr. Lembke—Injudicious selection—Division in the church—Controversy between Messrs. Rabenhorst and Triebner—Dr. H. M. Muhlenburg arrives at Ebenezer—Object of his mission—His prudent and judicious conduct—The grounds of dispute stated—Elders prefer charges against Mr. Triebner—Origin of the difficulty—Dr. Muhlenburg's efforts to reconcile the parties—His views of the case—Opinion of Mr. Triebner—Plan of settlement proposed—Reconciliation—Dr. Muhlenburg's reflections—His opinion of Mr. Rabenhorst—Exculpates him from all censure—His estimation of Mr. Rabenhorst as a man and as a preacher—Dr. Muhlenburg's labours among the Salzburgers—Saves the church property from alienation.

The death of Mr. Bolzius devolved upon Messrs. Lembke and Rabenhorst, his successors, the entire charge of the affairs of the colony. We have already seen that, owing to the emigration from Germany, and the rapid natural increase of the population, the field of ministerial labour had become very large, and the pastoral duties necessarily arduous. Now, that one of their number had been called to his reward, these labours would be very much increased, and their cares and anxieties greatly multiplied. It has already been stated, that some time previous to his death, Mr. Bolzius had assigned to Mr. Lembke the entire charge of the mill establishments, and all the property belonging to the congregations at Ebenezer. This was done in 1757. In 1767, Mr. Lembke made a similar transfer to Mr. Rabenhorst: this latter transfer was made two years after the death of Mr. Bolzius.

These two faithful men laboured harmoniously and successfully in the discharge of their heavy civil and religious obligations, and gave entire satisfaction to those with whose interests they were intrusted. It has been found impracticable to gather much information in regard to the administration of affairs at Ebenezer during the lifetime of Mr. Lembke. The most important measure was the building of the large brick church, which still stands near the banks of the Savannah river. A view of the church may be seen on the opposite page. The materials of which this church was constructed, were prepared for the most part among the Salzburgers themselves, but the funds necessary to defray the expenses of its erection were contributed by their friends in Germany. It is stated in Mr. Muhlenburg's journal, that the sum received for this purpose from Europe amounted to something over one thousand dollars, and Mr. Rabenhorst gave upward of one hundred and fifty dollars. The church is built of brick, eighty by sixty feet, and was originally designed for a two-story edifice. It is surmounted by a neat belfry, on the top of which is a swan, which was said to have been Luther's coat of arms, and is frequently placed on the spire of Lutheran churches in Europe.* The edifice is a plain but substantial one, and is in every respect creditable to those who planned and erected it. But reference will be made to it again.

It has not been found practicable to ascertain how long Mr. Lembke continued his labours among the Salzburgers; nor under what circumstances he closed his career. The most general opinion is, that he departed this life a short time before the Revolutionary War. Certain it is, that he was dead in 1774, when Mr. Muhlenburg visited Ebenezer. Although there are no means of ascertaining the particulars connected with his dying moments, it is not hazarding too much to assert, that like his predecessors, his end was peaceful and triumphant. This we have

---

* There is a tradition, that when John Huss, the Bohemian martyr, was burned by order of the Council of Constance, he remarked, "You this day burn a goose, (Huss signifying goose;) but a hundred years hence a swan will arise, whom you will not be able to burn:" in the Bohemian, Luther signifies a "swan."

a right to infer from his character. That he was an eminently pious man, is universally admitted by all who knew him. It was our privilege, in the years 1845 and 1846, to converse with a venerable father in Israel, (Mr. Gottlieb Snider,) who lived to the advanced age of more than *four-score years*, and who had known Mr. Lembke personally, and had often heard him preach. He bore strong testimony to the learning, piety, and zeal of Mr. Lembke, and seemed to regard him with the highest veneration. He stated, too, that this was the general estimate in which he was held by the entire congregation. No fears, then, need be entertained in reference to the end of such a man.

Upon the death of Mr. Lembke, the Rev. Christopher F. Triebner was sent over by the reverend fathers in Germany, as an adjunct to Mr. Rabenhorst. Mr. Tribner was a young man of fine talents, but very impetuous in his character, and seems to have possessed but a very small share of the humility and piety which characterized his predecessors. Shortly after his arrival he married a daughter of Mr. Lembke, who was also a niece of Mr. Bolzius. His selection as an assistant pastor at Ebenezer was attended with the most disastrous consequences to the congregation; for he succeeded in raising such turmoil and strife among the members, that Mr. Muhlenburg was sent on a special mission to Ebenezer, in 1774, to heal the difficulties which Mr. Triebner had occasioned, and, if possible, to save the congregation from ruin.

Dr. Muhlenburg arrived at Ebenezer in November, 1774, having been especially deputed by the Lutheran pastors in Europe (under whose spiritual care the Salzburgers had been placed) to investigate the grievances complained of severally by Messrs. Triebner and Rabenhorst. As was to have been expected from his wisdom and experience, Dr. Muhlenburg managed this unpleasant matter with a great deal of prudence and good judgment. His first step was to call upon the pastors personally, and after a friendly interview with them, to request that each one would furnish him with a written statement of his grievances. This was accordingly done, and each party presented a long list of complaints. It is not necessary to go fully into particulars, though the documents might be interesting, especially to the descendants of the Salzburgers. It must suffice to state, that Mr. Triebner accused Mr. Rabenhorst, among other things, 1. That Mr. Rabenhorst had appropriated to his private use certain lands and other property belonging to the church; 2. That by his mismanagement the mill establishments had greatly depreciated in value, and were nearly ruined; 3. That he had wilfully departed from the church regulations established by the fathers in Europe; 4.

That Mr. Rabenhorst's obligation for six hundred and forty-nine pounds was five years without date, and that the interest was computed sometimes at thirty pounds and again at forty pounds, whereas the Rev. Urlsperger fixed it at fifty-two pounds; 5. That Mr. Rabenhorst had assumed to himself the position and prerogatives of *first* pastor, and had attempted to exercise undue supremacy; 6. That Mr. Rabenhorst and his party, partly through craft and partly through violence, had obtained a majority of votes, and caused the church to be locked against Mr. Triebner and his party, &c. &c.

On the other hand, Mr. Rabenhorst complained, 1. That, shortly after the arrival of Mr. Triebner, he attempted to create distrust and dissatisfaction among the members, by accusing Mr. Rabenhorst of bad management of the schools, and of making unauthorized changes and innovations in other regulations; 2. That he had slandered the arrangement of the mill establishment, as though Mr. Rabenhorst intended it for his own use; 3. He denied that Mr. Rabenhorst had any legal call at Ebenezer; 4. He had refused to administer the Lord's Supper to Mr. Rabenhorst; 5. Besides the charge of dishonesty, he represented Mr. Rabenhorst as a false teacher, a pretender, and destroyer of the church; 6. He abolished the fellowship of colleagues to confer and pray with one another, lest his affected superiority might not be sustained; 7. When Mr. Rabenhorst went to Ebenezer to preach, Mr. Triebner invented all kinds of mischief and ill-will, ran out of church, laughed at the preaching, and occasionally criticised the sermon, &c. &c.

Besides these complaints drawn up by Mr. Rabenhorst, the deacons likewise presented charges against Mr. Triebner in writing, which were laid before Dr. Muhlenburg in due form. The principal were, 1. Ingratitude toward Mr. Rabenhorst, who had received him as a brother, and treated him with every mark of kindness; 2. Avarice or covetousness, in trying to get control of the church funds; 3. Anger and revenge; 4. Pride and arrogance; 5. Hatred, envy, and malevolence. There are specifications under each of these heads, but it is not necessary to state them. These charges were signed by the deacons, with this pointed remark:

"This is a faint outline of the image of our Evangelical Lutheran minister, Christopher Frederick Triebner. May God have mercy on him and each one of us!

JOHN ADAM TREUTLEN,
ULRICH NEIDLINGER,
CHRISTIAN STEINER,
JOSEPH SCHUBTREIN,
SAMUEL KRAUSS,
JACOB C. WALDHAUER.

It may be proper here to state, that one cause of the difficulty between these two ministers originated in an election which was held for church officers. Mr. Rabenhorst's party was successful, but their right to enter upon the discharge of their duties was strongly contested, and when they took possession of the church, they had to hold it by force and defend themselves with swords, &c. The deacons claiming office under Mr. Triebner, as representatives of his party, were, Messrs. John Caspar Wertsch, John Floerl, Christopher Krämer, Matthew Biddenbach, John Paulus, and Paul Müller.

Dr. Muhlenburg, having examined all the documents, and having in vain attempted to effect a private reconciliation between the parties, consented to hold a public conference with the pastors and their respective boards of deacons, and investigate fully all the matters in dispute. The 23d day of November was appointed for this purpose. Dr. Muhlenburg makes this minute in his journal under this date: "To-day, I expected severe and heart-rending labour, and found myself troubled and entirely unfitted for the work. The old and new vestry, witnesses of both contending parties, together with both the ministers, are to meet to attempt a reunion. I prayed to God secretly, but could obtain no confidence, and felt like a poor sinner who is being led forth to execution." * * * "I had previously advised my brother Triebner how, with a few words, he might end the complicated and perplexing strife, viz. if he would say before the meeting, 'I have erred, and ask your cordial forgiveness, and wherein you have wronged me, that I will forgive with all my heart and forget.' For, under all the circumstances, I could impartially learn that in many things he had acted unreasonably, not according to grace, but according to our depraved nature."

The journal of Dr. Muhlenburg contains a detailed account of the various propositions for a compromise, but it is not necessary to state the particulars. It is, perhaps, important to give Dr. Muhlenburg's view of the case, according to the impression made upon his mind. Speaking of Mr. Tribner, he says: "He endeavoured to defend himself against the charge of avarice, and his party testified very earnestly in his behalf. In regard to the remaining counts, various instances were adduced and testimony given. He endeavoured, however, partly to justify and partly to deny, and to turn it to the best advantage for himself, and began to weep, and said, to-day was the day of his visitation; he must suffer and leave it all to the righteous Judge. I aided as much as I could, with a good conscience, and said, that in strife and enmity, faults and errors of hastiness were converted into crimes, but where love reigned, they were covered up, or endured but for a little season. But as he thought he had not erred, on the contrary had acted according to grace, conscience, and the instructions of the reverend fathers, I therefore adduced certain points wherein he had erred, and said: 'That even a subject of grace carried within him the root or seed of all the aforesaid vices, and if he watched not, could soon be overtaken by them, and that we must avoid also the appearance of them.' He wept again, and said: Such vices as those mentioned were mortal sins, and if they could be proved against him, he would be unworthy of his office, much less could he continue a minister if the newly-elected vestrymen remained; he would rather remain by himself with his little flock. I told him, finally, that obedience and love had induced me to take this fatiguing journey to visit them, that, with the help of God, peace and unity might be restored. But if they were determined to continue in discord and be ruined, then my visit and experiment were ended; and to-morrow, with a sad and heavy heart, I would depart and report the result. I had hoped, by remaining over winter, that all things might yet be restored to order, but if this was the way, it was useless for me to stay. Mr. Wertsch and others said I should not adjourn yet, but try another proposition. I replied, that the following was my advice: 1. That they should bury all their former contentions and offences, and cordially forgive each other, as there were faults on all sides; 2. To open the Jerusalem church for Pastor Triebner, so that both ministers might, unitedly, perform their ministerial duties in the congregation; 3. I would endeavour, with the aid of the ministers, &c., to prepare a plan for the better conduct of the whole matter. Pastor Rabenhorst came to the rescue, and supported the proposition with a warm exhortation. I gave my hand to each one present, and said if in aught I had offended or wounded them, they should forgive me. Pastor Rabenhorst did likewise, and Pastor Treibner followed and said he would forgive his enemies, and would implore God to forgive them also; and thus we separated. Pastor Rabenhorst and I.ate at Mr. Triebner's, and at evening returned home. I was so tortured and worried in body and spirit, that I had to lie down. O Lord! how much has not the enemy of man already won, if he can effect a breach between ministers and colleagues in a church! What hateful mischief he does to the sheep, when he has disarmed the shepherds! How despised is the holy office and its dignity in the sight of Chamites and Canaanites, when they have seen the nakedness of the fathers, and scoff at it!"

It is gratifying to state that the judicious efforts of Dr. Muhlenburg to effect a reconciliation between these disaffected parties were happily crowned with a good measure of success, as will be seen from the above extract. But feelings of alienation grew out of these contentions, which were never fully pacified, and the bitter fruits growing out of this unfortunate rupture were seen for many years after. For it has been the sad experience of all who have ever had the misfortune to be connected, even remotely, with such schisms, that even though they may seem to be healed, the asperities of feeling which result from them are frequently only smouldered, and it requires a large measure of grace to entirely eradicate and destroy them. It is no wonder, therefore, that Dr. Muhlenburg, deeply sensible of the ruinous tendency of all such ruptures between Christians, should express himself so strongly in the latter part of the above extract from his journal.

In a subsequent part of his journal Dr. Muhlenburg states, that having examined all the church records, he was satisfied that "Mr. Rabenhorst did not acquire the ministers' plantation through fraud and evil practices, as Mr. Triebner and evil-disposed persons had complained; but that Mr. Bolzius rejoiced that it had been sold, and that Mr. Rabenhorst took it at £649 16s. 5d., with the consent of the reverend fathers in a regular manner, and gave his obligation for it; and the fund was thereby secured." This statement fully vindicates Mr. Rabenhorst from the most serious charge which Mr. Triebner and his associates brought against him. Further on in his journal, Dr. Muhlenburg, speaking of Mr. Rabenhorst, bears this strong testimony in his favour: "When I see with my own eyes, and hear with my own ears in intercourse, that the man possesses a heart of grace, excellent gifts to preach, and still more aptness to catechise; that he insists upon a new creature in Christ Jesus, upon radical repentance, living faith, and daily renewal; and that he adorns his sound doctrine with an edifying, sober, and godly life, &c.; when I reflect on all this, I must wonder in my simplicity, what could have been the preponderating reasons which prevented our reverend fathers from appointing Rev. Rabenhorst first preacher after the death of Rev. Lembke; and even induced them to place at his side, as second preacher, a young man who, although well-meaning and gifted, was nevertheless inexperienced, passionate, and a dangerous novice; and moreover to continue Mr. Rabenhorst as third preacher! Most heartily would I have regarded myself as fortunate, if the Lord had lent us in Pennsylvania a labourer like Mr. Rabenhorst, and I would rejoice even in my last days to be the adjunct of such a man. * * Although Mr. Rabenhorst had been most grossly wronged, and had been publicly assailed in honour, office, and reputation, yet he was the first, with tears, to extend his hand to his offender, to forgive every thing, and to ask forgiveness." Dr. Muhlenburg closes his investigation of this whole matter with these remarks: "In my humble estimation, Mr. Rabenhorst is the only man possessed of understanding and experience who, with Divine assistance, can save the Ebenezer congregations from destruction. If the reverend fathers will only appoint him first preacher, will hold Mr. Triebner tighter in hand, and honour Mr. Rabenhorst with a paternal and familiar correspondence, all may yet be well."

Dr. Muhlenburg remained three months in Georgia, during which time he preached frequently in all the churches of the Salzburgers—Jerusalem, Bethany, Zion, and at Goshen; and extended his visits also to Savannah. His journal contains a great many interesting details, which are, however, not necessary for our purpose. This sojourn among the Salzburgers was of incalculable benefit to the whole settlement. Beside effecting an amicable adjustment of the unfortunate breach which had occurred between the pastors and their respective adherents, his quick penetration led him to perceive, that in consequence of the manner in which the lands belonging to the churches at Ebenezer had been granted, the whole property was placed at the mercy of the Church of England, to be converted to the benefit of that church, whenever occasion might present. The words of the grant were, "In trust for a glebe for St. Matthew's *Parish*, for the use of the ministers of the Lutheran Church in Ebenezer." On this point Dr. Muhlenburg remarks: "The grant to Jerusalem church as the principal or mother church in the village of Ebenezer, is so strongly arranged and secured that no help is left for it. Mr. John Wertsch managed the matter entirely alone, and suffered himself to be outwitted. He regrets it, but that does not alter the case." This was also true in relation to the church and school-house called Bethany. The object was defined to be, "In St. Matthew's *Parish*, for the use of a *church* and school-house, and for the support of the minister and master thereof." Of this Dr. Muhlenburg says: "This is unwittingly cut out for the Church of England, as there is only *one church*, strictly so speaking, *established* in the British dominions."

Dr. Muhlenburg was seriously troubled (as well he might be) when he discovered the critical position in which these grants placed the church property at Ebenezer. He, therefore, visited Savannah, and had an interview with Mr. Habersham, the President of the King's Council, and Anthony Stokes, Esq., Chief Justice for the province, in which he represented the gross injustice and wrong which the Salzburgers were likely to suffer, unless these grants could be altered. He also drew up an able manifesto, in which he clearly set forth the just claims of the Salzburgers, and pointed out the distinctive *Lutheran* character of the churches which had been established at Ebenezer and its vicinity. The efforts of Dr. Muhlenburg to secure the rights of the Salzburgers were successful. The grants were accordingly altered, and the property forever secured to the Lutheran Church. For this act alone, the Salzburgers and their descendants, and in fact the whole Lutheran Church, owe Dr. Muhlenburg a lasting debt of gratitude.

CHAPTER VIII.

Dr. Muhlenburg still at Ebenezer—Church discipline—Views and practices of the founders of American Lutheran Church—Evils arising from want of discipline—False views on the subject—The discipline adopted at Ebenezer in 1774, and duties of pastors, officers, and church members defined—List of church members who signed the discipline, as certified by Dr. Muhlenburg—Settlements at Abercorn and Goshen—Mr. Knox buys the lands at Abercorn—Moravian missionaries brought over to preach to the Negroes—Labours of the Moravians at Goshen—Fears of Dr. Muhlenburg—Moravians not successful—Advice to them by one of the Salzburgers—Fears of Dr. Muhlenburg not realized—Moravians leave the settlement—Dr. Muhlenburg's successful labours at Ebenezer—He leaves Georgia and returns to Philadelphia—Condition of the congregations at Ebenezer—Reflections.

In another place reference has been made to the discipline which Dr. Muhlenburg drafted for the better government of the congregation in and around Ebenezer. It is, perhaps, appropriate that some extracts from that document should be here inserted, as this subject is properly connected with his visit to Ebenezer. The extracts may be regarded by some readers as rather too long, but they are made so purposely, to show what where the opinions of the founders of American Lutheranism upon the subject of church discipline. This is necessary for two reasons: 1. There are many *professedly* Lutheran preachers in the United States who, under a mistaken view of *Christian liberty*, have never attempted to throw any restraints around the deportment of the people of their charge. Hence, many Lutheran church members are very lax in their notions of Christian propriety, and participate in all the fashionable follies of life, seemingly without any compunctions of conscience. By this course of conduct the Lutheran Church has been injured very seriously in the estimation of other enlightened Christian denominations, and in many sections of country has become almost a by-word. Our church is regarded as a body of unconverted professors, whose lives are a scandal to the Christian name; and the impression has been made upon many minds, that we never have attempted to check the improprieties and immorality of which our members have sometimes been guilty, simply because we had no *discipline* which could reach and correct their misdemeanors. It is to be hoped that this stigma will now be removed, and that the Christian public will judge us more favourably in the future. 2. Some of our ministers, and many of our church members, have been disposed to look upon a judicious and rigid church discipline, as a "*new measure*"—an innovation upon the uses of our fathers. In some portions of the Lutheran Church, attempts have been made by designing men, to pander to the prejudices and corruptions of the human heart, by asserting that our pious forefathers never had any *discipline* in their churches; and that this movement to control the actions of freemen, by dictating to them what they should or should not do, would lead inevitably to the establishment of a censorship, which would ultimately destroy the rights of conscience, and bind the human mind in vassalage to the dictation of a haughty priesthood. Such were not the sentiments nor the practices of those godly men who laid the foundation of the Lutheran Church in America. They regarded a scriptural discipline, wisely and impartially administered, not only as absolutely necessary, but as fully sanctioned by Divine authority. And as far as their example furnishes a *precedent,* it forever silences the senseless ranting of those who seek to brand such measures as *innovations*, and who, to accomplish some ulterior design, would leave the church without a compass, to be driven about by the tempests of human passion.

Our illustrious fathers had wisdom and grace to perceive that the *moral power* of the church does not consist in its numerical strength, but in the piety and purity of its members. Hence, they planted themselves upon the precepts of Christ and the apostles; and by enforcing proper regulations in all their congregations, they sought to give character to the church, and to make the membership living witnesses to the elevating and controling influences of sound Christian principles. They had, too, the moral courage to do their duty faithfully in this particular. They had no fears in relation to their *popularity*, and never compromised their views of duty, nor shrunk from any responsibilities growing out of the faithful discharge of the obligations which they owed to Christ and the souls of their fellow-men. Would to God, their "mantle" had in all cases descended to their successors! But the reader may desire to see the discipline which was adopted and enforced in the early days of Lutheranism in America. Here is a portion of it. It will be seen that in some things it goes very minutely into detail, but it is not the less interesting on that account.

THE ELECTION OF DEACONS, &c.

"The election of deacons shall take place annually on Easter-Monday, as usual, in the most capacious church, where the whole congregation, consisting of all the regular and contributing male members of the Evangelical Lutheran Congregation in and about Ebenezer, which holds to the Augsburg Confession and Liturgy, and also to the old Discipline and Rule as described in Chapter I., is assembled. On the ensuing Sabbath, the church-deacons, elected by a plurality of the votes of the congregation, shall be presented publicly, at the service in the church in which they were elected, by one or other of the ministers, when they shall be reminded of the duties of their office, be received by taking of the hand, and their names recorded in the church-register. Previously, however, the deacons whose office has expired shall be dismissed with thanks and wishes of blessing.

"The meeting of the church-council shall be subject to the following rules, viz.: When necessary matters and business demand a meeting, the church-council shall be previously and publicly invited from the pulpit, and the time and place of meeting specified by the oldest minister, so that each member can make his appearance, and not absent himself without cogent reasons. If, however, the business will not admit of so long delay, the members shall be convoked by expresses. The oldest minister, who has for the longest period of time been in office in this congregation, and to whom its circumstances are best known, shall preside at every meeting of the council. Should he, however, be sick, or absent on necessary official engagements, he shall authorize his colleague to supply his place in the council. The elder minister, as president of the assembled council, shall have liberty to invite his junior colleague to all important meetings of the church-council, and permit him to keep on record the minutes or protocol, so that he may gain experience for the future.

"When the whole, or at least two-thirds, of the respective members of the church-council are present, the president shall open with a short ejaculatory prayer, and each member shall modestly take his seat; and the order of business shall follow thus: 1. The president shall make known the business concerning which it is necessary to consult and deliberate. 2. The president shall present one point after another, and allow each member to give his opinion and exposition of it. Whoever wishes to speak and offer his advice, shall rise and modestly give his opinion. No one shall interrupt another while speaking, and still less shall two persons speak at the same time. All undue, insulting, sarcastic, and abusive language and expressions must, in general, and especially in such assemblies, where matters affecting the honour of God, and the welfare of the congregation are considered, be avoided. 3. It is also very unbecoming in such meetings of council, for one individual to be sole spokesman, and arbitrarily wish to have every thing done according to the views which he conceives to be correct. 4. After each one has given his opinion and advice in regard to one point, the vote shall be taken upon it; the resolution made either unanimously or by plurality of vote, and be written down by the minister who records the minutes, and then read to the assembly, to ascertain whether it has been correctly recorded. 5. A resolution, however, in regard to weighty and important matters, cannot and shall not be considered valid, which is not unanimously passed, or, at least, by concurrence of the president and two-thirds of the regular members of the congregation. Matters of this kind are such, for example, as the building of churches and school-houses, the election or discharge of school teachers, the leasing or vending of mills or any other establishment. Should the church-council have come to a determination, and passed a resolution in reference to one or other such important matters, such resolution shall first be laid publicly before the congregation, and a week's time shall be given the congregation to reflect on it. Should it turn out, during this week, that either all or two-thirds of the regular members of the congregation are opposed and dissatisfied, for weighty grounds, the matter shall not be put in force, but shall again receive the deliberation and consideration of church-council. 6. After the session of the church-council is concluded, the president shall close with prayer, and see that the most necessary things in the minutes which were resolved for the welfare of the congregation, be properly transferred to the church-register.

"Should one or other member of the ruling church-council, viz. the ministers, deacons, trustees, deputy overseers or managers, deviate from our Evangelical Protestant religion, order, and worship, which are accordant with the Augsburg Confession, and go over to another religious denomination, or perhaps even give offence to our congregation by gross wickedness, (which, however, may

God in his mercy forbid!) and if such be plainly or sufficiently, convincingly, and indisputably proved by two or three reliable witnesses; and if the various degrees of admonition will not make an impression, or produce any reformation, he or they shall be expelled from the church-council, and shall have no part in any thing belonging to our congregation in and about Ebenezer, until a true return take place, and a reconciliation be effected with the congregation.

"As the laudable society in London for the Promotion of the Knowledge of Christ, out of affection toward the oppressed Protestants from Salzburg and Germany, has kindly undertaken, since the year 1733, to provide and compensate ministers and school-teachers who adhere to the Augsburg Confession, for the congregation which at this time was yet to be planted; and has also by certain agreements with a number of prominent ministers of the Evangelical Lutheran mother church, in Germany and England, viz. with Mr. Samuel Urlsperger, in Augsburg, Gothelf Augustus Francké, D.D., in Halle, and Mr. Frederick Michel Ziegenhagen, yet living, as very worthy members of the above-mentioned society, and their successors confirmed and established this privilege, and has actually until this time, for the space of forty-one years, afforded the same thing; therefore, the right to call a minister to Ebenezer congregation rests, upon the agreement of the laudable society, with the above-mentioned reverend fathers and those whom they are to choose as their successors in Europe, and shall continue so long as the aforesaid are not annulled, or until the Ebenezer congregation has become unworthy of such a favour.

"Should one or other Ebenezer preacher or teacher, secretly or openly, introduce and disseminate erroneous and soul-destructive doctrines, conflicting with the basis of the apostles and prophets in the word of God, contained in the Old and New Testaments, and opposed to our Augsburg Confession, (and other Symbolical Books); or give offences which may be really substantiated, and which have become public; or transgress by causing schisms and factions,—he shall first be examined by the other minister and pastor, together with two or three of the church-council who are experienced in the word and ways of God; and if found guilty, required to confess, deplore, and abhor such offences, and particularly to recall and expose the erroneous doctrines by manifesting sincere repentance. Should, however, said minister, after due representations have been made, not be disposed to fulfil the above conditions; and stubbornly and wickedly continue in such error, then the other minister and the whole church-council, with the assistance of intelligent and experienced church-members, shall once more investigate said offences and errors, direct the church-council to report the same to the reverend fathers, and await from them a full decision. In the mean time they shall suspend such minister from his office and service until the offences be removed; because in such cases delay is dangerous.

"It shall be the duty of the pastor of our congregation to teach and administer in our congregation, purely and without adulteration, publicly and explicitly, the doctrine of faith and the practical duties following therefrom; of our Evangelical Lutheran religion, and the two sacraments, according to the basis of the apostles and prophets contained in the Holy Scriptures of the Old and New Testaments, in which Jesus Christ is the cornerstone, (accordant with our Augsburg Confession and other Symbolical Books.)

"The qualifications and gifts requisite and necessary for our ministers and pastors, for the performance of the duties of their office, are amply described in the word of God, in the New Testament, the infallible rule, guide, and fountain of their faith, life, and conduct, according to their station, office and service. Matt. xxviii. 18–20; Mark xvi. 15, 16; Eph. iv. 11, 12; 1 Tim. iii. 2–13; Titus i. 5–11; 1 Pet. v. 2–4; James iii. 1; 1 Tim. iv. 10–13; 2 Cor. v. 17–20; vi. 1–10; Acts xx. 28; 2 Tim. iv. 2–5; 1 Cor. xii. 4, 5, 7; Rom. xii. 7, 8; John xiii. 34, 35; Matt. vii. 22, 23; 1 Cor. xiii. 1–10.

"They can also learn their duty from the documents containing their call and instructions, received from their reverend superiors.

"According to the ordinance introduced at the beginning, our Ebenezer congregation has had two churches, viz. the Jerusalem and Zion's churches, and has also one church in Bethany; and so long as there was, are, and will be two ministers, the whole congregation is and shall be jointly and associately supplied with the means of grace after the following manner: 1. The older minister shall conduct the worship at Zion's church every second Sabbath, until otherwise directed by the reverend directors; he shall also, if health and strength permit, deliver one catechetical sermon every week in the same place. Farther, he shall also, in accordance with the precedence and Christian example of the first ministers and his first appointments, have divine service, on different Sabbaths and week-days, in the German Evangelical Lutheran congregation at Goshen and in the town of Savannah. The other Sabbaths and fast-days he shall appropriate to holding service in the Jerusalem church. The second preacher, who at the present time lives in the little town of Ebenezer, near Jerusalem church, shall conduct worship in the Jerusalem church, until otherwise ordered by the reverend directors, on Sabbath and fast-days, so that the Ebenezer congregation shall lose nothing on those Sabbaths and fast-days on which the older minister has divine service at Goshen and Savannah. Furthermore, the second preacher shall also deliver a catechetical sermon weekly in the Jerusalem church; and as the members residing in Bethany are nearest to Jerusalem church, and belong to it, and as they have, with the approval of the first blessed ministers, built a church in Bethany, considering that the old, infirm, and sickly members and children can scarcely attend the Jerusalem church, and yet have need of spiritual nourishment, it was, therefore, resolved by the church-council, 'that the people in Bethany shall regularly have divine service, if possible, every fourth Sabbath by the preacher who lives nearest to them. Vid. minutes of January 12, 1774.' Yet this resolution shall not be enforced, except with the condition, that the minister receives the necessary travelling expenses, and entertainment for himself and horse; because, according to the teachings of Christ, the labourer is worthy of his meat and wages.

"According to the good regulation already introduced, the Lord's Supper shall be administered, if possible, every six weeks in our Ebenezer congregation after this manner, viz.: 1. It shall be published two weeks previously, after the morning service, in both churches or in one, when the whole congregation is assembled in it; and the names of such as signify their intention to commune shall be recorded by the respective minister or ministers. Should any of the members not be present when the announcement is made, and yet be desirous of participating, they shall be allowed to make known their intention at the service of the preceding week, or privately to one or other of the pastors. Both ministers shall mutually communicate to each other the names each one may have recorded, and confer betimes over them in a paternal and brotherly way, to ascertain whether there might be one or more among the number against whom complaint may exist, known either to the pastor himself by personal observation, or which information has been given by creditable testimonies. In such cases they must use particular wisdom and foresight, according to the rule of their Saviour and Master, in Matt. x. 16, so that they may deal impartially, without carnal affections and passions; that they may not judge according to hearsay; but confront accusers, accused, and witnesses, and, as the issue may be, either acquit the innocent or proceed with the guilty, according to the degrees of exhortation. Should, however, in this affair, important matters be affected, then the pastors shall have liberty to admit to their aid several intelligent and God-fearing members of the church-council. Neither of the two pastors shall, however, be permitted to exclude, upon his own responsibility, any one from participating in the Lord's Supper; but it shall be done with the knowledge of both, provided there be reasons and grounds sufficient which demand such procedure. And if it happen that any one has given offence to the congregation by gross and open sins and vices, and such persons or person has or have been brought to sincere repentance and sorrow on account of his or their sins, by the admonition and instruction of the pastors, through the word and Spirit of God; and if they evince an earnest desire, next to God, to be again reconciled with the congregation, then the church discipline shall be enforced as has been usual at other occasions, on the Sabbath on which the Lord's Supper is administered, as follows: The penitent or penitents shall be called out by name before the public assembly of the congregation, and commended to their compassionate intercession, and be again restored with appropriate admonition. In regard, however, to errors and faults committed through thoughtlessness, which occurred secretly and not publicly, and through which the congregation received no offence, the person guilty shall on no account be reprehended publicly from the pulpit, personally or by name, but shall be set aside privately by the pastor, and be directed to reform. Because, should any other method be pursued, imbittered feelings might be aroused, offence given, and injury done. The minister shall nevertheless retain perfect right and liberty to denounce each and every sin and deviation from the holy law of God, as is directed by the teachings of Jesus Christ and his holy apostles. The confession shall be held in both churches on Saturday morning, by both ministers. In case, however, one of the ministers should be sick, and the other thus be alone, it shall be held in the largest church, where all who have given in their names can be convened. The Lord's Supper shall, as usual, be administered in the most capacious church and by both ministers, viz.: the elements shall be consecrated and the bread distributed by the elder minister, and the consecrated cup shall be given by the junior minister. The collection, as directed, shall be taken up while the congregation is dispersing.

"The following rules shall be adopted in regard to the instruction and confirmation of young persons: 1. Parents, guardians, and masters shall be allowed to make mention of the young persons intrusted to their care, and send them to either of the two pastors nearest to whom they may live, or whom they may prefer; 2. Both parties shall employ the utmost fidelity, according to the grace which has been bestowed upon and received by them, to ground, through the love of Christ, the young souls intrusted to them, thoroughly, by the assistance and power of the Holy Spirit, in our evangelical doctrines of faith and duties of life, or in the order of salvation, or in the counsel of God conducing to blessedness, upon Jesus Christ, the rock of our salvation; 3. After this has been performed, and the time has arrived when they shall be publicly examined and tested, when they shall renew their baptismal vow and be confirmed, then each pastor may publish the time and day, and examine the little flock which he has instructed in one or other of the two churches, receive the vows of the faithful, and kindly invite his colleague and co-pastor to attend; because, by such a solemn act, faithful ministers and shepherds may be animated, encouraged, and excited to intercessions, if they have at all the spirit and disposition of Christ, the Lord of his own; 4. The persons newly confirmed by each minister shall be registered in a suitable church record, and preserved as a testimony to posterity.

"The order established by the first minister, with the approbation of the reverend directors, in regard to the public worship on Sabbath and fast-days in our Ebenezer congregation, shall remain undisturbed, and shall be observed in our church as follows: 1. At the usual time in the morning, the minister shall commence with the prayer from the London Liturgy; 2. The school-teacher shall read a chapter from the Holy Bible, following the prayer in order; 3. The minister shall announce a spiritual hymn from the Holy Hymn Book, according to its number, and also whether the whole, or (if only a part) how many verses shall be sung; 4. The minister shall read the Epistle or Gospel appointed for the day; 5. The hymn shall be again sung, it being previously announced as before; 6. The minister shall offer up an extemporaneous prayer, and end with the Lord's prayer; 7. He shall read the Epistle or Gospel, or text which forms the basis of his remarks; 8. He shall preach his sermon, and close it with prayer; 9. The general prayer from the London Liturgy shall follow, and be finished with the Lord's prayer; 10. All the necessary announcements shall be made, and concluded by an apostolic wish; 11. There shall be singing; 12. The congregation shall be dismissed with the Lord's benediction. The afternoon service shall be commenced, 1. By reading a chapter from the Holy Scriptures; 2. Singing; 3. The young persons and children shall rehearse what they have learned—passages from the little book of the blessed Tolner, the catechism of Luther, the order of salvation, or hymns; 4. Singing; 5. The minister shall offer up a prayer, and catechise the children, either on what they have rehearsed, or on the Epistle or Gospel read that day; 6. He shall close with prayer, and "Our Father," &c.; 7. Singing, and dismission of the congregation with the blessing of the Lord.

"Those who at any time shall be the ministers of our Ebenezer congregation, shall, according as God has given them grace, gifts, and experience, for which they shall daily implore the Lord and Master, be strenuously engaged for the general and particular salvation and education of the lambs and sheep intrusted to them, and purchased by the blood of Jesus Christ himself. They shall visit industriously the schools, as also the sick members, when and as often as they desire it, and supply them with the means of grace, so far as time, health, and strength will admit. In case one or other of the ministers is afflicted with sickness and confined, it shall be the duty of the other, who is well, as much as by the aid of God he may be able, amid the other necessary engagements of his office, to conduct the worship on the Lord's day in one or other, or both churches alternately, and serve and visit the filial or young congregation sprung from the parent congregation, on one or other day of the week, until the sick minister be restored. Further, the ministers and pastors shall also, according to the example of the first minister of the congregation, so pleasing to God himself, confer diligently, either orally or by writing, concerning official or casuistic cases which may be brought before them; the one serving the other with the gifts which he has received, and thereby manifest to the flock that, from thorough self-knowledge and just application of unction from on high, each regards the other as superior to himself; that they serve one Lord of all, and one congregation, and take heed unto themselves and the doctrine; that they preserve in a pure conscience the precious charge intrusted to them; and fight the good fight, so as to save both themselves and their hearers. 1 Tim. iv. 16. In this way, and not otherwise, can the will of God be accomplished, the wish of our fathers be fulfilled according to Psalm cxxxiii., their own hearts be rejoiced, the burden of their duties toward the congregation alleviated, and their conversation and exemplary walk become a wholesome terror to the obstinate, and serve as a blessing and comfort and means of growth in grace to the obedient sheep and lambs.

OF CHURCH MEMBERS.

"Whoever wishes to become and remain a member of our Evangelical Lutheran Church, holding to the Augsburg Confession and Liturgy, in and about Ebenezer, and have part in the spiritual and temporal benefits, privileges, and rights, must, in the first place, have been or be received within the covenant of grace by holy baptism, with the Divine Majesty of God the Father, Son, and Holy Spirit; 2. He must be or have been instructed for the participation in the Lord's Supper; he must be confirmed and received as a communing member; 3. He must, as much as possible, regularly attend to the hearing of the word of God, and participate in the Lord's Supper; 4. He must voluntarily contribute, according to his ability, of his gifts and merits toward the continuation and support of the evangelical worship of God, whenever and wherever the deacons may demand it; 5. He must not live in, or be found guilty of, prevailing sins and vices, contrary to the divine moral code or the ten commandments of God, nor indulge in the open works of the flesh enumerated in Gal. v. 19–21; 1 Cor. v. 1–12; vi. 9, 10; but he must conduct himself as a Christian, according to his calling and the doctrine of Jesus Christ; 6. In case, however, one or other member should be overtaken in faults, through the subtle artifice of Satan, of the flesh, and of the deceitfulness of the world, or, perhaps, even fall into great sins, and such failings or sins come to the knowledge of the ministers and pastors, then they shall first call these fallen souls to account, alone, with compassionate love and seriousness regarding them as wandering, lost, and wounded sheep, and admonish them to repent, point the sin and uncleanness again to the free and open fountain, and give them advice and direction how they, as lost sons and daughters, may again reach their home. Should this course prove fruitless, the pastors shall make still further attempts to retrieve them; and admit to their assistance two or three members of the church-council, who are experienced in the word and ways of God, and repeat the affectionate admonitions. And if this also prove abortive, then such persons, continuing in their sins, shall be cited to appear before the church-council and pastors, and the last admonition shall be applied. If, however, they refuse to appear and obey, their name shall then be recorded in the minutes of the congregation, and then have neither part, nor right, nor suffrage in the congregation, and its privileges and benefits, until, peradventure, by God's grace, long-suffering and mercy, for the intercession of Jesus Christ the Mediator, through the disciplining and gracious workings of the Spirit of God, true conversion takes place, and they give evidence of such by proofs, and withal, desire to be again received into the congregation; then they may be received, provided they acknowledge and confess, in open assembly of the congregation, the offences alleged, and ask forgiveness and reconciliation through the pastors.

"To all the above Fundamental Articles, Constitutions, and Rules, upon which and according to which a German Evangelical Lutheran congregation, composed of Salzburg emigrants and Protestants accompanying them, was founded, established, governed, and maintained (and shall in the future, through all time, be maintained and governed) in and about Ebenezer, in the Province of Georgia, (by virtue of the freedom of conscience granted by God and the constitution of Great Britain,) professing and adhering to the word of God and the Augsburg Confession, the ministers, pastors, and school-teachers who may at any time be in office, all the trustees, elders, deacons, each regular contributing, communing church member, mutually and deliberately bind themselves, with heart and hand and signature of their names; and that, too, with the express condition, that he or they who acts contrary to the above constitution, seeking in any way to annul or pervert it, shall have neither part or right, nor vote, nor pretension to the spiritual and temporal goods and benefits of the Ebenezer congregation.

Ebenezer, Georgia, December 14, 1774."

"That the above is a true transcript of the original Fundamental Articles, Constitution, and Rules, which were unanimously ratified by the church-council in public assembly at Ebenezer, with the signatures of their names, and also on the 26th of January, 1775, by the congregation in Jerusalem church at Ebenezer, plainly and distinctly heard and approved and confirmed by the signature of their names, is hereby testified and affirmed by Henry Melchior Muhlenburg, at the time Reverend of Evangelical Ministerium, Philadelphia, Minister Senior, and authorized agent of the Reverend Directors of the Ebenezer congregation, &c. &c."

The undersigned, respective members of the church-council, are the Reverend Ministers, the Trustees and Deacons, and appear in the original, subscribed as follows:—

Christian Rabenhorst,
Christopher Frederick Triebner, } PASTORS.

TRUSTEES.	DEACONS.
John Casper Wertsch,	John Adam Treutlen,
John Floerl,	Ulrich Neidlinger,
Joseph Schubtrein,	Jacob C. Waldhauer,
David Steiner,	John Kugel,
Conrad Rahn,	Christian Steiner,
Christopher Kraemer.	Samuel Krauss.
John Michael,	Veit Lochner,
John Paulus,	John Martin Paulitsch,
John Remshart,	John Paul Möeller,
Matt. Bedenbach,	Jacob Metzger,
Balthasar Rieser,	Jacob Mack,
Caspar Heil,	Philip Paulitsch,
John Haugleiter,	Michael Mack,
Charles McCay,	Christopher Rottenberger,
Lucas Zeigler,	Michael Reiser,
George Gruber,	John Schuele,
Christopher Oechsle,	John Adam Freyermuth.
Hans Jürk Winckler,	Jacob Tarringer,
John Martin Dasher,	Jacob Meyer,
George Schwinger,	John G. F. Zittrauer,
Israel Leimberger,	John G. H. Schneider,
John George Bentz,	John Justus Gravenstein,
Nicholas Michael,	John Rentz,
Jacob Housler,	John Heinley,
Solomon Schrempf,	John C. Oechsle,
Christian Dasher,	Nicholas Schubtrein,
Ernest Zittrauer,	Nicholas Helme,
Johannes Maurer,	George Gnann,

AND THEIR DESCENDANTS. 181

Jacob Buehler,
John Bollinger,
Ruprecht Zimmerebner,
Henry Ludwig Bentz,
John Steiner,
Daniel Burgsteiner,
John Christian Krinberger,
Daniel Weitmann,
Martin Dasher,
Mattheus Rahn,
John Gottleib Ott,
Israel Lackner,
Mathias Meyer,
John Kogler,
G. Israel Schmidt,
Nathaniel Ott,
Conrad Frank,
John Michael Oechsle,
John Metzger,
John Bolleinger,
Solomon Zandt,
John Adam Paulus,
Andreas Gnann,
John Rottenberger,
Michael Heisman,
Frederick Lackner,
Samuel Metzger,
Andrew Seckinger,
Benjamin Rieser,
John Sherraus,
Frederick Schrempf,
Jacob Mohr,
John Christian Buntz,
John George Maurer,
Israel Rieser,
John George Beckley,
John Scheraus,
Jacob Heinley,
Jacob Gnann,
Peter Freyermuth,
John Gottleib Neidlinger,
John Christian Gugel,
Abraham De Roshe,
Samuel Deppe,
Benjamin B. Glaner,
Jonathan Seckinger,
John Glaner,
John Gottleib Schneider,
Michael Halerer,
Frederick Helfenstein,
Jacob Metzger,
Mathees M. Schule,
Jacob Kiefer,
John Heckel,
George Zeigler,
Paul Fanck,
Sigismund Ott,
John Pfluger,
Andreas Seckinger,
Timotheus Lembke,
George Bechly,
John Rentz,
John Gottlieb Fetzer,
Joseph Schubtrein, Jr.,
Jacob Schmidt,
Emanuel Kiefer,
Israel Kiefer,
George Ditters,
Andreas Biddenbach.

This list of names shows that on the 16th of January, 1775, there were one hundred and twenty-four male members present at Jerusalem church, when the discipline was solemnly ratified and subscribed. There is no doubt that many of the members were absent; but still it furnishes sufficient evidence of the numerical strength of the congregation at that time. The list of names is inserted entire, as a matter of reference for the benefit of the descendants of the Salzburgers who still survive, many of whom will probably be gratified to have this opportunity to trace out their genealogy. Besides, it may be necessary to use it in noticing the dispersion of the Salzburgers into other portions of Georgia, and the changes which many of them have made in their church relations. For it will appear hereafter, that very many of the descendants of these men forsook the church of their fathers, and united with other communions. All that some of them carried with them was the *name* of their venerable ancestors: for the *Lutheran* Church they seem to have lost all affection and reverence. But we will dwell more fully upon this topic in its proper place.

There is one other historical fact brought to light in Dr. Muhlenburg's journal, which must not be omitted, and it will not be inappropriate to record it here. Reference has been made to the settlement at Abercorn, and the establishment of a Lutheran Church at Goshen. Dr. Muhlenburg states, under date, January 7, 1775:

"The so-called Abercorn was originally settled by Germans of our confession; gradually, however, it fell into the hands of two English gentlemen, who are now the proprietors, and cultivate the land with Negro slaves. The adjoining land, called Goshen on account of its fertility, was settled originally by our brethren in the faith; and our beloved ministers, Bolzius and Lembke, each patented five hundred acres of land, which were suitable for the cultivation of grain and rice. The faithful but poor brethren could not cultivate nor continue to hold them, and were compelled to sell them to an Englishman in Savannah, who was likewise forced to re-sell them to Mr. Knox, who keeps a large number of negroes and overseers upon them. There are about fifteen families of our German brethren in the faith still living at Goshen, having a small church and school-housé, who were served with the means of grace by the late ministers, and up to this time by Pastor Rabenhorst."

Dr. Muhlenburg further remarks, that while he was at Ebenezer two Moravian ministers arrived at Savannah, who had been brought over by Mr. Knox as missionaries, to labour among the slaves on his plantation. As a compensation for their services, Mr. Knox stipulated to give them one hundred and fifty acres of land, and to allow them the use of ten or twelve slaves to cultivate it. These Moravian brethren applied for the use of the Lutheran Church at Goshen to preach in. Dr. Muhlenburg seems to have had some fears in reference to their influence upon the Lutheran families about Goshen, especially in view of the distracted state of the Ebenezer congregations, growing out of the difficulty between Messrs. Rabenhorst and Triebner. Speaking of the presence of these missionaries at Goshen, he says: "I doubt not, according to their known method of insinuation, they will gain the most, if not all, the remaining families in Goshen, and will also make an attempt on Ebenezer, for their ways are well adapted to awakened souls. I have learned by experience that where strife and disunion have occurred in neighbourhoods and congregations, among the Germans in America, there black and white apostles have immediately appeared, and tried to fish in the troubled waters, like eagles which have a keen sight and scent. Well, be it so. He who controls all things has all power given unto him in heaven and on earth. He is the keeper of Israel, and never sleeps nor slumbers. What he ordains or permits must finally conduce to the glorification of his great name, when all his enemies shall have been placed beneath his feet."

The fears of Dr. Muhlenburg, in relation to the inroads which the Moravians might make upon the

Goshen church, were happily not realized. For, in another part of his journal, this minute is to be found under date of the 21st of January: "The Moravian emissary held his first meeting in the plantation last Sunday, and preached in broken English. He exerted himself also very much to build up his interests in the Lutheran Church there, or else to erect a church near it for himself. A person acquainted with the state of things told him, that the Ebenezer congregation and its associates had hitherto been served by regularly-called Evangelical Lutheran ministers and pastors, and as he had been called to instruct the Negro slaves, we wished him Godspeed and success in it; and if they had any superfluous time and strength, there were yet enough other inhabitants and Indians in Georgia, who were sitting in darkness and the shadow of death, and needed much help for instruction and conversion."

These missionaries were not, it would seem from this, as successful as they anticipated, and in a few years left the colony, and went probably to Pennsylvania. Goshen remained a part of the Ebenezer charge even after the Revolutionary War; but we shall speak of it more fully hereafter.

Dr. Muhlenburg fully accomplished the objects of his mission to Georgia. He succeeded in healing the breach between Messrs. Rabenhorst and Triebner, and restored harmony to the church. Besides which, he investigated thoroughly all the financial affairs of the congregation, took an inventory of the church property, had all the deeds and grants, &c. properly secured and recorded; and transmitted to the founders of the church in Germany a minute detail of all his observations and proceedings. During this visit, he performed a vast amount of labour, and displayed a degree of prudence and Christian fidelity which are worthy of all praise. His duties were frequently of the most delicate and embarrassing character, but he never shrunk from them; and while he always exhibited a nice regard for the feelings of those whose conduct he was sent to investigate, he never swerved from the path of duty, but performed his stewardship faithfully and conscientiously, and to the entire satisfaction of all parties. He left Savannah on the 20th of February, 1775, and arrived in Philadelphia on the 6th of March, after a tempestuous and rather unpleasant passage. The Salzburgers and their descendants should cherish the memory of Dr. Muhlenburg with lively gratitude. For, as has already been seen, he was not only instrumental in restoring harmony to the congregation: he saved the church property from being alienated, and by his presence and labours, and the introduction of a wholesome discipline, he prepared the way for the future peace and prosperity of the church. If, in after years, his wise counsels and godly conversation lost their influence among the Salzburgers, and they chose to walk according to their own vain and foolish imaginings, he at least must be exonerated from all censure, for he did every thing which human wisdom could devise and human agency could accomplish, to place the congregation at Ebenezer upon such a footing as would secure its permanent prosperity and success. The wisest and most judicious efforts are, however, sometimes unavailing to prevent the downfall of a church; especially is this the case, when God's people provoke his displeasure by disobedience to those laws which he has enacted for the regulation of their conduct. Wo to any people, when by their rebellious spirit they arouse the righteous displeasure of God! "Ichabod!" will be written upon their sanctuaries; and amid the storms of passion which ensue, their souls will be given up to spiritual leanness and barrenness.

CHAPTER IX.

Affairs at Ebenezer after Dr. Muhlenburg's departure—Rabenhorst and Triebner—Pastors cease to be Trustees, and the *trust* transferred to the church officers—Mr. Rabenhorst created *first* pastor—State of feeling between the two pastors—Inventory of church property—Its estimated value—Church funds—Views of the propriety of creating them—A case of necessity with the Salzburgers—General state of the colony—Prosperity of Ebenezer—A fancy sketch—Commercial relations of Ebenezer—Gradual extension of the settlements—New settlers come in—Commencement of the Revolution—Stamp Act and tax on tea—State of the public mind in the Province of Georgia—Position of the Salzburgers—Provincial Congress in Savannah—Salzburgers in that Congress—Majority of them side with the Colonists—Protest of a portion of the Salzburgers—Adherents to the Crown in St. Matthew's Parish—Patriotic and noble sentiments of the Salzburgers—Mr. Triebner sides with the Crown—Judicious course of Mr. Rabenhorst—His long and successful labours, and death.

THE departure of Dr. Muhlenburg from Georgia was universally regretted by all the Salzburgers, and particularly by Mr. Rabenhorst and his family. To this family he became very strongly attached, and he makes frequent mention of them in his journal, and especially of Mrs. Rabenhorst, whom he calls his "foster-mother," adding, "The king's daughter is all glorious within." "Like a precious gem, is so humble a soul." Mr. Rabenhorst was very deeply affected in separating from Dr. Muhlenburg. In him he had found a prudent friend, a judicious adviser, and a warm-hearted and affectionate brother. Besides, Dr. Muhlenburg seems to have formed a just estimate of the talents and sincere piety of Mr. Rabenhorst; and as there was great congeniality of spirit between them, they became united in the bonds of an indissoluble friendship. Mr. Rabenhorst was likewise apprehensive, from the known character of his associate, (Mr. Triebner,) that the absence of Dr. Muhlenburg would furnish an opportunity for new difficulties, if not for the opening of the old breach.

Against the recurrence of any further disruption between the two pastors and their respective parties, Dr. Muhlenburg had endeavoured to guard, as far as a wise foresight would accomplish such an object. He carefully investigated all the financial affairs of the church, and placed in the hands of the trustees a statement of the property belonging to the congregation, together with the deeds, grants, &c., and arranged that the trustees, and *not the pastors*, should as far as practicable superintend the management of all the temporal affairs of the congregation. He further inducted Mr. Rabenhorst as first pastor or senior minister, and made such an arrangement in reference to the relations which he and

Mr. Triebner should in future sustain toward each other, as to prevent any further jealousy or disaffection. With a man of Mr. Triebner's disposition it was, however, almost impossible to live upon terms of friendship, and for the simple reason, that he was in a great measure destitute of that spirit of Christian humility and brotherly love, which was necessary to make a "true yoke-fellow" in the gospel. Besides, the rupture between him and his colleague had been of such a character, that it was difficult, if not impossible, to induce a man like Mr. Triebner, having, it is to be feared, but a small share of grace in his heart, cordially and sincerely to forgive the past, and to become fully reconciled to his brother. If, therefore, there was no open hostility between the parties, the asperity of feeling on the part of Mr. Triebner was never fully subdued.

It has been stated that Dr. Muhlenburg made a careful investigation of all the property belonging to the church, at the time of his last visit to Ebenezer in 1774 and 1775. For the satisfaction of those who may feel interested in this matter, a copy of the inventory which he left is here inserted:

1. In the hands of Pastor Rabenhorst, a capital of 300*l*. 16*s*. 5*d*.
2. In the hands of John Caspar Wertsch, for the store, 300*l*.

3. In the mill treasury, notes and money, 229*l.* 16*s.* 2*d.*

4. Pastor Triebner has some money in hands, (400*l.*,) the application of which has not been determined by our Reverend Fathers.

5. Belonging to the church is a Negro boy at Mr. John Flöerl's, and a Negro girl at Mr. David Steiner's.

6. A town-lot and an out-lot, of which Mr. John Triebner has the grant in his hands.

7. An inventory of personal goods in the mills belonging to the estate.

8. And, finally, real estate, with the mills, 925 acres of land.

At a very reasonable estimate, this property must have been worth about twelve thousand dollars. To this sum additions were subsequently made, by donations from the patrons of the colony in Germany, and by legacies from private individuals; so that it is not assuming too much to say, that the church property could not have been worth much less than twenty thousand dollars.

It has been questioned by many wise and judicious minds, whether the funding of a large capital for the benefit of a congregation is to be commended. Whatever objections may be urged against this policy as a general rule, we think in the case of the Salzburgers it was not only wise, but absolutely necessary. Amid the persecutions which they had endured in the fatherland, their property had been confiscated, and they had been driven from their homes, and thrown upon the charity of their Christian friends. They came to America as exiles—poor, and houseless; and but for the liberality of their patrons in Germany and England, they could not have subsisted, much less could they have provided the means to build churches and schoolhouses and support their ministers. In their circumstances, the establishment of a *church fund* was an act of necessity; and though in other cases such a measure may be deemed objectionable, with them it was perfectly justifiable, as without it the colonial churches could never have been sustained. It is true, that when the descendants of the Salzburgers became able to support their pastors, at least to a considerable extent, they withheld their contributions, and relied too much upon the income of their funded capital; yet this dereliction of duty on their part, furnishes no just ground of objection against the provision which was made for the churches and their pastors in the infancy of the colony. The true policy for every church to adopt is, to support its pastor and to maintain itself by *voluntary contributions* on the part of its members. This is according to apostolic injunction, as well as the practice of the primitive church; and God seems wisely to have connected the spiritual prosperity of a church with the liberality of its members, in bestowing their worldly goods to the support of the cause of Christ. There is certainly a "withholding which tendeth to poverty," and it is only the "*liberal soul*" that is to "*be made fat.*" As a general rule, God has ordained that "they who preach the gospel shall live of the gospel," and a people assume a fearful responsibility who, while they enjoy the labours of a minister, seek to relieve themselves of the obligation to support him, by throwing him upon his own private resources. They thus rob the labourer of his just reward, and force him into some secular calling to gain a maintenance for himself and family, that the church, for which he is spending himself, is bound most solemnly and religiously to furnish. No church can expect to prosper, and be "enriched with all spiritual gifts," that pursues such a course. God will be honoured with the bestowal of our substance, as well as the dedication of our personal service to himself; and where the former is *intentionally* withheld, there is very little ground for hope that the latter will ever be acceptable. These remarks, however, will not apply to the first settlers at Ebenezer, how much soever some of their descendants may have been in fault.

The general state of the colony at Ebenezer was on the whole very favourable. It is true, as has been noticed, there were some unpleasant occurrences in the congregation, but they did not seem to affect very seriously the temporal prosperity of the Salzburgers. They prosecuted their various pursuits with their accustomed industry and perseverance, and their labours were abundantly rewarded. The town of Ebenezer attained about this time to the height of its importance. The population of the town proper was not less than five hundred persons. Almost every kind of trade was successfully carried on. The mechanic, the artisan, and the merchant followed their respective avocations with zeal and energy, and their thrift met with due reward. There is an old picture representing the appearance of Ebenezer at this period. It is a mere outline of the principal points in and around the town; but the Savannah river is distinctly delineated, and in the distance may be seen two schooners riding at anchor not far from "Ebenezer landing." This may be in some respects merely "a fancy sketch," but there is no doubt of the fact, that a regular trade was carried on between Ebenezer and Savannah, and perhaps also with Charleston, by means of these schooners or sloops. Through Savannah the people also conducted some foreign trade, for it has already been stated that silk was exported to England, and the Salzburgers were constantly receiving drugs and medicines and other supplies from Germany.

There was also a gradual increase of the population, and new farms were constantly settled in almost every part of the country. This was particularly the case in relation to the lands on the water courses, and along the main road leading from Savannah to Augusta, and which passed through Ebenezer. There was, however, with this increase of the population, a change in the character of the inhabitants. A number of settlers came over from Carolina, and some from other portions of Georgia. The majority of these, however, located in the upper part of the parish, or on its western borders, near the Ogechee river. Many of these settlers became among the most respectable and useful citizens in the parish, and the descendants of not a few are still residing in the counties of Effingham and Scriven.

New scenes, however, were about to be enacted in the Province of Georgia, and the Salzburgers were called upon to take part in some very important measures, and to mingle in strange and thrilling scenes. The passage by the British Parliament of the Stamp Act, the tax on tea, and the subsequent blockade of the port of Boston, because of the resistance of the people of Massachusetts to these unjust and tyrannical measures, had excited the indignation of all the colonies in America. The public mind in the Province of Georgia was, as a matter of course, considerably agitated in common with the people of the other colonies; and at an early period in this controversy Georgia declared herself opposed to the enactments of Parliament, and expressed, in unmistakeable language, her sympathy with her sister, Massachusetts. A Provincial Congress was held at Savannah on the 4th of July, 1774, consisting of delegates from the different parishes in the province. The Salzburgers could not remain indifferent or inactive spectators. When a call was addressed to the parishes, requesting them to send delegates to this congress, the Parish of St. Matthew promptly responded, and the following persons were duly chosen.* *John Stirk*, *John Adam Truetlen*, George Walton, Edward Jones, *Jacob Waldhauer*, Philip Howell, Isaac Young, Jenkins Davis, John Morel, *John Flöerl*, Charles McCay, *Christopher Craemer*. Thus the Salzburgers, or a very large majority of them, identified themselves with the cause of American Independence even in its very incipiency, and, as will hereafter appear, they bore their full share in all the dangers and sufferings of the struggle which ensued.

There was a portion of the Salzburgers, however, who (no doubt from conscientious motives) refused to unite in any remonstrance against the proceedings of the mother country, or to take any part in the revolutionary measures which were afterwards adopted. The following

---

* Salzburgers in italics.

document is inserted to show the feelings of these Salzburgers:

Wednesday, September 21, 1775.

We, who have just put our names to this paper, inhabitants of the Parish of St. Matthew and town of Ebenezer, think it necessary in this public manner to declare that about the 4th day of this inst. (August) we were told by certain persons that we must send a petition home to our king in regard to the Bostonians, to beg for relief, as a child begs a father when he expects correction; and that all those who would not join must sign their names, that they might know how many would be in this parish; and that should we decline what was recommended, we must expect the Stamp Act imposed upon us. By these and like flattering words we were persuaded to sign, but we find we are deceived, for that the people who met at Savannah on the 10th inst. did not petition our king, but made up a paper, which we think is very wrong, and may incur the displeasure of his Majesty, so as to prevent us from having soldiers to help us in case of an Indian war. We therefore disagree entirely from said paper, and do hereby protest against any resolutions that are, or may hereafter be, entered into on this occasion. Signed, Urban Buntz, George Gnann, John Paulus, George Gruber, Matthew Biddenbach, George Ballinger, John O. Rentz, George Buntz, John Pillager, Henry Ludwig Buntz, Jacob Metzger, John Metzger, John Adam Freymouth, Jacob Feberl, George Zittrauer, John Heckel, Solomon Zandt, Jacob Gnann, Jacob Kieffer, Christian Steiner, John Remshart, Israel Linlberger, Leonhart Krauss, George Bechly, Batlas Kieffer, Michael Mack, Jr., Peter Freyermouth, Solomon Prothero, John Gravenstine, Christopher Rottenberger, Andrew Gnann.

We, the subscribers, do hereby certify that we are against all resolutions: Philip Dell, Paul Pirick, Matthew Meyer, Jacob Meyer, John Maurer, George Maurer, Daniel Weitman, Martin Reylander.

These latter persons, at this time, belonged clearly to that class who advocated the doctrine of "passive obedience and non-resistance," recognising, no doubt, the divine right of kings, and yielding uncomplaining acquiescence in the will of their sovereign.

The views of these remonstrants were, however, subsequently very materially changed, and the majority of them espoused warmly the Whig cause, and took a very active part in favour of American Independence.

The adherents to the crown in St. Matthew's Parish proved ultimately to be comparatively few. Yet they were sufficient to create an angry controversy among the inhabitants, which imbittered their feelings, and interfered very materially with the peace and prosperity of the church. The largest portion of the Salzburgers espoused the cause of the colonies. They exclaimed, "We have experienced the evils of tyranny in our own land; for the sake of liberty we have left home, lands, houses, estates, and have taken refuge in the wilds of Georgia; shall we now submit again to bondage? No, never." A truly noble sentiment! and one which all the boasted patriotism of New England never surpassed. They had realized the sweets of freedom, they had sat beneath the tree of liberty, reposed in its shade, and partaken of its precious fruits; they therefore resolved that they would be freemen, and maintain their just rights at all hazards.

But they dreamed not as yet of the difficulties and privations which awaited them, nor the scenes of severe conflict through which they would have to pass. They were divided among themselves. Even one of their pastors (Mr. Triebner) openly espoused the cause of the king, and used all his influence to suppress the spirit of resistance to the usurpations of the British government, which was everywhere manifesting itself. And it was as much owing to his efforts, as to those of any other man, that the Salzburgers suffered so severely during the Revolutionary War. Mr. Rabenhorst pursued a more manly and judicious course, which was, however, to have been expected from his known character for prudence. If he did not openly espouse the cause of liberty, he did nothing to injure it. He laboured to calm the turbulence of passion, and endeavoured to enforce, by precept and example, the cultivation of a spirit of moderation and forbearance among those who had taken opposite sides in this controversy. This, however, was impossible in the very nature of things; and it was perhaps fortunate for him, that in the midst of the commotion and the scenes of strife which ensued, he was called by the great Head of the church to receive his reward in heaven.

It has been found impracticable to ascertain

the precise time when Mr. Rabenhorst departed this life, nor any of the particulars connected with his death. He arrived at Ebenezer in 1752, and probably served the congregation about *twenty-five years*. His character for piety, learning, Christian humility, and unyielding devotion to the cause of Christ was fully established, and the testimony of his life is the best guarantee that he closed his earthly pilgrimage in full prospect of a better inheritance. His remains were deposited in the cemetery connected with Zion's church, about four miles below Ebenezer. It was near this church that Mr. Rabenhorst always resided, the other pastor being settled in Ebenezer.

The influence of Mr. Rabenhorst's example upon the Salzburgers was very salutary; and, but for the counteracting effect of Mr. Triebner's efforts and deportment, he would have accomplished a vast amount of good. Even amid the adverse circumstances which surrounded him, he did very much for the spiritual welfare of the congregation; and the pious Salzburgers in Savannah, and throughout his whole charge, held him in very high esteem. But, like his worthy colleagues, Bolzius and Lembke, he passed away from earth, and now sleeps calmly among those for whom he laboured well and profitably for a quarter of a century.

CHAPTER X.

Descent of the British upon Georgia—General Provost takes Savannah—British posts along the river—Mr. Triebner takes the oath of allegiance to the crown, and conducts troops to Ebenezer—A garrison established under Major Maitland—Proclamation issued by Major Maitland—Some of the Salzburgers take "protections"—Majority of the Salzburgers Whigs—Governor Treutlen—Holsendorf—John and Samuel Stirk—John Schnider—Strohaker—Jonathan and Gotlieb Schnider—Jonathan Rahn—Ernest Zittrauer—Joshua and Jacob Helfenstein—Sufferings of the Salzburgers during the war—Tories—Eichel and Martin Dasher—Marauding parties—Frederick Helfenstein and his two sons—General Wayne—The Salzburgers forced to abandon their homes—Sufferings at Ebenezer—Prisoners—Sergeants Jasper and Newton—Sacrilegious act of the British toward the church at Ebenezer—Other acts of cruelty—Mistaken policy of the British—Sad influence of the licentiousness of the British troops upon the morals of Ebenezer—Pastor Triebner—His removal to England and death—General character of the pastors at Ebenezer—Triebner an exception—Dispensations of Providence—General Wayne attempts the reduction of Savannah—British troops withdrawn from Ebenezer—General Wayne makes his head-quarters there—British evacuate Savannah—Salzburgers return to Ebenezer—Scene of desolation—Condition of the church—Congregation without a pastor—Petition sent to Germany—Dr. Muhlenburg's concern for the Salzburgers—A minister visits Ebenezer—Dr. Muhlenburg's letter—Vindication of Mr. Triebner—Pastor to be sent in the spring—Despondency among the Salzburgers—Darkness begins to disappear—New pastor about to be sent.

THE Revolutionary War commenced in 1775. But it was not till 1779 that any demonstration was made against Georgia. In that year, General Provost, acting under instructions from Sir Henry Clinton, made a descent upon Georgia, and met with comparatively little resistance. He made his head-quarters at Savannah, and proceeded to establish posts along the western bank of the Savannah river. When Mr. Triebner heard that General Provost was in Savannah, he waited upon him, took the oath of allegiance to the crown, and advised that Ebenezer should be occupied by royal troops. This was accordingly done, and Mr. Triebner had the honour (?) to conduct a detachment of British soldiers to Ebenezer. These troops were under the command of Major Maitland. Upon arriving at Ebenezer, they threw up a redoubt within a few hundred yards of the church, with a view to fortify their position and guard against a surprise. The remains of this fortification are still standing.

Upon arriving at Ebenezer, Major Maitland issued a proclamation to the inhabitants of St. Matthew's Parish, offering the protection of the British arms to all who might be disposed to take an oath of loyalty and allegiance to the crown. Many of the Salzburgers, influenced by the advice and example of Mr. Triebner, accepted this offer, and obtained certificates guaranteeing protection to themselves and to their property. The majority of the Salzburgers, however, warmly espoused the Republican cause. Those who figured most conspicuously were John Adam Treutlen, rebel governor; William Holsendorf, a rebel counsellor; John Stirk, rebel colonel; Samuel Stirk, rebel secretary; John Schnider, planter; Rudolph Strohaker, butcher. Beside these, mention should be made of Jonathan Schnider, J. Gotlieb Schnider, Jonathan Rahn, Ernest Zittrauer, Joshua and Jacob Helfenstein, and others. Most of these worthy men served faithfully in the struggle for independence, under General Wayne and other officers in the American army, and their names deserve to be perpetuated with the long list of worthies who distinguished themselves by their devotion to the cause of liberty.

The citizens of Ebenezer and the surrounding country were made to feel very severely the effects of the war. The property of those who did not take the oath of allegiance was confiscated, and they were constantly exposed to every species of insult and wrong from a hired and profligate soldiery. Beside this, some of the Salzburgers who espoused the cause of the crown became very inveterate in their hostility to the Whigs in the settlement, and pillaged and then burned their dwellings. The residence on the farm of the pious Rabenhorst, was among the first that was given to the flames.

Among those who distinguished themselves

for their cruelty, was one EICHEL, who has been properly termed an "inhuman miscreant," whose residence was at Goshen; and MARTIN DASHER, who kept a public-house five miles below Ebenezer. These men placed themselves at the head of marauding parties, composed of British and Tories, and laid waste every plantation or farm whose occupant was even suspected of favouring the republican cause. In these predatory excursions the most revolting cruelty and unbridled licentiousness were indulged, and the whole country was overrun and devastated. *Dasher* seems to have distinguished himself fully as much as *Eichel*, though perhaps he was not quite so cruel. He had stolen some cattle from a poor widow, and General Wayne, while occupying Ebenezer, sent him word that if he did not restore them to her in person, he would have him taken into custody and gibbeted. This threat had the desired effect, and *Dasher* became less troublesome to his neighbours.

Mention has been made of Mr. Frederick Helfenstein, who settled at Goshen. He had acquired some property before the war commenced, and might have been considered in comfortable circumstances. It is known that he owned a large tannery in successful operation, a good farm, and several valuable Negroes. Of all this property he was dispossessed by the Tories, (or Cow-boys, as they were then called,) and he was left penniless to begin the world anew. Thus it would seem that his misfortunes did not cease even after his settlement in Georgia. Yet he never deserted the Whig cause, and furnished, in the persons of his sons, several bold soldiers during the war. Two of them joined a troop of cavalry under Colonel McCoy, and subsequently served under General Wayne. When General Wayne, at the close of the war, returned to Pennsylvania, (his native State,) these two brothers, Joshua and Jacob Helfenstein, accompanied him, and it is more than probable that from them the Helfenstein family in Pennsylvania is descended, several of whom are now distinguished preachers in the German Reformed Church. In Georgia the name has been changed to Helvenston. Mr. John C. Helvenston, of Macon county, Georgia, and his brother, residing in Florida, no doubt belong to the same family. Mr. Frederick Helfenstein died at Goshen at the advanced age of eighty-three, and his wife, who survived him many years, at the extreme old age of *ninety-three!*

The Salzburgers, nevertheless, were to experience great annoyances from other sources. General Clinton, as before stated, had directed that a line of British posts should be established all along the western bank of the Savannah river, to check the demonstrations of the rebel forces in Carolina. Under these circumstances Ebenezer, from its somewhat central position, became a kind of thoroughfare for the British troops in passing through the country from Augusta to Savannah. To the inhabitants of Ebenezer, particularly, this was a source of perpetual annoyance. British troops were constantly quartered among them, and to avoid the rudeness of the soldiers and the heavy tax upon their resources, many of the best citizens were forced to abandon their homes, and settle in the country, thus leaving their houses to the mercy of their cruel invaders.

Besides all this, they were forced to witness almost daily acts of cruelty practised by the British and Tories toward those Americans who happened to fall into their hands as prisoners of war; for it will be remembered that Ebenezer, while in the hands of the British, was the point to which all prisoners taken in the surrounding country were brought, and from thence sent to Savannah. It was from this post that the prisoners were carried who were rescued by Sergeant Jasper and his comrade, Newton, at the "Jasper Spring," a few miles above Savannah.

There was one act performed by the British commander which was peculiarly trying and revolting to the Salzburgers. Their fine brick church was converted into a hospital for the accommodation of the sick and wounded, and subsequently it was desecrated by being used as a stable for their horses. To this latter use it was devoted until the close of the war and the removal of the British troops from Georgia. To show their contempt for the church, and their disregard for the religious sentiments of the people, the church records were nearly all destroyed, and the soldiers would discharge their guns at different objects on the church; and even to this day the metal "*swan*," (Luther's coat of arms,) which surmounts the spire on the steeple, bears the mark of a musket ball, which was fired through it by a reckless soldier. Often, too, cannon were discharged at the houses; and there is a log house now standing not far from Ebenezer, which was perforated by several cannon shot. In short, it was the policy (an unwise one, truly) of the English officers at this post, as it was at every other which they occupied, to make their power felt, and by mere brutal force to awe the colonists into subjection. The Salzburgers endured all these hardships and indignities with becoming fortitude; and though a few were overcome by these severe measures, yet the great mass of them remained firm in their attachment to the principles of liberty.

One of the most serious consequences which resulted to Ebenezer and the neighbourhood, from the occupancy of the town by the British, was the sad state of morals which ensued. The soldiers were licentious in the extreme, and tippling-houses were established for their accommodation in several parts of the town. These became the resort for the soldiers and many of those Salzburgers who espoused the royal cause, and thus habits of intemperance were introduced, and the once sober and moral Germans soon learned to imitate the vicious practices of their corrupt and debased English associates. It was bad enough to desecrate the church, to devastate the country, and to drive off the inhabitants. These were, however, light evils compared with the poisonous moral influences which were spread among those who remained, by the vicious practices which are always more or less incident upon the soldier's life in the camp. These effects were seen and felt many years after the Revolution terminated.

It might be interesting to some, to insert a detailed account of the events which are said to have occurred at Ebenezer during the war, but many of them rest upon rather questionable authority, and are, besides, not of much historical value. The most important to our narrative is the part which was taken by Mr. Triebner, the pastor at Ebenezer. He seems to have remained unmoved amid all the wrongs which the Salzburgers suffered from the British; and when the war terminated he accompanied the English troops to England, where he continued to reside until he attained the advanced age of seventy-eight years. It was a wise movement on his part to leave the country in company with the English troops; for in view of the extreme lengths to which he went in carrying out his Tory principles, it is certain that the Salzburgers would never afterward have tolerated him. It was therefore a fortunate thing for him, that he found an asylum in England, where he could end his days in retirement and comparative peace.

The departure of Mr. Triebner occasioned no regrets among those Salzburgers who had sympathized with the Whigs of the Revolution, and we doubt very much if his friends cherished any particular desire to retain him. His appointment as one of the pastors at Ebenezer was very unfortunate in every respect, but it furnishes another mournful evidence of the fallibility of human judgment. The patrons of the Salzburgers, in Germany, exercised always, as they supposed, a wise discrimination in selecting pastors for the Ebenezer congregations; and it is worthy of remark that this was the only instance in which their judgment was at fault; but alas! what mournful consequences resulted even from this one mistake! It was, however, permitted for some wise purpose; and although with our present darkened vision we cannot comprehend the design which God contemplated, it is the duty of the Christian to bow in humble submission, and believe that the glory of God will be promoted even by those events in the history of the church which are seemingly the most adverse. Sometimes he permits an ungodly minister to creep into a church, to test the stability of his people in the trial of their faith and patience. Sometimes he orders it as a punishment for the want of faithfulness in the discharge of their Christian duties. But, whatever may be the design of such occurrences, it is for us always to feel persuaded that God will not forsake his church, and that even "the gates of hell shall never prevail against her."

In the year 1783 the American troops, under General Wayne, attempted to recover Savannah from the British. General Clarke, who commanded the royal troops in that city, called in his outposts, and made preparations to defend his position. The British troops being thus withdrawn from Ebenezer, General Wayne established his head-quarters there. Between the 12th and 25th of July, 1783, all the English forces stationed at Savannah, amounting to twelve hundred royalists and regulars, besides women, children, Indians, and Negroes, sailed from the port of Savannah; the garrison having capitulated to General Wayne and other American officers. Thus Georgia, after having been three years, six months, and thirteen days in possession of the British, was abandoned after an inglorious attempt to subjugate her people to the control of the mother country.

As soon as the British left Georgia, the Salzburgers had an opportunity to return to their much beloved Ebenezer. This many of them did; but alas! what a scene of desolation was presented! Many of their dwellings had been burned, others had been very much injured, their gardens were completely destroyed, and the general aspect of the place so entirely changed that they could scarcely realize that here they had once had their homes, in which they and their children had dwelt in safety and peace, and that around those homes had clustered the warmest sympathies and most ardent affections of their hearts. They, however, went to work immediately to repair their houses, and to restore, as far as they might be able, order out of the general ruin which everywhere prevailed.

One of the first objects to which the pious Salzburgers directed their attention, was the renovation of their church. This they found in a most deplorable condition. True, they were not compelled to adopt the lamentation of the prophet: "Our holy and beautiful house, where our fathers praised thee, is *burned up with fire;*" but they could say, "all our *pleasant things* are *laid waste.*" It has already been stated that the British had converted the church into a hospital, and subsequently into a stable for their horses For this latter purpose they continued to use it until their departure from Ebenezer. As a matter of course, the Salzburgers found it in a foul and most disgusting state; and to render it again decent and fit for use as a place for divine worship, was a task almost equal to cleansing the famous "Augean stables." But although there was no Peneus whose waters they could cause to flow through their church, yet by industry and perseverance they removed the filth which had accumulated, repaired the edifice, and having completely renovated it, they once more assembled for the worship of God. Amid the angry contentions, and the scenes of strife and carnage incident upon the war, many of them had remained faithful in their devotion to their divine Redeemer, and to the religion of their fathers. Even when they were scattered abroad, and were driven from place to place by their enemies, they assembled in groups for the purpose of prayer and mutual edification. Now that their church was restored to them, they longed ardently to meet in the sanctuary with the solemn assembly, and worship according to the forms which had descended to them from their ancestors, and which were hallowed by so many endearing associations. But who shall call them to the house of God? The faithless Triebner had abandoned them; the pious and beloved Rabenhorst was sleeping "his last sleep," and there was nowhere to be found any one to sympathize with them in their distress, or to succour them in this the hour of their greatest need. They were made to realize that they had been left in a state of spiritual orphanage. They were without a pastor. If there was a time, since their arrival in Georgia, when they stood mostly in need of a wise and faithful minister, it was at this juncture. But alas! they knew of no man speaking their language, and sympathizing with them in this their day of severe trial, who would be willing to become their spiritual shepherd, and "lead them into the green pastures, and beside the still waters" of life.

In their destitution they naturally turned their attention to the much-loved fatherland. The elders of the church called together the scattered members of this once large and interesting flock, and banding themselves together as brethren, they renewed their covenant engagements with God, and then addressed an affectionate letter to the reverend fathers in Germany, humbly but earnestly requesting that a pastor might be sent over "to break unto them the bread of life." A fraternal correspondence was opened, and their patrons in Germany expressed not only their warm sympathy with the Salzburgers in their present distress, but their determination to send them a suitable minister as soon as one could be obtained.

Dr. Muhlenburgh also interested himself on behalf of the Salzburgers. He wrote to Germany, urging the necessity of prompt action on the part of the church there in sending a preacher to Ebenezer. These efforts were not in vain, as shall presently be seen. But while they were pending, a Lutheran minister visited the churches at Savannah and Ebenezer, (for they had both suffered alike during the war,) and he was temporarily employed until the congregation could be supplied from Germany. The following letter, written by Dr. Muhlenburg to the Hon. Mr. Davis, will show what the friends in Germany were doing. It also contains some other facts which will be read with interest. The letter, it will be noticed, was written in 1784, just after the close of the war.

"*New Providence*, April 19, 1784.

"Dear Sir:—As to the accounts concerning the circumstances of the Ebenezer congregation, with which you have been pleased to favour me, I am very much obliged to you for your confidence and ancient friendship. It seemed to me somewhat strange and unexpected, when I heard that the house on Mr. Rabenhorst's plantation had been burned down, and that the congregation had hired a young minister from Germany. On the same day that your letter arrived, I received an important one from Germany, from the unwearied benefactor, Rev. S. Urlsperger, D.D., and President of the Protestant Evangelical Consistory in Augsburg, containing, among others, the following facts:

1. The Rev. Mr. Triebner has, since his arrival in England, honestly paid the principal and interest of the three hundred pounds sterling belonging to Ebenezer church, (unto the Rev. S. Urlsperger,) which the deceased Mr. Caspar Wertsch owed him. Also, whatsoever Mr. Triebner himself owed to the said President he has discharged, and is acquitted.

2. Moreover, the Rev. Dr. Urlsperger offers, that if some one or other of the Ebenezer congregation may have a just and lawful claim against Mr. Triebner, if it be laid before him lawfully proved and attested, it shall be duly paid.

3. He would, during the winter season, endeavour to find out and call a faithful and suitable minister for Ebenezer congregation, and had such a one already in view, to be sent in the spring to Ebenezer, if it pleased God to grant his blessing to it.

4. The reverend fathers will grant the interest of the capital which lays upon the estate of the late Rev. Rabenhorst toward the support of the new minister, and therefore the said principal ought to be well secured.

5. The said fathers have asked the honourable Society in London, whether they would be pleased to continue their benefactions toward supporting a minister and schoolmaster at Ebenezer? and have received for answer, that the Society could not extend their benefactions except to British subjects, and had now to provide for a multitude of poor objects.

6. The reverend President mentions that he has forwarded a letter to the wardens and elders at Ebenezer, which I hope has arrived, and will no doubt give them satisfaction and comfort, so that I have only to add my due respects.

Your well-wishing friend and humble servant.

HENRY M. MUHLENBURG."

"*To the Hon. Mr. Davis.*"

This letter entirely removes all suspicion in reference to the supposed dishonesty of Mr. Triebner, in the management of that part of the Ebenezer church fund which he controlled; and also exonerates Mr. Wertsch from all blame in regard to the *three hundred pounds* which he held as a store-fund. It is important, as showing that the aid which the " Society for the Promotion of Christianity" had extended to the Salzburgers, was withdrawn immediately upon the establishment of the independence of the States. The Salzburgers were no longer *"British"* subjects, and of course, were removed beyond the charities of the Society. Further, it proves, that even after the Revolution the reverend fathers claimed and exercised the right to appoint the pastor for the Ebenezer congregation, and this right was duly admitted by the wardens and elders of the church. Thus the dependence of the Salzburgers upon the church in Germany for ministerial service, as well as for pecuniary aid, continued until the year 1785, about which time a new pastor arrived in Georgia.

Up to this time the prospects of the Salzburgers had been very dark, both as regards their temporal and spiritual interests. They recovered rather slowly from the sad effects of the war. But they never suffered themselves to despair. They had been disciplined in a severe school, and had learned that it is unwise to yield to the force of circumstances, how forbidding soever they might be. They therefore laboured on patiently and perseveringly, hoping for happier and more prosperous days. They believed, too, that their benefactors in Germany would not be unmindful of their spiritual destitution, and with prayerful and believing hearts they looked to God, to send them, through these benefactors, a faithful and godly minister—one who would come imbued with the spirit of his station, and preach to them that word which had been their chief solace in the hours of their deepest calamity. Their prayers were heard, and in due time their pastor came. And thus, as the darkest clouds which obscure the sun are nevertheless tinged by some of his golden rays, adding even beauty to the darkness, so they were enabled to discover, amid the murky clouds which seemed to overhang their prospects, some bright indications of the divine favour, which filled them with holy joy, and afforded them the earnest that a brighter and better day was about to dawn upon them, and that they should yet see the glory of God as they had seen it in the sanctuary, an denjoy once again, not only temporal but spiritual prosperity.

CHAPTER XI.

The arrival of a pastor anticipated—Solicitude on the subject—The Rev. John Earnest Bergman arrives at Ebenezer—His early history—His qualifications for the ministry—State of affairs at Ebenezer and Savannah—Mr. Bergman's defects—Parochial schools—Mr. Bernhardt—Mr. Probst—Mr. Ernst—Increase of pastoral labours—Church in Savannah—Letter from Mr. Scheuber—Correct views of the sacraments—Usages of the Lutheran Church—Mr. Bergman's marriage—His family—Mr. Bergman as a scholar—His correspondence—Parsonage at Ebenezer—Bishop Francis Asbury—His letter to Mr. Bergman—Improvement in temporal affairs—Bad habits among the Salzburgers—Want of church discipline—Disaffection toward the church—Members withdraw—Ebenezer bridge—Ebenezer becomes the county site—Effects of this measure—County site changed to Springfield—The mills—Demand for English preaching—Letter from Bishop Asbury—Mistaken policy—Methodists in Savannah—Obligations of the Methodists to the Lutheran Church—Rev. Hope Hull—Jonathan Jackson—Josiah Randle—John Garvin—Rev. S. Dunwoody—First Methodist Society in Savannah—Mr. Bergman relinquishes the church in Savannah—Letter to Rev. H. Holcombe—Savannah church without a pastor—Rev. S. A. Mealy—Salzburgers in other churches—Jesse Lee visits Ebenezer—Mr. Bergman curtails his labours—"Bethel" church erected—Personal difficulty—Letter of Rev. J. McVean—Efforts to proselyte—Lax state of morals—Want of discipline—Mr. Bergman's grief at the condition of the colony—External prosperity—Spiritual declension—Death of Mrs. Neidlinger—Mr. Bergman's health declines—His death.

THE Salzburgers, particularly the pious portion of them, received with great satisfaction the intelligence that their brethren in Germany were interesting themselves on their behalf, and they hailed with great enthusiasm the prospect of being soon favoured with the services of a devoted and well-qualified pastor. The news of his appointment had reached them through the letter of Dr. S. Urlsperger to the wardens and elders of the church, and they awaited his arrival with great anxiety; and yet their wishes on his behalf were not unmingled with deep solicitude. Although they had the fullest confidence in the wisdom and prudence of their German benefactors, their sad experience in the case of Mr. Triebner had justly excited their fears, lest the newly-appointed minister should disappoint their expectations. There is always one inevitable and painful result growing out of the improper conduct of ministers: it excites suspicion against the innocent; and where a pastor has proven himself unworthy of the confidence of a church, his successor will always be regarded with mistrust, until he has established his claims to the esteem and respect of his people by his unimpeachable deportment. This, however, a truly pious minister will soon accomplish; for although men are sometimes slow in yielding their prejudices, true merit and integrity of character will dispel all doubts and evil surmising, and win the respect and love of the virtuous.

At length the wishes and prayers of the Salzburgers were answered by the appearance of their new pastor. The person sent over by the directors in Germany was the Rev. JOHN ERNEST BERGMAN, a young man of decided talents and extensive literary acquirements. Mr. Bergman was a native of Peritsch, in Saxony. In 1776, he entered the university at Leipsic, where he was graduated with distinguished honour. He was ordained by the Evangelical Seniors of the Lutheran Church, in the Duchy of Augsburg, on the 19th of July, 1783. This was once Protestant territory, but was surrendered by Prussia, and came under the jurisdiction of Bavaria.

It has not been ascertained from what position he was called when he was chosen pastor at Ebenezer; this, however, is not important. He arrived in Georgia in the spring of 1785, and entered zealously and actively upon the discharge of his duties. These he was to find numerous and arduous, and often a source of deep anxiety and perplexity.

Mr. Bergman found both the temporal and spiritual affairs of the Salzburgers in a very unfavourable condition. The town of Ebenezer had been almost entirely deserted during the war, and many of the settlements were nearly broken up. The people, therefore, had to commence life almost anew; and, as a matter of course, their pecuniary circumstances were very much embarrassed. Besides this, the whole congregation had been in a great measure scattered; their records were either lost or very much mutilated; the members had not only greatly declined, but many of them had entirely departed from their Christian profession. This was not only true of the congregations in and about Ebenezer; it was equally so in relation to the Salzburgers in Savannah. Mr. Bergman was greatly grieved at the desolation which met his eye on every side, and at times he was well-nigh giving up in despair all hopes of restoring order and organizing the churches upon a permanent footing.

He possessed, however, many requisites for the arduous work which was before him, though in some respects he was deficient. He was young, and though not endowed with a vigorous constitution, yet he was a man of energy and great industry. Besides, he possessed more than ordinary intellect, which he had cultivated with great assiduity. It is questionable whether, in point of learning, he was equalled by either of his predecessors; and the manuscripts he executed bear ample testimony to his extensive acquirements and untiring diligence in the acquisition of knowledge. As a pulpit orator he is said to have been above mediocrity, and always commanded the attention and respect of his hearers. He lacked, however, one very important ingredient in the character of a minister, to make him successful. He had *no knowledge of men and things.* In other words, he was a perfect novice in all matters of business, and seemed not disposed to cultivate any intercourse with society, except in as far as he was forced to do so in the discharge of his duty. In his feelings he was too exclusive, and did not mingle enough with society to qualify him for very extensive usefulness. His books were his companions, and he sought his chief enjoyment in the retirement of his study.

Under these circumstances, it was not to be expected that Mr. Bergman would achieve as much for the Salzburgers as he might have done, if his disposition had led him to cultivate a freer intercourse with his parishioners. Still he was instrumental in effecting much, especially for the spiritual improvement of the people.

Mr. Bergman, among other measures, endeavoured to revive the parochial school at Ebenezer. A young man by the name of Bernhardt was sent over from Germany as a teacher, but owing to his levity of disposition and insubordination, he gave Mr. Bergman a great deal of trouble. Mr. Bernhardt was in a year or two dismissed, and Mr. Probst was appointed as his successor. Mr. Probst occupied this position until 1796, when Mr. G. Ernst became the teacher. With him terminated the *parochial* school, although private schools were subsequently taught at Ebenezer.

Mr. Bernhardt removed to Carolina, where he was converted, and subsequently became a useful minister in the Lutheran Church. He was the father of the late Rev. David Bernhardt of the South Carolina Synod, whose memory will long be cherished by the church and all who knew him.

The ministerial labours of Mr. Bergman were much more arduous than those of his predecessors. It will be remembered, that up to the Revolutionary War, the Salzburgers had always had two, and in some instances three, pastors. But the pecuniary affairs of the congregation becoming somewhat deranged, and the "Society for Propagating Christian Knowledge" having withdrawn its aid, the funds were found insufficient to maintain more than one minister. It was thus made the duty of Mr. Bergman to cultivate, as far as practicable, this field, which at one time gave full employment to not less than two pastors. He was, however, not discouraged, either by the extent of the field before him, or the demand upon his mental and physical energies. He immediately entered upon a systematic arrangement of his labours, by which he hoped to be able to supply not only the churches in and about Ebenezer, but also the one in the city of Savannah. In a very short time he was enabled to furnish all these churches with regular preaching, apportioning his time between them as equally as circumstances would permit.

The congregation in Savannah, though much injured by the war, kept up its organization, and some of its members appear to have been devotedly pious men. By a portion of this congregation Mr. Bergman's labours were highly appreciated, and for a time he was instrumental in affecting much good among them. In December, 1786, he communicated to the elders of the church in Savannah his intention to visit them and administer the Lord's Supper. The following letter, written to him in reply by one of the elders, will be read with interest:

"*Savannah,* December 29, 1786.

DEAR SIR:—In a letter of the 26th inst., I understood that if it suited the German congregation in Savannah, you intended to come down and celebrate the Sacrament of the Lord's Supper on Sunday, the 7*th of January.* In consequence of such intimation, I acquainted the elders and wardens, who, with one voice, acquiesced in it, and agreeably to their resolution gave notice, in yesterday's letter, to Mr. Probst. But this day, several other members of the congregation, not being properly prepared for so solemn an act in religion, wish beforehand to hear a few sermons tending toward this object, in order to prepare themselves more fully for this sacred duty; and consequently they prefer to postpone receiving the Lord's Supper until Easter, or thereabouts.

In the mean time, reverend sir, you are expected on Saturday, the 6th of January next, to give the congregation a forenoon sermon on repentance, and Mr. Probst, who, if he should fail in his appointment at Ebenezer, may give a sermon in the afternoon; and if his oration is liked by the congregation, may perhaps prove him an establishment in this place, in case he should be disappointed with you. There will be on the Sunday appointed a full congregation, if the weather permit. God grant you may be satisfied with your appointment, and the congregation with you, in which I hope you will not fail; and in that case you might even enjoy a heaven on earth.

You have my best wishes for your welfare and happiness, and I have the honour, for the first time, to subscribe myself with sincere regard and profound respect, your most humble servant,

JUSTUS H. SCHEUBER."

From this letter it will be seen that the church in Savannah was duly organized in the year 1787, having a full board of elders and wardens. It is further manifest that there must have been a favourable state of religious feeling among the members, as evinced by the holy reverence which they seemed to cherish for the ordinances of God's house, and their unwillingness to partake of those ordinances except after due meditation and self-examination. This speaks well, at least, for the devotional feelings of a congregation; and when such sentiments are cherished, they cannot fail to produce the most salutary influence upon the character and life. This is a peculiarity of the Lutheran Church, and arises from the wise and wholesome usages which the founders of Lutheranism established both in Europe and America. The course of catechetical instruction prescribed by our ritual, and the *preparatory services* which are held in our churches prior to the administration of the Lord's Supper, are admirably calculated to inspire the heart with a holy veneration for that most solemn and instructive sacrament. It is to be regretted that some of our churches have manifested a disposition to depart from this ancient landmark of Lutheranism.

About the year 1792, Mr. Bergman married Miss Catherine Herb, sister of Mr. Frederick Herb, of Savannah. By this marriage Mr. Bergman had four children, only one of whom, his eldest son, Christopher F., survived him. This, for him, was a very happy and advantageous union. And perhaps much of his success in after life may justly be attributed to the influence of this most excellent lady. She seems to have possessed very remarkable business talents; and it is said that her husband committed to her the entire management of all his domestic matters, even giving up to her the receipt and disbursement of all his funds, while he devoted himself exclusively to his literary pursuits. These were very extensive, and embraced a wide field. History, philosophy, the various departments of natural science, classical literature, all engaged his attention, and in each of them he attained to very considerable proficiency. As a thelogian, he was especially well read, having acquired a thorough knowledge of the Hebrew, Arabic, and several other oriental languages. His correspondence, too, was very extensive, and he was honoured with the confidence of some of the most remarkable men of his day; among whom, were Bishop Asbury, of the Methodist Episcopal church; Dr. R. Furman, pastor of the Baptist church in Charleston; the Hon. R. Wayne, and the Rev. Messrs. Holcombe, McVean and others, of Savannah.

His home at Ebenezer was the receptacle of every preacher who might chance to visit that neighbourhood; and in his Christian intercourse with his ministerial brethren of other denominations, he seems to have won their confidence and Christian regard. Bishop Asbury, on several occasions, sojourned at the parsonage at Ebenezer, and between him and Mr. Bergman there existed the warmest Christian affection; and the good bishop held Mr. Bergman in such high regard that he honoured him with his correspondence. The following letter is in point.

"*Wilkes county, Georgia*, December 5, 1800.

"My Dear and Greatly Respected Friend:—Grace, mercy, and peace be multiplied to you and family. When I come to Georgia, I remember you if I do not see you. For a few years past I have not been able to preach or write as formerly. Shall I pity or envy you in your solitary life. It must cheer up your mind to converse with a friend on paper. I thank you, kind sir, for the friendly letters you have sent me, and the notice you have taken of Elder Lee. This year hath been marked with divine glory; my colleague, Bishop Whatcoat, and self have travelled from Baltimore, in the month of May last, to the east of Boston, west as far as Kentucky and Cumberland in Tennessee, South Carolina, to this State, making near three thousand miles from the General Conference. The revival of religion that began with the year, became very great; so that the eastern and western shores of Maryland, Delaware, and Pennsylvania, have felt the holy flame; the high probability is, that one or two thousand souls have been under the operations of grace. The preachers caught the divine influence at the General Conference, where more than one hundred ministers assembled, and thus it ran, two, three, four, five hundred miles. You have heard of the revival of religion among the Germans in the west of Pennsylvania, Maryland, and Virginia, by the instrumentality of the venerable Otterbein,* and an ancient patriarchal man, Martin Beem, once a Menonist minister; but he received the Methodists about twenty years ago. He was cast out by the Menonist. God has given him to see his children's children brought to Christ, and peace upon Israel. At seventy, he is brisk as a boy, and travels very extensively; for in appearance he is like old Moses or Aaron with his long beard. Oh! my dear friend, if you was among the thousands in Pennsylvania of Germans to labour, and travelling night and day, you might have a happier soul and a brighter crown. A late Dr. Lodly was in some part of Holland almost useless; he was sent for to New York, and the first sermon he preached in the Low Dutch Church, Madam Livingston, and several reputable women were convinced. They said it was like a new gospel; he continued in usefulness till the Revolutionary War; then he was forced to retire, when his labours were lost as at the first. I was told he had intimations of what

---

* Mr. Otterbein was a very pious minister of the German Reformed Church.

was to befall him in both changes. Thus a Wesley, and some of the Moravian brethren appeared to be buried for a time at and about Savannah. And some godly men have lived in parishes and congregations in England, with small prospects of good. Before I close this letter I must give you a sketch of the marvellous work of God. For two weeks, we trust one or two hundred souls were wrought upon at the General Conference in Baltimore. At the yearly Conference at Duck creek, Delaware State, one hundred and seventeen came forward to join the church,—the fruit of four days' and nights' labour. The brethren did not leave the house of God day nor night; this was in a small village, and fifty had been added previously, since the commencement of the year. The return was three hundred in society, as made last June to me; and the work is spreading all around that place, through the whole peninsula of Maryland and Delaware. We have travelled so rapidly and extensively, letters could not reach us well, till we came to our yearly conference in Camden, South Carolina, January 1, 1801. In Cumberland, State of Tennessee, God has wrought among the Presbyterians; five godly ministers are entered into the spirit of the work,—a Mr. Craighead, Hodge, Rankin, Mr. Goady, and McGee, and the stationed preachers among the Methodists, and some eminent local preachers. Judah doth not vex Ephraim; they live and love as brethren; they hold sacramental meetings four days and nights, all the ministers present; it is in the woods; no house will contain the people, wagons, food, fires, some ten, twenty, thirty, fifty, and one hundred miles from home; they begin at high noon, preach and pray until evening, then retire to refresh with food; and come again, and continue the whole night, and souls are born to God at the solemn hours of night,—seven, eight, nine, ten, twelve, one o'clock, till morning. It hath been judged, that the congregation have contained from five hundred, to one and two thousand people, and eight or ten ministers; and at a meeting Bishop Whatcoat and myself attended, near twenty ministers present,—Presbyterians,

Methodists, and Baptists; souls have professed to find the Lord from twenty-five to forty-five, and as many as one hundred at a meeting. The probability is that between three and four hundred have been brought to Christ in the course of this summer and fall, and the work was going on when we came from the settlement. The ministers promised to send me a correct account of the work of God. We hope to be able to publish the workings of God with souls. I hope and trust five or six thousand souls are, and will be formed of God on this continent in 1800, among the different societies of professing Christians. I shall make no apology for my long letters, but the cause of God, love to you, and my joy that I have to hear and see my poor labours are not in vain, and other ministers, and other societies have Jehovah with them. I am in the thirtieth year of my labours in America, besides about nine years in travelling and local labours in England.

"I am, with great respect, yours in Christ,
FRANCIS ASBURY.'

The temporal affairs of the Salzburgers commenced improving gradually; and the population which, during the war, had been somewhat diminished, began to increase steadily, and to assume a somewhat more permanent character. Their spiritual interests, too, assumed a more favourable aspect, though Mr. Bergman found many just causes of complaint. Some of the members of the church had fallen into rather loose habits of living, and the establishment of one or two drinking shops at Ebenezer, exerted a most injurious influence upon the morals of not a few. Mr. Bergman remonstrated against such conduct, but he was, perhaps, rather two mild and lenient in the enforcement of the church discipline, to effect much of a reformation. Still the church made some progress, while it must be admitted that the tone of piety was far below what it had been in former years.

Mr. Bergman kept up a regular course of catechetical instruction in all his churches, and endeavoured to indoctrine the young people of his charge in the principles of our holy religion, as taught in our standards; and there were many, who, under his instructions, became devotedly pious and exemplary Christians. But even in his time, a spirit of indifference to the *Lutheran* church began to manifest itself among some of the descendants of the Salzburgers, which was afterwards to result in the withdrawal of not a few of them from the church of their fathers. It will be necessary, however, to dwell more at large upon this topic hereafter.

It is not deemed important, nor would it be practicable, to attempt a regular chronological history of the Salzburgers from this period, nor, indeed, is it necessary; for there were not many occurrences of striking interest during the life-time of Mr. Bergman. The most prominent, however, will be noted as far as reliable data can be obtained. After a settlement assumes a permanent character, it is not to be expected that many incidents will happen of sufficient moment to make them worthy of historical record. The reader will, therefore, not expect any thing like detailed narrative in the further prosecution of this work.

It has been stated that Mr. Bergman was in correspondence with a number of distinguished ministers and other gentlemen, and some of their letters are extant; but their publication would only swell this volume without increasing its interest. It might be mentioned that many of these letters furnish intelligence in reference to the progress of religion in different parts of the United States, and perhaps a few extracts may be given from some of them hereafter.

Mention has been made of the erection of a bridge over Ebenezer creek, and the making of a causeway through the swamp. The first bridge, however, was a very humble and unpretending structure, and answered only a temporary purpose. Mr. King, who owned most of the land north of Ebenezer creek, applied to the Legislature, in 1791, for a charter for a causeway and toll bridge. The charter covered a period of *thirty years*. In 1824, (24th of April) the Trustees of the Lutheran church purchased, at public sale, Mr. King's interest, which was for the unexpired term of *nine* years, for the sum of *eighteen hundred dollars*. With the bridge the Trustees obtained *sixty-five acres* of land. A new bridge was erected by Messrs. William and Lewis Bird, in the fall of the same year, at a cost of four hundred and ninety-nine dollars. The Trustees obtained a renewal of the charter in 1824 for *thirty years.* Mr. C. F. Bergman, in a note in his journal, estimated that the income from the bridge for nine years would amount to about five thousand dollars. Whether or not this expectation was realized, it would be difficult to ascertain; though it is certain, that the Trustees did realize at first a handsome profit upon the investment. Within the last fifteen years, however, the bridge and causeway have been rather a tax upon the church, as the inferior court of Effingham county authorized the opening of a public road from Sister's Ferry, on the Savannah river, by way of Springfield, on to the city of Savannah. This measure has cut off nearly all the travel from the old Augusta road, and the toll-gate does not now pay expenses.

In 1796, Ebenezer was made the county site, and the Legislature appointed commissioners to select lots for the court-house and jail, and also to provide for the support of an academy. This academy was intended as a *county* institution. There was already a *parochial* school at Ebenezer, under the care of a competent teacher. The instructions, however, were given almost exclusively in the German, and did not meet the wants of the community, which even at this time had become measurably Anglicized.

The selection of Ebenezer as the county site was the second experiment to procure a suitable location. The public buildings were erected at Tuckasee-King, in 1784, near the present line of Scriven county; but as this movement did not suit the wishes of the people, Ebenezer was selected. It would have been well for the Salzburgers if their town had never been made the seat of justice. There are always men of debased morals collecting at a county site, who drink, gamble, and indulge in almost every species of vice; and these influences did not fail to effect the Salzburgers, some of whom were, alas! too easily seduced from the right way. Fortunately for them, however, Ebenezer was found to be not sufficiently central; and, in 1799, Springfield was made the county site, and continues so to this day.

It has been stated, that during the life-time of the first pastors, mills had been erected, and several tracts of land were granted for the benefit of the church. During the war, nearly all these "mill establishments" were materially injured, and they subsequently were allowed to go to decay. In 1808, the congregation applied to the legislature for leave to sell their glebe land. This request was granted, and the proceeds were placed in the treasury of the church. The congregation by degrees disposed of all its real estate, and the money was invested in bonds and mortgages, from the interest of which the pastor's salary, and the current expenses of the church were paid. This plan is pursued to the present day.

The interests of the churches, both at Ebenezer and Savannah, began to demand that a portion of the services should be held in English. Many friends of the Lutheran church saw this, and felt it, and urged upon Mr. Bergman the importance of attempting to qualify himself to preach in that language; but it was with great difficulty that he could at first be brought even to consider the subject. In this he certainly acted unwisely, as will appear hereafter. An extract is here given from a letter of Bishop Asbury to Mr. Bergman, a part of which bears upon this very subject. The letter was written from Georgetown, in 1803. After stating the wonders which God was working in various parts of the country in the conversion of sinners, the bishop says:

"I am not without expectation of visiting Savannah and Ebenezer next December. I shall take an assistant with me, and, if I could find a decent family, that had the form of godliness, with whom I could lodge, and a house to preach in, we would perhaps spend a week. But I shall be unwilling to preach in Cloud's or the Baptist church. If you have a church in town, I would borrow that. I am sorry you do not attend some of the camp-meetings. Our yearly conference will be held in Augusta, January 1, 1804. There I hope to see you. *I think as you are not advanced in age, if you wish to be extensively useful, you ought by all means to learn English to preach, as well as to write. By close application and some little assistance, you would soon gain a good accent and pronunciation. In learning to preach English you will open a door to preach to thousands in this country; besides you will get good as well do good.* I hope that you have a clear witness of your redemption in Christ, and that you walk closely with God, and are seeking freedom from all sin. When I read in Mr. Wesley's journal, of the holy men once at Ebenezer, I hope you will be their faithful successor. Oh! may the good will of Him that dwelt with Moses in the bush be with you, and the dew of heaven upon your dwelling-place.

"I am, as ever, your friend and brother.

FRANCIS ASBURY."

From this letter it will appear that good men in other denominations, who really wished well to the Lutheran church, saw that our ministers, who persisted in adhering to the German language, pursued a ruinous policy, while they circumscribed greatly the sphere of their own usefulness. Would to God, that our forefathers could have been truly wise on this subject. It will also be seen, that up to this date the Methodist's had no church in the city of Savannah, and Bishop Asbury asked the use of the Lutheran church. This is a fact worthy of notice. There is no doubt that the use of the church was cheerfully granted, and thus, as Lutheran emigrants from Salzburg were measurably the instruments in Mr. Wesley's awakening, and Luther's preface to the Romans the means of his conversion, the Lutheran church in Savannah was employed by the first Methodist bishop in America to promulgate the doctrines of the venerable Wesley. From all this it is apparent that Methodism owes many obligations to the Lutheran church, which it is to be regretted have not always been duly remembered and reciprocated.

It is proper here to remark, that as early as 1790, the Rev. Hope Hull was sent to Savannah to propagate the doctrines of the Methodist Episcopal church. He preached a few years in a chair-maker's shop belonging to Mr. Lowry; but, in consequence of the violent opposition raised against him, he met with very little success. In 1796, Jonathan Jackson and Josiah Randle made another attempt, without any better results. In 1800, John Garvin commenced preaching. He induced a few persons to attend his meeting, but never succeeded in organizing a society. The next attempt was by Mr. Cloud, whose extravagances increased the prejudices against the Methodist; and it is probable that it is to this Mr. "Cloud's house" that Bishop Asbury refers in the foregoing letter. In 1806, Rev. Samuel Dunwoody was sent to Savannah. By assiduous effort he organized a society, and the members after many severe trials succeeded in erecting a small house of worship, which was called Wesley Chapel. This was the origin of Methodism in Savannah.

Nothing of much importance occurred among the Salzburgers until about the year 1804, when Mr. Bergman relinquished the charge of the Lutheran church in Savannah. In a letter written to the Rev. Mr. Holcombe, pastor of the Baptist church in that city, he assigns the reasons which had induced him to take this step. The letter is dated July 4, 1804. In that letter he says: "In Germany both Protestant churches (Lutheran and Reformed) have become measurably corrupt, through false teachers creeping into the church, whose bad qualities are described in Paul's letter to Timothy, and in the Epistle of Peter. These teachers impiously deny all the fundamental doctrines of our salvation, which is in Jesus Christ. The Germans who have come to this country in late years have imbibed these false principles, and cannot bear sound doctrine, leading also a perverse life. Besides this, I cannot see any fruit of the gospel preached to them; and some impious men, longing for riches, are insolent enough to impute to me motives which I never entertained. Further, I am bound to stay at Ebenezer, because my frail constitution will not longer endure the fatigue of journeying so often to Savannah. Consequently, when I visit Savannah hereafter, it must be on week-days."

In another letter addressed to the same gentleman, Mr. Bergman remarks: "I have not (as has been falsely charged) denounced good morals or external religion, as it is termed. I agree with the good Cardinal Bellarmine, who, while he apologizes for good works, concludes that it is safest and best to put all our confidence in God's grace and Christ's merits. And when I pray that I may be numbered among God's elect children, I desire that he would deal with me, not according to *my merits*, but according to *his grace*. Yet some wicked persons whom I refused to admit to the Lord's table, have accused me of advocating Antinomian sentiments. And a man by the name of Salvinger, who resides near the 'White Bluff,' defamed my name in the Savannah market, as did also one Elliott, once a schoolmaster at White Bluff, and afterward at Goshen, to whom I refused the Lutheran church at Ebenezer. The whole Lutheran church in America needs a reformation. There are many pious people in Germany, and some of them come occasionally to this country, but for the most part they are only nominal professors, and cannot endure sound doctrine. Hence the trouble in many of our German churches."

The motives which prompted this step were certainly pure, and the reasons assigned justify the course which Mr. Bergman pursued. It is, however, probable that he did occasionally visit the church in Savannah, and perform services for the benefit of the few pious persons who still adhered to the true doctrines of the Reformation. However, as the services were all held in German, the young people belonging to the congregation gradually withdrew to attend English preaching in other churches, and in a few years Mr. Bergman ceased altogether his ministerial labours in Savannah, and the Lutheran church was closed, and no successful attempt was made to revive the congregation until the year 1824, when the Rev. S. A. Mealy of Charleston, assumed the pastoral charge,—not, however, until many of the descendants of the Salzburgers had been induced to leave the church of their fathers, and connect themselves with other Christian denominations. The records of all the Protestant churches in Savannah will show that much of the most valuable material from which their societies were organized, was of Lutheran origin. And this same sad story must be told in reference to the Lutheran population in every important city in our Union. It is, however, far better that these precious souls should find spiritual pasture somewhere, and be made the heirs of eternal life, than that they should wander about without a spiritual guide, exposed to the wiles of Satan and the craftiness of ungodly men.

It was about this time that the Rev. Jesse Lee, one of the pioneers of Methodism in the United States, visited Ebenezer, and spent a few days with Mr. Bergman. The interviews seem to have proved a source of mutual edification to these pious men. Mr. Lee, speaks of this visit in a letter addressed to Mr. Aurelius of New York, and expresses himself as having been very favourably impressed with the piety and learning of Mr. Bergman. It is a pleasing fact, that every one of the first pastors at Ebenezer (Mr. Triebner only excepted) commanded the confidence and esteem of the ministers in the other evangelical churches, showing very clearly that their learning and irreproachable Christian character had gained for them a most enviable reputation among the wise and good. But still, their piety and learning did not exempt them from the attacks of the vicious and profane; and, as has already been shown, they were often made the objects of vituperation. It was, however, fortunate for them that they were sustained in all their trials by a consciousness of their own integrity, and the assurance of the divine approbation. These are ever the Christian's chief solace amid the reproaches of the censorious, and the scoffs and derisions of the profligate and worldly; and but for the "sweet peace" which the soul derives from a sense of its own rectitude, cheerless indeed would the path of the faithful minister as he mingles with the cares and perplexities of life. But amid the conflicts of human passion which meet him on every side, and the buffetings and derisions of a world lying in wickedness, he may ever and anon hear the cheering and animating voice of the Saviour, "Lo! I am with you always!" "My peace I give unto you." "Be of good cheer! I have overcome the world." Thus he passes on through life, ever reposing his confidence in the great captain of his salvation, and sustained by the hope that his labours and toils shall terminate in a rich and glorious reward, which shall amply compensate him for all the afflictions incident to his earthly pilgrimage.

The labours of Mr. Bergman were somewhat curtailed by relinquishing the charge of the Lutheran church in Savannah; and it has already been stated, that the church called Bethany had been in a good measure abandoned. It became necessary, however, to erect a new church near "Jack's branch," about four miles northwest of Springfield, the county site. This church was called "*Bethel.*" It was demanded by the emigration to that neighbourhood of a number of families who had formerly resided near Ebenezer, and were members of the congregation at that place. Yet no new organization was attempted; and, even to this day, the members residing near Bethel continue their connection with the parent-church at Ebenezer. This was a judicious movement on the part of Mr. Bergman, as it was the means of saving to the Lutheran church many families who might otherwise have connected themselves with other denominations.

Among the difficulties connected with his labours, Mr. Bergman mentions several of a *personal* character. One of these was with Colonel W., who resided near Sister's Ferry. The nature of the misunderstanding is not stated, nor is it necessary at this late day to attempt to investigate it. Colonel W. had been a soldier in the Revolutionary War, and was a man of influence; hence, Mr. Bergman was troubled because of the rupture which had taken place, and corresponded with the Rev. John McVean on the subject. *Mr. McVean* was stationed in Savannah as pastor of the Methodist Episcopal church. An extract from his letter to Mr. Bergman on this subject is here inserted, to show the excellent spirit by which he was actuated. Besides, it contains a great deal of wholesome Christian advice, which it would be well for every one to remember and practice. He says:

"I am truly sorry for the misunderstanding between you and Colonel W., and sincerely wish it were otherwise. I know it is painful to human feelings to receive injuries from the quarter from whence they were least expected; but our Saviour suffered in the same way, and good men often do and may expect to suffer. May I be permitted to suggest a plan of reconciliation? When I do so, I need only quote Scripture to you, without any comment. First, 'If thy brother trespass against thee, go and tell him his fault between him and thee alone; if he shall hear thee, then thou hast gained thy brother.

Matt. xiii. 15; v. 23. Do, my dear sir, have the honour and the comfort to be the first to make peace: love will conquer the stoutest. Suppose you were to take up the cross and go some serene and clear morning and breakfast with Colonel W., and bind and tie his hands, and feet, and heart, and tongue with cords of love and with pious loving conversation and admonition; this will do. This method I am certain will succeed, and under its influence even the 'lion will become a lamb.'

"Yours in Christian love,

JOHN McVEAN."

It is believed that this advice was taken, and friendly relations were again established between these parties.

In addition to the sources of trouble which have already been stated, one which was very trying to his feelings was the disposition manifested by some of the descendants of the Salzburgers to forsake the church of their fathers. The Methodists and Baptists began to preach in various portions of Effingham county; and, in several instances, members were drawn off from the Lutheran church, who, with their families, formed a nucleus for the organization of other churches differing from the Lutheran, if not in any essential doctrinal views, yet in their uses and form of church government; and it will appear hereafter, that, but for the material which the Salzburgers furnished to the other denominations which have sprung up in Effingham county, they could never have had any existence. This is true, particularly, in relation to the

Methodist and Baptist churches, and it is a fact susceptible of proof, especially in relation to the Methodist church, that their very best members, both as to piety and influence, are those who descended from the Salzburgers. Mr. Bergman saw the course which things were taking in this respect, and he might have checked it, at least measurably, by introducing the English language into the church service, and by bestowing a little more attention upon the spiritual wants of his people; but, with all his piety and learning, his views were not sufficiently *practical.*

There was, however, another cause operating, to produce alienation of feeling on the part of those who felt it their duty to cultivate a spirit of genuine piety; and that was the lax state of morals in which many of the members indulged, and the want of proper church discipline. The discipline was there, but it was a *dead letter.* Mr. Bergman either did not, or could not enforce it, and many of the members became very irregular in their habits, so that their conduct was a just cause of offence to the more godly and consistent part of the congregation; and many were constrained from a sense of duty to flee from associations which they felt were baneful, and to seek others, more congenial to their feelings, and better calculated to aid them in the cultivation of their hearts and the fuller development of the

Christian character. It is not admitted that such a course of conduct is justifiable under all circumstances, and should not be adopted except in extreme cases; and only after every means has been tried to effect a reformation. Then our own safety may require us to separate ourselves from those "evil communications" which may tend to corrupt our religious principles.

The state of the churches was a source of deep sorrow to Mr. Bergman. In his letters to his friends, he complained of the fruitlessness of his labours, and seemed wellnigh to despair of ever accomplishing any permanent good. His personal piety was evidently of a high order, and in this respect he was well calculated to be a teacher in divine things; but still, he appears to have been unable to wield that moral influence which was necessary to suppress every species of vice among his people, and induce them to aim at an elevated standard of piety.

Thus things continued to progress from year to year; and though the outward prosperity of the colony was increasing, the population multiplying, the people acquiring wealth and seeking new means of advancing their worldly interests, yet there was a gradual but manifest decline in the piety of many of the Salzburgers, so that the language of Jeremiah to Israel might very justly be applied to the descendants of the Salzburgers; "Yet I planted thee a noble vine, wholly a right seed; how then art thou turned into the degenerate plant of a strange vine unto me?" Jer. ii. 21. Nevertheless God had not left himself without witnesses.

In the midst of all his other trials, Mr. Bergman was about to experience a heavy bereavement, in the loss of his only daughter, Ann Catharine, consort of John Neidlinger. She was born January 1, 1795, and married September 18, 1814. In her sixteenth year she made a profession of religion, and connected herself with the Lutheran congregation at Ebenezer, according to the established usages of the church. Her marriage seems not to have been a judicious one, and proved a source of grief to herself and her family. Her death occurred on the 31st of January, 1819, she being in her twenty-fifth year. Her brother has these notes in his journal in reference to her decease: "When her mother first came to her, she said: 'Mother, are you not sorry for your poor child?' (alluding to her bodily suffering.) She continued: 'I am going to my dear Redeemer. My Redeemer will have mercy on me. I am quite happy and easy, my Saviour has strengthened me, I feel not the least pain.' She expired without a sigh or a groan, calmly commending her spirit into the hands of her divine Saviour."

This sad event cast quite a gloom over the

family, and it is to be hoped that the dispensation was sanctified to all who were afflicted by it.

A few years subsequently to the death of his daughter, Mr. Bergman himself was removed from the vineyard of the Lord. This occurred on the 25th of February, 1824. Mr. Bergman had served the congregation at Ebenezer with great faithfulness, but his labours seem not to have been duly appreciated, and there had evidently been a retrograde movement in the congregation, and the moral and religious aspect of the colony was far from being favourable. Yet his labours were not in vain. God gave him many seals to his ministry, some of whom still live to bless the church and the world by their pious and exemplary deportment. The labourer was gathered to his reward in peace and holy triumph, after having spent *thirty-six years* of unremitting toil in the Master's vineyard. His remains were buried in Ebenezer Cemetery, and there, with hundreds of the pious Salzburgers, he rests in hope of a better resurrection. "He was a good man and full of faith."

CHAPTER XII.

Gloomy prospects at Ebenezer—Rev. C. F. Bergman—His early religious sentiments—Calvinistic tendency—Attends the Georgia Presbytery—Letter to Rev. M. Rauch—Conflicting views—Becomes a member of Presbytery—Receives a call to St. Matthew's Lutheran Church—Dr. J. Bachman visits Savannah and Ebenezer—Interview and correspondence with Mr. Bergman—Mr. Bergman changes his views, joins South Carolina Synod, and becomes pastor at Ebenezer—His piety and qualification for the work—State of the congregation—Methodist and Baptist churches organized—Methodist church at Goshen—Rev. J. O. Andrew—Delusion—A false messiah—Strange scene at Goshen—Sad results—Rev. L. Myers locates at Goshen—His character, labours, and death—Temperance movement at Ebenezer—Mr. Bergman introduces English preaching—His marriage—His children—Temporal and spiritual prosperity—Emigration of Salzburgers to other counties—Church in Savannah—Rev. S. A. Mealy—Rev. N. Aldrich—New church in Savannah—Rev. A. J. Karn—German congregation—Rev. W. Epping—Disaffection at Ebenezer—Other churches built up by Salzburgers—Mr. Bergman as a scholar—Trials—Indifference to education—Mr. Bergman's sickness and death—Rev. J. D. Schenck—Rev. E. A. Bolles—Difficulties at Ebenezer—Rev. P. A. Strobel—Death of Mrs. Bergman—Rev. E. Kieffer—Rev. G. Haltiwanger—Rev. J. Austin—Present condition of the church—"Father Snider."

THE condition of the colony at Ebenezer, on the death of Mr. Bergman, was gloomy indeed. Owing to the establishment of the independence of the States, the "Society for Promoting Christian Knowledge" had ceased to extend any aid to the Salzburgers, and as the congregation at Ebenezer had made some changes in the administration of its affairs, the church no longer looked to their friends in Germany to supply them with a pastor. Their friend and faithful adviser, Dr. Muhlenburg, was dead, and there was no Lutheran Synod in the South from which they could expect to receive any aid. It is true, Mr. Bergman had left a son, *Christopher F.*, a young man of deep piety and of extensive learning, acquired mostly under the instruction of his father, and to him the people naturally looked as the successor of their late venerable pastor. His mind, however, was turned in a different direction.

Young Bergman seems in early life to have imbibed strong Calvinistic sentiments. This, no doubt, was the result of his reading. He had made himself familiar with the writings of Scott, Henry, Doddridge, and other eminent divines of that school, and he appears to have adopted the doctrine of the "Divine Sovereignty" and the doctrine of "grace," as taught in Calvin's institutes. So far had he gone in embracing these tenets, that he attended several sessions of the Georgia Presbytery, one in Abbeville South Carolina, in 1821, one in Augusta in 1822, and the other at Darien in 1823. At this latter meeting he presented a Latin exegesis on this question, "An Christus sit Deus verus." The exegesis was received with great favour by the Presbytery, and Mr. Bergman was examined as to his personal piety, and upon natural and moral science. This examination was highly creditable, and furnished unmistakable evidence of fine order of intellect and very extensive acquirements. Mr. Bergman was consequently duly licensed as a Presbyterian minister. In his father's congregation, he had occasionally exercised his gifts in preaching the gospel, but it was not with a view to become the pastor of the church. This may be learned from the following extract of a letter addressed to Rev. M. Rauch in Orangeburg, South Carolina, and dated September 7, 1821.

"I have been for a while past revolving the question within myself, on the propriety of my assuming the pastoral relation in connection with our society. It is not very material whether we are denominated Calvinistic or Lutheran, provided the gospel be preached in purity and according to its true intent and acceptation. As to the exposition of the doctrine of grace, we need only refer to impartial history to discover that Luther maintained it no less strenuously than Calvin himself, differing only in a few slight shades. The fact is this, there are mysteries in revelation which a finite mind is incapable of resolving on any known principles.

"If I say, 'Christ is the propitiation for the sins of the whole world,' the question arises, 'Why then are not all saved?' because they do not believe; but then 'faith is the gift of God.' It is the word of God that we believe, when *he* has said, that nothing debars us from salvation but unwillingness or dissimulation. If, then, this desire and inclination be implanted in us by God's Holy Spirit, we shall of course be saved. Our salvation must be gratuitously bestowed, if by free grace.

"The difficulty that presents itself on the other hand is no less formidable. The only way to extricate ourselves is to receive the sacred Scriptures as we find them, and not confine ourselves to abstract systematic reasoning. The Scripture is the best interpreter of itself.

"Yours sincerely,
CHRISTOPHER F. BERGMAN."

In this state of mind Mr. Bergman continued in the Presbyterian church until the year 1824. In the mean time he was invited to take charge of the Lutheran church in St. Matthew's Parish, South Carolina, which, however, he declined. In 1824, Dr. Bachman, pastor of the Lutheran church in Charleston, went to Savannah with a view to attempt a reorganization of the Lutheran congregation in the latter city. Dr. Bachman extended his visit to Ebenezer, and had an interview with Mr. Bergman. This interview, in connection with a subsequent correspondence between the parties, gave a new direction to the theological views of Mr. Bergman. He embraced cordially the doctrines of the Lutheran church; and, in November, 1824, was received in connection with the Evangelical Lutheran Synod of South Carolina and adjacent States, and solemnly ordained a minister of the gospel. He immediately assumed the pastoral charge of the congregation at Ebenezer.

To the discharge of his duties as a pastor, Mr. Bergman brought a mind well stored with varied and useful learning, and a heart deeply imbued with a spirit of Christian humility and unfeigned piety. In his tastes he was, perhaps, rather too refined for the particular sphere in which he moved. He had been a close student of nature, and his journal furnishes abundant evidence of a rich exuberance of sentiment, chastened, however, by a strong religious sentiment. His cast of mind was, perhaps, rather melancholic, but yet he seems always to have cherished an unwavering confidence in God, which cheered and animated him, even under the most trying circumstances. Still, there was a natural timidity and reserve in his character, which operated somewhat to his disadvantage as a pastor.

When he assumed that relation at Ebenezer, he found the congregation in a declining condition. This, as has been stated, was occasioned in part by the want of proper discipline, and also by the too long use of the German language. These causes induced many of the descendants of the Salzburgers to forsake the church of their fathers, and unite in the organization of other societies. Methodist and Baptist churches sprung up in various parts of the county, and the preachers of these denominations seemed to labour with great zeal to proselyte the members of the Lutheran church and their families. In this they were only too successful. In the neighbourhood of Goshen, Mr. David Gougle and his family, with several others, were induced to join the Methodist society; and, as they were allowed the use of the Lutheran church at Goshen, in process of time the church itself was transferred to the Methodist Conference, and is held to this day as their property, though the *swan* still surmounts the spire, clearly showing what was *originally* the character of the church.

The Methodist church at Goshen was organized about the year 1822. The Rev. James O. Andrew (now Bishop Andrew) was at that time stationed in Savannah, but occasionally, and perhaps statedly, visited Goshen. It was under his ministry that this society was formed, though the transfer of the property did not take place for several years afterwards. Among the first members of this society, were, besides Mr. David Gougle, his daughters, Mrs. Nowlan (wife of Major Nowlan) and Mrs. Charlton, and the husband of the latter, Major John Charlton.

There is a singular incident connected with the history of this church at Goshen, which it may be proper to insert here. The facts are given, but, out of respect to the feelings of their families, the names of the parties are suppressed.

Two gentlemen, Mr. D— and Captain W—, labouring under a strange hallucination, imagined themselves called, by a special revelation from heaven, to preach the gospel. By dwelling too much upon this subject, they ultimately became somewhat monomaniac, and announced themselves respectively as John the Baptist and the Messiah. They made an appointment to preach at Goshen, but owing to their insane pretensions, the elders closed the church against them. Nevertheless, they attended at the church at the time appointed, and announced to the large congregation assembled, that, as an evidence of the divinity of their mission, the doors and windows would fly open miraculously, precisely at *twelve o'clock*. But their prediction was not verified, and they were compelled to leave the assemblage, being deeply mortified at their disappointment. Of course, the whole affair proved a miserable farce. Mr. W—— left his house the next day, under great mental excitement, and wandered about in the woods until he died from hunger and exhaustion. Apart from this strange delusion, he is represented as having been one of the best and most exemplary men of his day, and was even honoured with a seat in the Legislature. Mr. D——, who had once been sheriff of Effingham county, after being immersed some three or four times, connected himself with the "Bible Christians or

Campbellites." He still lives, and is man of great integrity, and possesses many fine traits of character.

In the neighbourhood of Goshen resided the Rev. Lewis Myers, a venerable local preacher of the Methodist connection. He was admitted a member of the South Carolina Conference in 1799, and continued in the itinerancy until about the year 1823, when he settled with his family at Goshen in Effingham county. Father Myers occupied a very conspicuous place in the Methodist church. He was stationed at one time in Charleston, South Carolina, and frequently received the appointment of presiding elder. He travelled extensively in South Carolina and Georgia, and by his zeal and piety always secured the confidence and esteem of those who formed his acquaintance. After he located, he laboured diligently in the cause of his Master. He was a warm friend of Sabbath-schools and the temperance cause, and gave to both the full weight of his influence. In his domestic relations, he was dutiful and affectionate, and very social in his feelings. He always candidly reproved faults when he discovered them, but the reproof was tempered with kindness, and no one could fail to see the spirit of the honest, uncompromising Christian in every act of his life. He reared an intelligent and respectable family, most of whom are still living.

Father Myers was attacked with paralysis in 1848, from which he never fully recovered. In 1849, he removed with his family to Springfield, where he resided until his death, which occurred in 1851.

Mr. Bergman entered upon his duties at Ebenezer with zeal, and with a full determination to discharge his obligations to his people in the fear of God; but he soon found that he was to meet with serious opposition in carrying out some of his measures of reform. He had seen that intemperance was prevailing to rather too great an extent among the people of the county, and that some of his own church-members were not as free from this sin as he had a right to expect. He therefore felt constrained to reprove this vice from the pulpit, and to suggest the propriety of organizing a temperance society. This measure met with very few advocates, and it is said that one of his members rebuked him publicly, in not very mild terms, for his temerity in attempting to correct this evil. He was not, however, driven from his purpose.

Mr. Bergman continued to preach at Ebenezer, at Bethel, and occasionally at Zion's, and he introduced the use of the English language in all the churches. This, together with the better enforcement of the discipline, had a beneficial influence upon the spiritual interests of the church, and the cause of true piety seemed generally to revive. Still there was much apathy and indifference among a large portion of the members.

In 1825, Mr. Bergman was married to Miss Mary C. Flerl, second daughter of Mr. Israel Flerl, a lineal descendant of the Salzburgers. This lady, in point of mind and disposition, was well calculated to become the companion of such a man as Mr. Bergman, and their union was a source of mutual happiness and comfort. By this marriage, Mr. Bergman had three children, only one of whom survived him; a daughter, who died, however, in 1837.

There is nothing of special importance to notice in the general condition of the descendants of the Salzburgers during the ministry of Mr. Bergman. In their temporal interests they were very much prospered; and, on the whole, the church had made some improvement in spirituality.

There was, however, manifested by many of the Salzburgers, a disposition to emigrate to other sections of Georgia. Some had removed to Scriven, and other families had located in Lowndes and Thomas counties; and in fact, the descendants of the Salzburgers, if we had the means to trace them up, could no doubt be found in many States of the Union, from Pennsylvania to Louisiana, and in nearly one-third of the counties of Georgia; though, it is true, in most cases, in rather an isolated condition;

still they retain their names and their general characteristics.

Reference has been made to the church in Savannah. The congregation, since the elder Bergman relinquished his charge, had greatly declined, though there were some pious families who still adhered to our confession. In 1824, Dr. Bachman of Charleston succeeded in reorganizing the church. He found the families of Mr. Frederick Herb, Mr. Snider, Mr. Haupt, Mr. Spann, Mr. Gougle, Mr. Felt, Mrs. S. Cooper, Mrs. N. Weriman, and Mrs. L. Cooper, and some others who were still attached to the Lutheran church, and were disposed to unite in an effort to resuscitate the congregation. The effort was successful.

The same year, the Rev. Stephen A. Mealy, a native of Charleston, South Carolina, and a licentiate of the South Carolina Synod, was induced to remove to Savannah and assume the pastoral charge of the church. Mr. Mealy had the pleasure to see the church attain to considerable respectability, both as to piety and numbers. He served this people with great usefulness until 1839, when he accepted a call from St. Matthew's Church in Philadelphia, and removed to that city.

Mr. Mealy was succeeded by Rev. N. Aldrich of Charleston. Mr. Aldrich removed to Savannah in 1840. Up to the year 1843, the congregation had worshipped in a small wooden church which had been erected before the Revolutionary War. As, however, the city of Savannah was rapidly improving, and the congregation had increased in wealth and intelligence, a fine brick edifice eighty-eight by fifty-six feet was erected, at a cost of fifteen thousand dollars. The church was dedicated in the fall of 1843, on which occasion the pastor was aided by Rev. Dr. Bachman of Charleston.

Mr. Aldrich continued in Savannah until the year 1850, when he was succeeded by the Rev. A. J. Karn, who still sustains the pastoral relation. Mr. Karn labours with great acceptance to the people of his charge. The congregation is rapidly improving, and has been blessed with several gracious revivals, which have brought many members into the church. This congregation occupies, at this time, a very favourable position in the estimation of the Christian community of Savannah, and is making itself respected by the happy influence that it is exerting upon the moral interests of a large portion of the community. Within the last two years a German congregation has been organized, which bids fair, under the divine blessing, to accomplish much good for the large German population which is now to be found in that city. The German congregation is at present supplied by the Rev. W. Epping. These two churches, acting as they do in concert, are well adapted to meet the wants of the English and German Lutherans in Savannah, and important results may be confidently expected from them. May great grace abide upon them, and may God continually add to their number scores and hundreds, who shall be saved in the great day of rejoicing.

It has been deemed proper to make this reference to the Lutheran church in Savannah, because it was originally organized by emigrants from Salzburg, and was for many years a constituent part of the pastorate at Ebenezer. Great changes, however, have taken place in the congregation. Very few of its present members are descended from the original stock, and the church has become entirely anglicized. In fact, it has been so ever since 1824, when Mr. Mealy became the pastor. Having said this much in relation to Savannah, it is time to return to Ebenezer.

It has been stated that many of the descendants of the Salzburgers had abandoned the church of their fathers, and had aided materially in the organization of other churches. In Savannah, in the Episcopal church, the Methodist Episcopal church, and the Baptist church, many of them may be found. This is particularly the case in reference to the Methodist church. There we find the Remsharts, the Sniders, the Heidts, and others; some of them men of wealth and influence. This is, however, more especially true in relation to Effingham county. Prominent among the Methodists may be seen the Hineleys, Sherraus, Bergsteiners, Scheubtrines, Neidlingers, Zittrauers, Mingledorffs, Oechleys, (now spelled Exley,) occasionally a Rahn, a Gnann, a Zettler, and some of the descendants of the Gougels, including the Charltons, Remsharts, and others. In the Baptist church, there are occasionally a Rahn, some of the Dashers, Waldhours, Wisenbakers, Bergsteiners, &c. &c. These families constitute, for the most part, the most conspicuos and wealthy members in the churches to which they respectively belong. Their withdrawal from the Lutheran church was certainly a serious loss; but it is consoling to think that they still form a portion of the great army of our common Lord, and in their new spheres of action are contributing materially to push forward the triumphs of the cross. Though, therefore, they have "gone out from us," we can heartily wish them God-speed, even though it may not be proper to endorse the propriety of the course which they pursued, in abandoning the church of their fathers, especially as they cannot find in other communities any thing which is sounder in faith, or wiser, or more judicious in discipline and church government, than existed in the church which they left. And if reform was needed, they who were the first to perceive the necessity, were under the greatest obligation to labour with the most untiring zeal and energy to effect it.

These disaffections among the Salzburgers toward the Lutheran church, many of which occurred in the lifetime of Mr. Bergman, proved a source of great grief to him; and although he had a consciousness that he did his duty faithfully, yet he was pained at the results, even though he was not the cause of bringing them about.

The younger Bergman presided over the spiritual interests of the Ebenezer congregations for about eight years. If there was any fault of which he was guilty, it was too close attention to his literary pursuits, to the neglect of pastoral visitations and the serious injury of his health. He evidently was a very close and industrious student, and he laboured to acquire a thorough knowledge of every department of science and literature. He has left a number of treatises on various subjects, including botany, meteorology, astronomy, natural philosophy, history, poetry, belles lettres, &c. Beside which he kept a diary in which are carefully and minutely noted all the important events that happened in our own country and throughout the world, as far as they came to his knowledge. His acquirements in the languages and mathematics were extensive; and what is remarkable, his entire education was obtained in his father's study. But his paternal instructor was well fitted for the task, being himself a man of very extraordinary attainments.

Among the other causes of regret to Mr. Bergman, was the indifference which many of the Salzburgers began to manifest on the subject of education. It had been an object with all the pastors at Ebenezer, to keep up good parochial schools at each of the churches, and for many years this was successfully done. Even after the Revolution, when the elder Bergman came over from Germany a teacher accompanied him, as has been stated, and the school at Ebenezer was reorganized and sustained for many years. But as the Salzburgers began to remove from Ebenezer and settle upon their farms, they gradually lost their interest (or at least in a good measure) in the subject of education, and many of them permitted their children to grow up in comparative ignorance, having very little more than the *rudiments* of the plainest English education. In this the people have been very culpable, especially as there is a fund belonging to the church for the education of those children whose parents may see proper to avail themselves of it.

About the year 1830, Mr. Bergman's health began to decline; and it became manifest to his friends and himself that his constitution was seriously impaired. Nevertheless he endeavoured to perform his duties faithfully and cheerfully, as far as his strength would permit. In the early part of the year 1832, it was evident that the season of his probation and ministerial usefulness was drawing to a close. About the 1st of March he was compelled to desist from all active employments, and about the middle he was confined to his bed. He became so reduced in the course of a week that he could not speak above a whisper. Thus he continued gradually to waste away until the 26th of March, 1832, when he was gathered to his rest in peace. A short time before his death he regained sufficient strength to be able to converse with a ministerial brother, (Rev. S. A. Mealy) to whom he remarked: "If it is the divine will, I am prepared and would rather go now. I feel that for me to depart and to be with Christ, is far better. I think I can truly say, for me to live is Christ and to die is gain. Blessed be the God and Father of my Lord Jesus Christ, I have no doubts. . . . I look into the grave without alarm. I believe I can say without dread, to 'corruption thou art my father, and to the worm thou art my mother and sister.'" He then repeated with great energy, while his face was irradiated with a heavenly smile, the Christian's hymn of triumph:

> " Cease, fond nature, cease thy strife,
> And let me languish into life.
> * * * *
> Lend, lend your wings, I mount, I fly!
> O grave, where is thy victory?
> O death, where is thy sting?"

With this language upon his lips, he gently fell asleep in Jesus, and was gathered to his fathers like one "who lies down to pleasant dreams." On the 27th of March he was buried in Ebenezer cemetery, adding another to the pious and truly godly men who repose in that ancient and venerable receptacle of the dead. The congregation, as an evidence of the high regard which was cherished for him, erected a suitable tablet to his memory in the cemetery at Ebenezer.

The Rev. John D. Scheck succeeded Mr. Bergman. Mr. Scheck is a native of Maryland. In 1831 he removed to South Carolina, and connected himself with the Lutheran Synod of that State. During the first year of his ministry he missionated among the destitute congregations in the bounds of the synod. He then accepted a call to the charge of the Lutheran church in St. Matthew's Parish, Orangeburg District, South Carolina. From this charge he removed to Ebenezer, and served the congregation until 1838, when he resigned and removed for a brief period to Alabama. Mr. Scheck's labours were duly appreciated by a large portion of the congregation, and it is believed that his preaching was blessed to the edification of not a few. Nothing, however, of special importance occurred during his connection with the church.

While Mr. Scheck was pastor, his health and that of his family suffered very much during their residence at Ebenezer, from the miasma arising from the river and swamps. It became necessary, therefore, to build a new parsonage in the pine land, about three miles from Ebenezer. This house has been the permanent residence of the pastors ever since, and has proved to be one of the healthiest locations in all that country. At the suggestion of Mr. Scheck, the congregation likewise improved the church, placing in it a new pulpit after the modern style, and in other respects rendering the church more comfortable and tasty in its exterior and interior appearance.

In 1838, the Rev. E. A. Bolles of Charleston, South Carolina, received and accepted a call to the Ebenezer charge. Mr. Bolles had been a private student of Dr. Bachman's, and subsequently spent two years in the theological seminary at Lexington, South Carolina. Upon leaving the seminary he removed to North Carolina, where he remained a year, prior to his location at Ebenezer. Mr. Bolles was for several years successful as a pastor, and made many warm friends at Ebenezer. However, in 1842, an attempt was made to introduce and enforce the new discipline, adopted by the Synod of South Carolina, which was warmly opposed by a large number of the members, and resulted in a schism, which wellnigh rent the church in twain.

For this measure there was really no necessity. Those who attempted to introduce the new discipline were no doubt influenced by the purest and best motives, but they evidently acted unadvisedly. A reform in the church was greatly needed; but those who favoured it, did not adopt the most judicious course to effect their laudable object. If they had examined the archives of the church, they would have found a discipline already in existence far superior in *every respect* to the one which they proposed to introduce, and by planting themselves upon that, they might very easily have accomplished their purpose; and while, by this course, they would have fortified their own position, they might have disarmed the opponents of the discipline of their most powerful arguments against the measure. The new discipline was evidently adopted unconstitutionally, and it was well for all parties that this controversy was amicably settled. This was accomplished through the agency of Dr. Bachman of Charleston, then President of the Synod. In 1843 he visited Ebenezer, and calling the whole congregation together, the matters in dispute were all discussed and an adjustment effected, which was satisfactory to the great majority of the members. A few, however, still remained disaffected, and several left the church. The strife had been very severe, and various documents had been presented to the synod, setting forth the views of the respective parties; and it was accomplishing much for the church, when, after all the crimination and recrimination which had occurred, the dispute was settled upon any terms whatever. There was a union effected, but it is to be feared it was not a very cordial one.

Mr. Bolles continued at Ebenezer during the remainder of this year; but in 1844, he relinquished the position and removed to his native city. After a short sojourn there, he accepted a call to the Beth-Eden charge in Newberry District, South Carolina. He is now an agent for the American Bible Society in South Carolina, in which position he is rendering good service to the cause of Christ.

After Mr. Bolles removed from Ebenezer, the congregation extended a call to Rev. P. A. Strobel, at the time principal of a female seminary in Savannah. Mr. Strobel is a native of Charleston, South Carolina, and a graduate of the theological seminary at Lexington, South Carolina. The call was accepted, and Mr. Strobel served the congregation for four years and a half.

During Mr. Strobel's stay at Ebenezer, a new

church was built on the Middle Ground Road, near the Ogeechee River. This church was designed for the accommodation of those members who had removed so far from Ebenezer that it was impracticable for them to attend preaching at the parent church. It is believed that this measure was the means of saving many members to the Lutheran church, who would otherwise have been lost to it, and it also carried the means of grace to a very destitute neighbourhood.

Mr. Strobel continued at Ebenezer until the commencing of the year 1849, when he removed to the city of Macon, and accepted an appointment as missionary to the few Lutheran families who reside in that city. After labouring in this field a year, with some prospect of success, it was found impossible to prosecute the mission successfully, and it was abandoned. The Lutherans in Macon are mostly Germans, and their attachments to the church of their fathers are not strong enough to induce them to make the necessary sacrifices to build up a congregation. Those who make any pretensions to piety at all, have become pew-holders and worshippers in other churches, and they could not be induced to unite cordially in the enterprise of erecting a Lutheran church.

The congregation at Ebenezer was without a regular pastor for more than a year, after Mr.

Strobel removed to Macon. In the mean time the Rev. Ephriam Keiffer served them as a temporary supply. Mr. Keiffer was a descendant of the Salzburgers, and had united with the church in the lifetime of the elder Bergman. Being a man of ardent zeal and devoted piety, he felt it to be his duty to do something to promote the spiritual welfare of the church. Encouraged by the pastor, he was induced to hold prayer-meetings and deliver exhortations, whenever an opportunity was afforded him. He took great interest in the Sabbath-school, and acted as superintendent for many years. He was at length prevailed upon to apply for license to preach. This was readily granted; for although his education was rather limited, yet he was a man of excellent natural abilities, and his good sense and upright and consistent deportment compensated for many other deficiencies.

While the congregation remained vacant, Mr. Kieffer was prevailed upon by his brethren to discharge the duties of a pastor, until one could be obtained. With great reluctance he complied with the wishes of the congregation, and served them until the beginning of the year 1851. During this year it pleased God to call him away from the scene of his earthly labours. After an illness of several weeks, he expired at his residence in Effingham county, closing his career with great serenity of mind, leaving to his family and the church the rich legacy of an unblemished Christian character.

The Rev. George Haltiwanger became the pastor at Ebenezer in 1851. Mr. Haltiwanger is a native of Lexington district, South Carolina, and a graduate of the seminary at Lexington. Possessing naturally a good mind, which he has cultivated with some care, and imbued with a spirit of deep piety, he is well calculated (if any man is) to succeed in this somewhat difficult charge. For it is a melancholy truth, that of late years the congregation at Ebenezer has become rather hard to suit with a pastor. Mr. Bolzius served them for thirty-two years. Mr. Rabenhorst for more than twenty years. The elder Bergman for *thirty-six years*. And the younger Bergman for eight years. And it is worthy of remark, that all the pastors at Ebenezer, up to the time of the younger Bergman, (with the exception of Mr. Triebner,) sustained the pastoral relation until they were removed by death. Since the demise of the younger Bergman, however, up to this date, a period of twenty-two years, four changes have been made, showing an average of a little more than *four years* for each pastor. It cannot *always* be the fault of the minister; the people must necessarily be more or less to blame, and it would be well for them to inquire seriously, prayerfully, and candidly, in how far they have *unneccessa-*

rily rendered the situation of the pastor such, as to constrain him to leave the congregation, for his own peace as well as that of the church. A congregation will be made to feel, sooner or later, the baneful effects arising from so many changes, especially when they are demanded, not so much by any want of faithfulness on the part of the minister, as by a restless, fault-finding, and captious spirit on the part of the people.

Thus far, Mr. Haltiwanger has succeeded in giving general satisfaction to the people; and there seems to be a more general interest manifested on the subject of religion, than for several years. Since his removal to Ebenezer, a new church has been erected near the old site of Bethel, three miles above Springfield, which is very creditable to those who built it. In this neighbourhood, particularly, the members have always been noted for their piety and the harmony which prevails among them. It may, in fact, be regarded as the most interesting and flourishing part of the congregation, and this in no doubt attributable to the spirit of union which always prevails among them.

In this neighbourhood lived and died the venerable J. Gotlieb Snider. He was a soldier in the Revolutionary War, having served his country faithfully under General Wayne. Father Snider lived to be nearly ninety years of age. He was contemporary with Messrs. Lembke, Rabenhorst, and Bergman, and lived until the year 1848. He was a man of ardent piety, enlarged benevolence, and strong practical views. By his beneficence he relieved many a widow and orphan, and sought to render himself a benefactor to all who needed his assistance. As he advanced in life, the evidences of the divine favour seemed every day to become brighter, and his faith and hope increased as he approached the end of his long and eventful life. He delighted to speak of the early days of the colony; of the prosperity of Ebenezer; of the large and attentive congregations that once assembled in the old church; of the piety of the pastors and the spirituality of their flock; and while he dwelt upon these scenes, his eyes would fill with tears and his countenance beam with holy joy, as he would remark, "Oh! I shall soon see many of these pious, good old friends in heaven." He died in full prospect of an inheritance among the saints in light. May the savour of his holy life never be entirely lost!

The congregation at Ebenezer, under the judicious management of the Rev. G. Haltiwanger, is making decided advancement. There has been a steady increase of the membership, and a gradual progress in the spirituality of the church. The people are beginning to manifest more enlarged views of Christian duty, and an expansive benevolence, which augur well for the future. As some evidence of this favourable change, the church has been recently thoroughly renovated. The brick floor has been removed, and a plank one substituted. Neat pews have taken the place of the old-fashioned "benches," and both the interior and exterior of the venerable "Jerusalem" church have been greatly improved. One alteration has, however, been made, which is objectionable. The "swan" which once stood upon the spire of the church has been taken down, and its place is now occupied by a "fish." This is in bad taste. If, as has been stated, the swan was Luther's coat of arms, it should have been permitted to remain as emblematical of the distinctive character of the church. Besides, in view of the many thrilling associations connected with *that* swan, it ought never have been removed. It should have stood there as a kind of heirloom, connecting the present with all the glorious and inspiring recollections of the past: reminding us ever of the immortal Reformer, and the soul-elevating doctrines he proclaimed; in defence of which the Salzburgers were exiled, and for their propagation and maintenance erected that time-honoured temple upon the banks of the beautiful Savannah. Let that "fish" come down, and let the old swan resume its accustomed place. It stood there for more than a century, solitary and alone, weathering every storm, a witness to all the varied incidents which have marked the history of the colony. Amid the decay of generations and the mutations of society, it has been a silent yet eloquent monitor, reminding us of the noble moral heroism of our ancestors, and bidding us emulate the example of those whose attachment to a pure and heavenly faith made them the victims of a dark and murderous spirit, and drove them upon a "willing pilgrimage" in search of that "holy ground" where, unawed by human cruelty and a blind superstition, the soul might unfold its pinions and soar aloft to hold sweet and unfettered communion with the "Father of spirits."

In addition to these improvements in the church edifice, other measures have been adopted to advance the interests of the church, which cannot be too highly commended. The congregation have agreed to call and support an adjunct pastor; and the Rev. Jacob Austin, a recent graduate of the seminary of Lexington, South Carolina, has already entered upon his duties in that relation. Under this arrangement it would really seem that nothing can be wanting, as far as human instrumentality is concerned, to secure the permanent prosperity of the congregation. By a proper division of labour, and by harmonious and judicious effort on the part of the associate pastors, the several congregations can be supplied with preaching upon almost every

Sabbath. Catechetical instruction and pastoral visitation, those very important agents in ministerial success, can be regularly and systematically employed; and the descendants of the Salzburgers may yet, under the blessing of God, witness a return of that glorious period in the history of the church, when under the instruction of two pious and faithful pastors, the prayer-meeting, the catechetical lecture, and the ministerial conference shall be resumed, and the shepherds, being themselves nourished with "the pure milk of the word," and "enriched with all spiritual grace," shall be the better prepared to lead this precious flock into "the green pastures and beside the still waters," and God shall be *their* God, and dwell with them, even as he dwelt with their fathers.

CHAPTER XIII.

The town of Ebenezer—Its present appearance—The results of this experiment at colonization—The colonies in New England, Virginia, and the Carolinas—Royal Historical Society of Austria—Inquiries as to the fate of the Salzburgers answered—Religious and social influence of the Salzburgers upon the other colonists—Religious sentiments of the first pastors—Dr. Hazelius's testimony—Present condition and pursuits of their descendants—Effingham county—General reflections—Conclusion.

To one visiting the ancient town of Ebenezer, in the present day, the prospect which presents itself is any thing but attractive; and the stranger who is unacquainted with its history would perhaps discover very little to excite his curiosity or awaken his sympathies. The town has gone almost entirely to ruins. Only two residences are now remaining, and even one of these is untenanted. The old church, however, stands in bold relief upon an open lawn, and by its somewhat antique appearance seems silently, yet forcibly, to call up the reminiscences of former years. Not far distant from the church is the cemetery, in which are sleeping the remains of the venerable men who founded the colony and the church, and many of their descendants, who, one by one, have gone down to the grave, to mingle their ashes with those of their illustrious ancestors.

Except upon the Sabbath, when the descendants of the Salzburgers go up to their temple to worship the God of their fathers, the stillness which reigns around Ebenezer is seldom broken, save by the warbling of birds, the occasional transit of a steamer, or the murmurs of the Savannah, as it flows on to lose itself in the ocean. The sighing winds chant melancholy dirges as they sweep through the lofty pines and cedars which cast their sombre shades over this "deserted village." Desolation seems to have spread over this once-favoured spot its withering wing, and here, where generation after generation grew up and flourished, where the persecuted and exiled Salzburgers reared their offspring, in the hope that they would leave a numerous progeny of pious, useful, and prosperous citizens, and where every thing seemed to betoken the establishment of a thrifty and permanent colony, scarcely any thing is to be seen except the sad evidences of decay and death.

While surveying this scene, one is almost instinctively led to inquire what advantages have accrued to the Salzburgers and their descendants, or to our State, by their removal from their fatherland and their settlement in Georgia? Have the results of this experiment been such as to compensate in any good degree for the large expenditures of money and the various sacrifices which were necessary to the establishment of this colony? These questions are very proper, and it is hoped that in answering them some rays of light will illume the rather cheerless picture exhibited above.

An interest in the history of the Salzburgers has been manifested, not only in the United States, but also in Europe. A year or two since, a letter was received by the Governor of Georgia from the Secretary of the Royal Historical Society of Austria, in which information was sought in reference to the fate of this interesting people. Among the questions proposed were the following:—Did the Salzburgers retain their language? Did they ever change their religion? To what extent did they diffuse themselves in Georgia and other portions of America? Did they exert any influence upon the civil institutions and the religious character of the state? Some of these questions have already been answered. It has been shown that the Salzburgers gradually acquired the use of the English language, and in 1824 it was formally adopted in public worship in all the congregations in and about Ebenezer. It has also been stated that many of the Salzburgers forsook the church of their fathers at various times, and united with other denominations. Nevertheless, the great bulk of their descendants have remained faithfully attached to the religion which their ancestors professed with so much moral heroism amid the severest persecutions in their native land, and to enjoy which, without molestation, they cheerfully submitted to every form of suffering and privation, and even to banishment and death. The other questions remain to be discussed. Various considerations render it necessary that they should be briefly considered before this little volume is brought to a close.

There is a commendable curiosity which prompts many to desire to know to what extent the descendants of the Salzburgers have been multiplied? What is their general character for intelligence and morality? What are their pursuits? To what extent and in what departments of life have they become distinguished? And, in short, in how far have they exerted any beneficial influence upon the social and religious character of the state? Besides, there are many men so decidedly utilitarian in their views, that they regard no enterprise as worthy of commendation or patronage which does not promise great practical benefits to all who are in any wise associated with it.

In addition to this, the history of the colonies planted in New England, in Virginia, and the Carolinas, will no doubt suggest similar inquiries. The Puritans, as has been stated, left the impress of their character indelibly fixed upon all their institutions. By their industry and indomitable energy, they felled the forests, and, amid almost inconceivable hardships and dangers, brought under successful cultivation a somewhat rocky and barren soil; making it yield them not only the necessaries, but even the comforts and luxuries of life. They planted churches and established colleges and schools, many of which remain, until this day, the lasting monuments of their piety and enlightened liberality. In process of time, they engaged in extensive and successful commercial enterprises; and having built up towns and cities, and settled most of the adjacent territory with an energetic, intelligent, and virtuous population, they sent out their descendants to almost every portion of our country; and wherever the sons of New England are found, they are generally the pioneers in commerce, in education, and, in short, in every thing which tends to elevate individual character and promote the best interests of the state. No one can with truth deny that from the Pilgrim Fathers there has descended a long list of worthy names who have adorned the various professions, given dignity to our public councils by their wisdom and eloquence, and contributed their full quota to the development of every thing that is truly great or glorious in national character.

This is equally true of the colonies of Virginia and the Carolinas. The descendants of Cavaliers who settled the " Old Dominion," and the Huguenots of Carolina, not only built up permanent and extensive settlements, but they also, in the course of time, spread themselves over many parts of our widely extended domain; and everywhere, they are distinguished for lofty intellect, profound statesmanship, heroic bravery, uncompromising attachment to principle, and an ardent love of virtue and of liberty. Nor have they failed to contribute largely to every enterprise which was in any wise calculated to increase the commercial importance, develop the agricultural resources, and secure the safety and prosperity of the country. It may be truthfully asserted that their history, and that of their descendants, furnish some of the brightest and most glorious pages which adorn the annals of our country. This is true, not only of their struggles and successes, and the many thrilling incidents connected with their colonial history; it is equally true in relation to the war for Independence, and the bright recollections which the Revolution awaken, as well as the conspicuous part which they have acted in all the affairs of our government, in every period of its existence. With these considerations pressing upon the mind, the inquiries which have been suggested in relation to the Salzburgers are both natural and pertinent, and it is proposed to answer them as far as may be practicable.

It would be unreasonable to expect that the Salzburgers and their descendants should occupy as prominent a place on the page of history as the other colonies, and for reasons which are very satisfactory. Their language being entirely different from that spoken in the province of Georgia, together with their somewhat peculiar habits, kept them rather isolated from the other inhabitants, and made them measurably a distinct colony. Besides, as their location prevented them from becoming a commercial people, and as they confined themselves almost exclusively to the pursuits of agriculture, they did not possess those facilities for extending their settlements and increasing their wealth and their influence, which were enjoyed by the other colonists. It should be remembered, that they were poor, houseless wanderers, who were sent to Georgia upon the charity of their Christian friends in Europe; and, for many years after their arrival, their poverty prevented them from doing more than simply providing a competency for their families..

Besides this, the climate was unfavourable to the rapid increase of population; and, during the first years of the colony, many of the Salzburgers fell victims to the fevers and other diseases which are always more or less incidental to southern latitudes, especially when the forests are newly cleared. It is true, there were many accessions to their numbers by way of emigration, during the first four or five years after the planting of the colony; yet, from the causes already mentioned, the Salzburgers did not multiply very rapidly, and their settlements were confined to a limited portion of the state.

It is nevertheless true, that, as far as their circumstances would permit, they made every effort to identify themselves with the interests of the province, and contributed to the best of their ability to promote its prosperity. If they did not become as distinguished as the other colonies in commerce and wealth, and if they did not occupy so important and influential a position, and if their descendants did not become as renowned in the cabinet and the field as the sons of New England, Virginia, and the Carolinas, or even as some of the sons of Georgia, yet there is much in the character and history of the Salzburgers, which would adorn the annals of any country.

This is true, not only of their transatlantic history, with its many incidents of holy devotion to the faith of the gospel, under the most studied and revolting persecutions; it is likewise true of them after their removal to America. In circumstances of the severest trial, whether suffering from fatigue or hunger, or lying prostrate under the influence of fatal diseases, they evinced a degree of Christian fortitude which did not fail to make a most favourable impression upon their neighbours. If, then, they had done nothing more than simply to set an example to the other colonists of holy living, and of patient, uncomplaining resignation to the divine will; if the only record which could be made of them was, that they were consistent Christians, "and adorned the doctrines of God their Saviour in all things;" the moral influence of even such a record, would entitle them to distinction among the benefactors of their race. That such was their character, is abundantly proven by all who knew them; and in every sketch of the early history of Georgia, honourable mention has been made of the piety and purity of life exhibited by the Salzburgers, and especially by their pastors. It may be necessary, however, to refer to this subject again.

In the civil and military affairs of the colony, many of the Salzburgers became conspicuous. When, in 1775, the Provincial Congress assembled in Savannah, to adopt measures to protect the Province against the unjust and arbitrary legislation of the Mother Country, St. Matthew's Parish, was represented in that Congress, in part, by John Stirk, John Adam Treutlin, Jacob Waldhauer, John Flerl, and Christopher Cramer, all of whom were Salzburgers. Mr. Truetlin also filled the office of Provincial Governor, and in all the proceedings which were adopted for the preservation of the liberties of the Province, the Salzburgers heartily concurred.

When the Revolution commenced, as has already been shown, they took a very decided stand in favour of the cause of liberty. In the list of persons proscribed by the British Parliament as Rebels, occur the names of the following Salzburgers:—J. A. Treutlin, Rebel Governor, Col. John Stirk, William Hobzendorf, Rudolph Strohaker, Samuel Stirk, George Wyche, John Schnider, and others. From this it will be seen, that in the very incipiency of the Revolution, they arrayed themselves on the side of the Colonists, and were willing to incur all the risks connected with that struggle. In every emergency they contributed what they could to the relief of the Colony, promptly and cheerfully making every sacrifice, and performing every duty which seemed to be demanded by the welfare of the Province. And, in proportion to their ability, no portion of the population did more to advance the various interests of the country. In short, they became fully identified with the Whigs of the Revolution, and in all the dangers and sufferings of that memorable epoch in our country's history, they bore their full share. When the war terminated, they went to work, patiently and zealously to cultivate the soil, to improve their homesteads, and to repair, as far as practicable, the injuries which their settlements had suffered, and to restore to the Colony the prosperity which it had enjoyed prior to the war. In these purposes they persevered, and in process of time they were successful in regaining much that had been lost during those troublesome times; and they saw their settlements extending, and their descendants multiplying, until they spread themselves over the whole of the county of Effingham, and even into many of the adjacent counties.

It is proper, before a more minute sketch is given of the condition and pursuits of the Salzburgers, that something should be said in reference to their religious character, and the doctrines of which the pastors at Ebenezer may with propriety be said to have been the exponents. This is deemed important, not only as illustrative of the moral influence which the Salzburgers may be supposed to have exerted upon the other Colonists; it is necessary, especially to the Lutheran Church, as it will exhibit in a proper light, the religious views of the founders of American Lutheranism, upon some of the cardinal doctrines of Christianity. This is rendered the more important, because of the tendency of too many professing Christians in the present day, to what has been very properly called "sacramentalism," or the settling down in a cold and lifeless orthodoxy. It is hoped that, by exhibiting in a prominent light the teachings and experience of the pastors who had the spiritual oversight of the Colony of Salzburgers, many false impressions which now exist in relation to the distinctive doctrines of the Lutheran Church will be removed, and it will be made to appear that our pious ancestors were the friends and advocates of a vital, soul-renewing, and soul-pervading Christianity. A sickly sentimentality, which seeks to substitute a speculative philosophy, or a formal Christianity, for the power of a living, active faith, received no countenance from them. True, they were "symbolists," in a restricted sense, because they subscribed to the Augsburg Confession, and the other symbols of the Lutheran Church; but they never gave undue importance to the ordinances of religion, while they taught, both by precept and example, that true Christianity is a heavenly principle implanted in the soul by the Holy Spirit; and that, whenever it is experienced, it produces a new creation, and conforms the soul to the image of Him by whose spirit we are renewed, and made the partakers of a divine inner life.

As illustrative of this view, an extract is subjoined from Dr. Hazelius's history of the American Lutheran Church. He remarks:—" From the journals of the ministers labouring among the Salzburgers, it is evident that their aim was to direct their flock into the narrow path that leadeth unto life. Though they were anxious to influence the members of their church to the observance of an external decorum, and to submission to good church discipline; and though, according to the testimony of their neighbours, the inhabitants of the villages round about them, and those of Savannah, as also to that of the colonial government, this congregation was distinguished in that respect; and though the pastors were also desirous that the people should be duly affected by the preaching of the word,— yet it is evident, from every statement they make, that they were labouring to impress this truth deeply on the minds of the people, that neither an external observance of order, nor an excitement of mere animal feelings, insures us the high title of being the sons and daughters of God; but the approach of the heart and mind to the character of our great prototype, the Lord and Saviour Jesus Christ, as well as to have a conscience void of offence before God and man."

In this connection, it may be appropriate to make a few brief extracts from the letters and journal of Mr. Bolzius. In one of his letters he remarks:—" We acknowledge, to the praise of God, that piety and contentment still reign among us, as even strangers are willing to acknowledge. . . . . Among our congregation are many men and women who are truly converted to God, and who walk in the truth, and are an ornament to our office, and humble assistants in the discharge of our duties." In his journal he makes these minutes:—" Careless and froward men are indeed presuming upon Christ and his merits, without seeking conversion, but *he* calls those only who labour and are heavy laden; and if they come to Christ, anxious for their soul's salvation, the tempter will endeavour to deprive them of the grace in Christ. We ought, however, to lay firm hold on him and his merits, because he is not only the beginning, but also the finisher of our faith, and his honour is concerned to finish the work he has begun." . . . . In another place he remarks:—" It is terrible indeed to offend God with wilful sins, and to sin in hopes of his mercy. . . . . Thousands are going to hell while flattering themselves with this delusive promise; and even when the eyes of some are truly opened and their hearts converted to God, and they have received the pardon of sins in the order of true repentance and faith in Christ, God nevertheless frequently causes them to feel the heinousness and guilt of sin."

Mr. Bolzius, in that part of his journal in which he furnishes an account of the illness and death of his colleague, Mr. Gronau, seems desirous to lay peculiar stress upon the evidences which Mr. Gronau furnished of his acceptance with God, and his hope of a better life. This is his language: "The time of Mr. Gronau's illness has been a source of edification to us who were daily about his person. His heart continually enjoyed communion with his Redeemer. Nothing troubled him, for he tasted the reconciliation with God, and the joy and peace of the Holy Ghost. He fell asleep, and entered into the joy of his Lord, full of peace."

It would be easy to furnish many such extracts, all going to show that the first pastors at Ebenezer were men of devoted piety, and that they were not only themselves the subjects of the renewing, transforming power of the Holy Spirit, but that in all their preaching, as well as in their private instructions, they laboured to inculcate a religion which "new creates the soul" in the likeness of God, and produces a radical change in our whole moral constitution. So that, under the influence of this new principle, we become the children of God, receive "the spirit of adoption," and are enabled "to walk in all his ordinances and commandments blameless."

This is true not only of Messrs. Bolzius and

Gronau, but also of Messrs. Lembke, Rabenhorst, and Bergman. It is true, there are very few facts in the history of the two former which have been preserved, but enough is known to warrant the opinion just expressed. Those who knew Mr. Lembke personally, bear testimony to his humble piety and faithful dealing with the souls committed to his trust. Mr. Bolzius, in his journal, speaks of "the excellent spirit" which Mr. Lembke always exhibited, and commends him for his unremitting diligence in the discharge of every duty. This was likewise the case in relation to Mr. Rabenhorst. Not only does Mr. Bolzius speak favourably of him for his zeal, humility, and great diligence as a pastor, but Dr. H. M. Muhlenburg, in his Journal of a Voyage to Georgia, mentions him in the most flattering terms, as a man and a Christian, and especially as a faithful and devoted pastor. Dr. Muhlenburg instances as a peculiarity in Mr. Rabenhorst's preaching, that he insisted on the doctrine of the *new birth*, and was decidedly evangelical in all his views and feelings. The same statement may be made of Mr. Bergman.

From all this it will appear, that the religious sentiments inculcated by the pastors at Ebenezer, and which they enforced by their own experience and example, were decidedly in favour of practical, experimental godliness. They believed and taught that *true* religion has its seat only in the soul which has been born from above; that in every soul thus renewed Christ dwells by his Spirit, imparting new life and energy to our spiritual nature; and thus becoming the great fountain of our strength, and hope, and joy, he reigns in us as the grand controlling motive of all our noblest purposes and loftiest aspirations, and leads us from one attainment in righteousness and holiness to another, until we are made meet for "the inheritance among the saints in light."

In fact, the whole of the early history of the Salzburgers is but an exemplification of this great doctrine of Christianity. This was true of them while they dwelt in their native valleys and mountains. It was for their bold and uncompromising attachment to a pure and holy faith—a "faith that works by love and purifies the heart"—that they became the objects of the most cruel and unrelenting persecutions. For maintaining this faith they were driven from their country and their homes, and cast upon the charities of their Christian brethren. Amid scenes of the severest trial and suffering, they demonstrated the sustaining power as well as the comforting influences of that heaven-born Christianity, for the enjoyment of which "they took gladly the spoiling of their goods," and became pilgrims and sojourners in the earth. When the good providence of God delivered them from the hands of their enemies, and brought them safely to a land where they could enjoy their religion unawed by human restraint, they erected their temples, and from their pulpits, and by their examples of holy living, and their peaceful and triumphant death, they furnished fresh evidences of the importance of this great fundamental doctrine in the Christian system. If, then, the history of the Salzburgers, both in Europe and after their removal to Georgia, had done nothing more than furnish illustrations of the reality and the power of this vital principle of Christianity, they would be justly entitled to a prominent place among those who, by becoming living witnesses to the truth of Christianity as a renewing and sustaining principle, have furnished some of the strongest encouragements to our faith and hope, and some of the most powerful incentives to the conscientious discharge of Christian duty, even under the most adverse circumstances. That such was the influence which the Salzburgers exerted is proven by the testimony of Wesley and Whitfield, and all who had an opportunity to acquire a correct knowledge of their religious opinions and character; and whenever the Christian shall search the records of the church in modern times to discover instances of moral heroism in the maintenance of our holy religion, and of humble, devoted piety, the history of the Salzburgers may be confidently appealed to as furnishing some of the brightest and most striking examples.

This is likewise true of the social influence which they exerted. In their habits they were frugal, temperate, and industrious. They knew very little of the artificial wants of life, and hence were easily contented when supplied with its necessaries. Having an unwavering confidence in the providential care of their heavenly Father, they laboured cheerfully and hopefully amid the most discouraging circumstances, and thus set an example to the other colonists which was not without its influence. As a consequence, the colonial authorities frequently commended their habits of diligence, sobriety, honesty, and general virtue. To the cultivation of their lands and the improvement of their homesteads they devoted themselves with great assiduity, so that they became successful farmers, and their settlements were always spoken of as models of neatness, and their farms furnished the best specimens of profitable tillage. In their intercourse with the other colonists they exhibited a friendly and peaceable disposition. In their business transactions they were generally just and upright, and never compromitted their Christian integrity for any temporary worldly gains. In all the relations of life they were dutiful, and sought to display the influence of Christianity in so regulating human conduct as to make our social intercourse a source of happiness as well as of mutual improvement. To such an extent did the spirit of peace reign among them, that for many years they had no courts of justice, and referred all disputed matters to the arbitration of their pastors and the elders of the church. It is a remarkable fact in the history of Effingham county, that there has generally been so little litigation among the inhabitants, that until within the last few years, it was a rare thing for a session of the Superior Court to continue more than two days. From these statements, it is manifest that the influence which the Salzburgers exerted upon the religious and social interests of the colony were decidedly beneficial, and their conduct in these particulars will ever form a bright page in the colonial history of Georgia.

It would be difficult to ascertain to what extent the descendants of the Salzburgers have been multiplied, and in what localities they are to be found. Their principal settlement is in Effingham county, Georgia, which constituted formerly a part of the parishes of St. Philip and St. Matthew. This county was the seat of the colony when the Salzburgers emigrated to Georgia. It has the Savannah river for its eastern boundary. The length of the county is thirty miles, and its breadth sixteen, and it contains about four hundred and eighty square miles.

The principal streams, besides the Savannah and Ogeechee rivers, are the Big and Little Ebenezer, Turkey Branch, Jack's, Lockner's, and Kogler's creeks, or more properly branches. The population is about four thousand, including one thousand six hundred slaves. Of the white population, fully nineteen-twentieths are the lineal descendants of the Salzburgers; and it is pleasing to state, that they retain many of the characteristics of their forefathers. They are for the most part an industrious, frugal, and peaceable people, and are doing much in developing the resources of their county.

Their chief pursuits are the tillage of the soil, and the getting of wood and timber for the Savannah market. They have been successful in raising silk on a small scale, and in the cultivation of the sugar-cane. The majority of them make their own sugar and syrup, and some of them produce these articles for market. They also pay considerable attention to the rearing of cattle and poultry, and the raising of fruits and vegetables, for which they always find ready sale in Savannah. Their lands, for the most part, are not well adapted to cotton, and hence but little is cultivated: the annual average amount being about three hundred and fifty bales, and a very small portion of this is produced by the Salzburgers. The articles to which they direct their attention are rice, corn, rye, peas, potatoes, and wheat. The two latter, under the system of culture adopted by the Salzburgers, succeed admirably well. It is often the case that thirty bushels of wheat are obtained from an acre, though this is very far beyond the average crop.

Besides the pursuits of agriculture, many of the Salzburgers are excellent mechanics, and there is a family that has become celebrated for the manufacture of copper bells. These bells always command a higher price in Savannah than any which are imported either from Northern or European markets. Some of the Salzburgers have also become distinguished merchants. In the city of Savannah many of them are settled, who have been very successful. Among these are the Rahns, the Sniders, the Heidts, the Zittrauers, the Herbs, the Gougles, the Remshardts, the Neidlingers, the Ihleys, and others. It is not known that any of them have become distinguished in the professions.

It is necessary to state, that the descendants of the Salzburgers (as has been already intimated) settled in many of the counties of Georgia, and some of them removed to South Carolina, Alabama, Florida, and even to Pennsylvania and Ohio. In Liberty and Lowndes counties, Georgia, may be found the Dashers, the

Waldhauers, the Weisenbakers, and others. In Macon county the Helfensteins, (now Helvenston;) in other portions of the state, the Haugleiters, the Scheubtriens, the Hineleys, the Exleys, and the descendants of the Sniders, who have intermarried with other families in the state. It would be impossible, however, to give any thing like an accurate account of the diffusion of the Salzburgers, and this hasty sketch must suffice.

It has been remarked that very few, if any, of the descendants of the Salzburgers, ever became distinguished in the professions. This may be owing in a great measure to the fact that, as a general thing, the standard of education among the descendants of the Salzburgers has been rather low, especially in the last fifty years, though it is believed that latterly there has been some improvement in this particular. Besides this, very few of them seemed to have any taste for literary pursuits; and having no college, and very few good scholars, there was an absence of all those stimulants which are necessary to quicken the intellect into vigorous exercise, and excite that ambition for literary fame which leads the mind to thirst after professional distinction. The tastes and educational biasses of the Salzburgers seem always to have led them to prefer the quiet and unobtrusive, though not less useful and honourable, pursuits of agriculture. In the retirement and comparative seclusion connected with the culture of the soil, and kindred employments, they find their chief enjoyment; especially as this mode of life seems of all others the best adopted to the fostering of that pious and contemplative spirit which has ever been one of their peculiar characteristics. In this connection it may be proper to state a somewhat remarkable fact, that not one of the *descendants* of the Salzburgers ever aspired to the ministry in the Lutheran Church, and not one of them ever became the pastor at Ebenezer, except the Rev. C. F. Bergman. But even he can hardly be classed among the Salzburgers. It is true that his father was pastor at Ebenezer for thirty-six years, but yet he was a native of Prussia, and had no identity with his congregation except that growing out of the pastoral relation.

The present condition of the descendants of the Salzburgers, especially in Effingham county, may be regarded on the whole as rather favourable. In their temporal affairs they are prosperous, perhaps as much so as at any former period, and there is a gradual improvement in their intelligence and social habits. They are becoming by degrees more interested in the cause of education, and books and periodical literature are sought with considerable avidity. As a consequence, there has been an improvement in their manners and social habits, and there is reason to hope that in these particulars an advancement will be made in each successive generation, so that they may keep pace with the citizens of other portions of the State in every thing that tends to refine and elevate. These desirable ends can be attained, if proper efforts are made to establish and sustain neighbourhood schools, under the management of competent teachers. This has for years been a great deficiency among the Salzburgers. It is true there is a most excellent classical academy at Springfield, the county town, but this does not and cannot meet the educational wants of the community generally. Upon this subject, so very important to the best interests of every people, there has been manifested an indifference which is any thing but commendable. No community can expect to prosper long, or to retain any of the elements necessary to its advancement in true greatness, that does not cherish a just appreciation of the advantages of a liberal system of education. It matters not how favourable the state of religion among any people may be; unless their mental development corresponds in some good measure with their religious privileges, their piety will degenerate into a blind devotion, or run into some of the numerous forms of fanaticism or delusion which are always addressing themselves to the over-credulous and unwary. It is to be hoped, therefore, that a more enlightened policy will obtain among the descendants of the Salzburgers, in reference to the importance of furnishing to their offspring the necessary educational facilities. For this they have a precedent in the example of their forefathers, for it has been made to appear that they entertained correct views upon this subject, and regarded the schoolmaster and the parochial school as only next in importance to the pastor and the church.

The state of religion among the descendants of the Salzburgers may be said to be encouraging. Among a portion of them, rather lax views are entertained on the subject of experimental piety, and as a consequence their religion consists more in a "formal godliness," and a decent morality, than in that inward work of the Spirit which converts the soul, and, by purifying the fountain of human actions, conforms the life to the requirements of that law which is "holy and just and right." Yet, even in this particular, there is much cause for encouragement. Within a few years, there has been a manifest change in the religious sentiments of not a few, and there is reason to believe that a more devotional spirit is gradually, though perceptibly, prevailing among them. True, the standard of piety is far below what it ought to be, and what it was in the early days of the colony; but still in the congregations there are many devout Christians, the savour of whose conversation is exerting a silent but powerful influence upon the moral interests of the church and the community generally. It is confidently hoped that this influence will continue to extend itself until the present generation, and those which may succeed it, shall make the highest attainments in moral excellence, and imbibing more and more of the Spirit of Christ, shall become as distinguished for their spirituality and holy living as were the godly men who in the fear of God, and from a sincere love to a pure Christianity, laid the foundation of the colony. There is ground for this hope, in the fact that the Salzburgers are enjoying the labours of two pious and devoted pastors, whose teachings and example, under the Divine blessing, have already exerted a very happy influence, and afford promise of greater results for the future. Besides this, it is not to be supposed that the great Head of his church will permit this vine, which he himself planted and watered and nourished for so many years, to wither and decay. The pious care with which it has hitherto been cultivated, and the genial showers of grace which from time to time have poured upon it, will, it is believed, produce an abundant harvest, to the praise of his name, who has declared in relation to his church:—"Behold! I have graven thee upon the palms of my hands, and thy walls are ever before me." From this people there shall no doubt yet come forth many who will become living witnesses to the converting power of the gospel, and to the faithfulness of that God who safely led their fathers through scenes of the darkest persecution and distress, and gave them, both in the land of their nativity and the land of their adoption, so many signal evidences of his love and fostering care. Such *will be* the case if the descendants of the Salzburgers are not recreant to the history of their fathers, and insensible to all those noble impulses which prompt mankind to venerate and to imitate the virtues of a noble ancestry. That they had an ancestry whose history is luminous with every thing that is attractive in humble and consistent piety, or stimulative in moral heroism and uncompromising attachment to religious principle, cannot be questioned. Surely, then, if there is any inspiration in the records of the virtuous and holy dead, if there is any thing suggestive of lofty purpose, of love for God and his truth, and of zeal to promote his glory in the education and proper development of our own spiritual natures, or in the religious advancement of our race, the example of the Salzburgers cannot and will not be lost. The seeds of virtue and true religion may for a season seem to be destroyed, or they may be buried amid the rubbish of a formal Christianity, or chilled by the blighting influence of a cold orthodoxy, but such is the inherent, vital energy of truth, that it will break through all these obstacles, and triumphing over every opposing influence, produce its legitimate fruits in the hearts and lives of men, and thus vindicate its claims to their confidence and homage.

It is the object and the earnest prayer of the humble author of this volume, that the history of the Salzburgers may be productive of some such beneficial results. If so, he will feel that the time spent in the preparation of this work has been most profitably employed. While he laboured at Ebenezer in the pastoral office, he delighted to visit the cemetery where sleep the remains of the venerable Bolzius and Gronau, and the many holy men who founded the colony at Ebenezer. Standing in that sacred receptacle of the dead, and musing upon their example of ministerial fidelity and of entire consecration to the cause of Christ, he has felt rebuked for his own imperfections, and has had the desire kindled in his heart to become a more devoted Christian and a more faithful and successful ambassador of the Lord Jesus Christ. Alas! how far do many of us, both in our experience and practice, fall below the example of the pious founders of our Lutheran Zion! and how infinitely far do we fall below His example, "who loved us and gave himself for us!" If such reflections are awakened as shall lead to some practical benefits to the Salzburgers and others, this history will not have been written in vain. That such will be its influence, is confidently hoped; and in this confidence it is sent forth, with the prayer that God may make it a source of instruction and edification to all who may read it. Surrounded as we are by temptation to sin, and by the seductive charms of a corrupt and corrupting world, we need constant stimulants to our virtues. Where can we more appropriately look for such incentives than in the faith and zeal, the holy fervour and consistent piety, of those Christians who, by their devotedness, have illustrated the truth, the excellency, and the moral sublimity of our holy religion? Such incentives are furnished in the HISTORY OF THE SALZBURGERS. As we dwell upon the incidents of this history, and the many instances which it furnishes of the power of our holy religion to sustain and comfort under the most trying and adverse circumstances of human life, and to prepare the soul for a peaceful and happy triumph over death, hell, and the grave, may our faith in that religion be confirmed, may our zeal and love and hope be quickened into livelier exercise, and thus may we be better qualified for the trials and responsibilities of life, and prepared to join "the general assembly and church of the first-born, whose names are written in heaven!"

THE END.

STEREOTYPED BY L. JOHNSON & CO.
PHILADELPHIA.

Appendix

LIST OF RECORDED MARRIAGES OF MEN WHO ARE LISTED IN STROBEL'S HISTORY.

(Taken from the "Ebenezer Record Book.")

Matthew Bedenbach [Bittenbach] to Anna Paulus, Nov. 7, 1770.
Matthew Bendenbach [Bittenbach] to Apelonia Kieffer, July 28, 1778.
Jacob Buehler to Christine Elizabeth Bechtol, July 6, 1773.
John Christopher Buntz to Hannah Elizabeth Hangleiter, March 13, 1778.
Daniel Burgsteiner to Mary Daescher [Dasher], April 11, 1769.
Christian Desher [Dasher] to Anna Christine Mayer, Feb. 19, 1754.
John Floerl, Jr., to Hannah Elizabeth Brandner, Jan. 15, 1765.
John Floerl, Jr., to Dorothea Kieffer, Feb. 22, 1774.
John Adam Freyermuth to Mary Elizabeth Buehler, Dec. 16, 1766.
Peter Freyermuth to Anna Catherine Groll, May 23, 1769.
Benjamin Glaner to Hanna Margaret Bach, Feb. 7, 1775.
George Gnann to Anna Franciska Rottenberger, Jan. 22, 1771.
Jacob Gnann to the widow Mary Margaret Depp, Jan. 23, 1759.
Jacob Gnann to Hannah Metzger, April 6, 1773.
John Justus Gravenstein to Catherine Bidenbach, Feb. 22, 1763.
George Gruber to Elizabeth Schwartzwalder, Nov. 14, 1758.
John Michael Haberer [Halerer] to the widow

Anna Eva Weidman, Feb. 26, 1771.
John Heckel to Hannah Margaret Heinrich, April 9, 1771.
Jacob Heinley [Heinle] to the widow Christine Meyer, Dec. 12, 1769.
John Heinley [Heinle] to Mary Kogler, Feb. 19, 1760.
J. Israel Kieffer to Hannah Margaret Schubtrein, July 6, 1773.
John Jacob Kieffer to Dorothy Reuter, March 24, 1767.
Christopher Kraemer [Kramer] to Catherine Hengleiter [Hangleiter], March 1st, 1774.
Samuel Krauss to Judith Floerl, Jan. 24, 1764.
J. Fredrick Lackner to Johanna Margaret Schubtrein, March 8, 1774.
Christian Israel Leimberger to Apollonia Dauner, Aug. 28, 1764.
Gabriel Maurer to Anna Eigel, Feb. 13, 1760.
John Maurer to Mary Magdalene Zant [Zandt], Feb. 24, 1767.
John Maurer to the Widow Anna Mueller, July 1, 1777.
John George Maurer to Mary Sybille Saecht, March 27, 1775.
Jacob Meyer [Meier] to the widow Juliana Schmidt, Jan. 22, 1771.
Nicholas Michael to Hannah Elizabeth Gugel, Jan. 28, 1772.
Jacob Mohr to the Widow Elizabeth Walliser, March 2, 1758.
John Oechsle [Exley] to Elizabeth Gress, Dec. 16, 1766.
John Martin Paulitsch to Ursula Schwinthofer, April 22, 1754.
John Paulus to Mary Ursula Groll, April 1, 1755.
John Remshardt to Anna Margaret Mueller, Feb. 14, 1764.
John Rentz to Barbara Unselt, Nov. 26, 1754.

John Scherraus to Anna Mary Mohr, Feb. 20, 1759.
John Schneider to Catherine Grimminger, June 7, 1758.
John George Schneider to Barbara Schneider, March 21, 1758.
Frederick Schrempf to Sarah Dixon, Feb. 3, 1770.
George Schwaiger [Schweiger] to the widow Margaret Zittrauer, May 19, 1761.
Joseph Schubtrein to Agnesia Ott, July 6, 1773.
J. Nicholas Schubtrein to Margaret Haussler, Nov. 11, 1772.
Nicholas Schubtrein to Anna Mary Zuercher, July 4, 1758.
Andrew Seckinger to the Widow Agnes Ziegler, May 17, 1756.
John Seckinger to Anna Barbara Huber, Sept. 29, 1767.
Christian Steiner to Dorothy Farr, Dec. 16, 1760
David Steiner to Margaret Zimmerbner, Feb. 1, 1763.
John Adam Treutlin to the widow Ann Unselt, Jan. 14, 1778.
Jacob Caspar Waldhauer to Agnesia Ziegler, June 27, 1758.
Daniel Weitman to Miss Salime . . . . (?), Oct. 28, 1777.
John Caspar Wertsch to Hannah Elizabeth Gronau, March 14, 1758.
Solomon Zant [Zandt] to Elizabeth Kieffer, March 24, 1767.
Solomon Zant [Zandt] to Dorothea Reiser, Jan. 3, 1775.
John George Zeigler to Anna Catherine Rau, June 1, 1756.
Luke [Lucas] Ziegler to Salome Zettler, June 25, 1765.
Ernest Zittrauer to Hannah Reiter, Oct. 2, 1770.
John George Zittrauer to Catherine Brandwein, May 19, 1761.

Index

Note: Those names marked with an asterisk are listed in Coulter, E. M., and Albert B. Saye, eds., A List of the Early Settlers of Georgia.

Abercorn, settlement of, 131, 182, 183
Adam, Wolff, Salzburg magistrate, 34
Aldersgate, street in London, 82
82
Aldrich, Rev. N., 259
Alps, 41
Alps (Norric), 42
Alps (Rhetian), 42
Alps (Swiss), 26
Amatis, Nicolas, 129
Andrew, Rev. James O., 254
*Arnsdorff, John Peter, 112
Asbury, Bishop, 227-230, 235-236
Attila, 42
Augsburg, city of, 43, 50
Augsburg Confession, 50, 93
Austin, Rev. Jacob, 276
Austria, Emperor of, 35
Austria, upper, 41, 42

Bachman, Dr. John, 7, 252, 259, 260, 268
Baden, city of, 43
Bancroft, *History of the United States*, 24, 80
Baptist Churches, 244
Bavaria, 41, 49, 50
Bavarian Dukes, 42
Bechly, George, 181
Beckley, John George, 181
Bedenbach, Matthew, 180
Bentz, Henry Ludwig, 181
Bentz, John George, 180
Berchtolsgaden, town of, 47

Bergman, Christopher F., 226, 250-253, 257, 263-266
Bergman, Rev. John Ernest, 220-248
Bergsteiner, Matthias, 112
Bergsteiner, family, 262
Bernhardt, Mr., 222, 223
Bethany Church, 106, 131
Bethany School, 162
Bethel Church, 242
Bethesda Orphanage, 110
Biddenbach, Andreas, 181
Biddenbach, Matthew, 155
Boehler, Rev. Peter, 79
Bolleinger, John, 181
Bolles, Rev. E. A., 267, 269
Bollinger, John, 181
*Bolzius, Rev. John Martin, 23, 54, 55, 61, 68, 69, 86, 101, 103, 104, 105, 110, 113, 114, 118, 120, 123, 132, 134, 145, 148, 292, 293
Bradford (Puritan), 23
*Brandner, Matthias, 112
Brassus, Rev. Anthony, 27
Brewster (Puritan), 23
Briscen, Suffragan of, 41
British Troops, 206
Bruckner, George, 112
Buehler, Jacob, 181
Buntz, John Christopher, 181
Burgsteiner, Daniel, 181

Calvin, John, 21
Camuse, Jacques, 129
Carver (Puritan), 23

312

INDEX 313

Charles II, 44
Charles V, 50
Charles IX, 21
Charleston, S. C., 59
Charlton, Major John, 254
Chiemre, Suffragan of, 41
Church Council, list of, 180
Church of England, 20
Church of Rome, 21, 25, 27
Clarke, General, 210
Cloud, Mr., 237
Coligny, Admiral, 21
Constance, Council of, 150
Cooper, Mrs. L., 259
Cooper, Mrs. S., 259
*Cornberger, John, 112
Cornish, Capt. Joseph, 75
Council of Constance, 150
Cramer, Christopher, 196, 287
*Crause, Leonard, 112

Dasher, Christian, 180
Dasher, John Martin, 180
Dasher, Martin, 181, 204
Dasher, family, 262, 299
Dauphine Mountains, 26
Davis, Jenkins, 196
Deacons, election of, 167
deMedici, Catherine, 21
Depp, Samuel, 181
De Roshe, Abraham, 181
Ditters, George 181
Dover, city of, 55
Dreisler, Rev. Ulrich, 24
Driesler, Rev. Ulrich, 85, 118
Dunbar, Mr., 61
Dunwoody, Rev. Samuel, 237

Ebenezer, 25, 63, 64, 65, 67, 80, 81, 85, 86, 87, 88, 92, 100, 102, 105, 106, 109; prosperity of, 108; residents of, 112

Ebenezer Creek, 65, 66, 91, 92, 129, 130, 132
Ebenezer (New), 90
Ebenezer (Old), 89
Edward VI, 20
Effingham County, 64, 67, 195
Effingham, Lord, 64
Eichel, Mr., 204
Eichelberger, L. (D.D.), 7
*Eischberger, Ruprecht, 112
Elliott, Mr., 239
Emigrants' Song, 39
England, 20, 21, 43
Epping, Rev. W., 260
Ernst, G., 222
*Ernst, Joseph, 112
Exley, family, 262, 300

Felt, Mr., 259
Fetzer, John Gottlieb, 181
Fler! [Floerl], Mary C., 258
*Floerl, Carl, 112
Floerl, Israel, 258
*Floerl, John, 112, 155, 287
France, 21
Francke, Rev. Gotthelf Augustus, 93, 110, 114
Frank, Conrad, 181
Frankfort, 53
Frederica, town of, 84, 85, 100, 118, 119
Frederick-William, Elector of Brandenburg, 33
Frevermuth, John Adam, 180
Freyermuth, Peter, 181
Friessingen, Suffragan of, 41

Garvin, John, 237
Gascoine, Captain, 76
Gaudolph, Bishop Maximilian, 30
Georgia Historical Society, 24

INDEX

Glaner, Benjamin B., 181
Glaner, John, 181
Gnann, family, 262
Gnann, Andreas, 181
Gnann, George, 180
Gnann, Jacob, 181
Goshen Church, 131, 183
Goshwandel, Mrs., 68
Goshwandel, Thomas, 112
Gougel, family, 262
Gougle, David, 254, 299
Gravenstein, John Justus, 180
Gravesend, England, 76
Great Britain, 20
Great Embarkation, 75
*Grimminger, Andreas, 112
*Gronau, Rev. Israel Christian, 23, 54, 55, 62, 86, 101, 111, 120, 123, 292
Gruber, George, 180
*Gruber, Peter, 112
Gugel, John Christian, 181
Gurk, Suffragan of, 41

Habersham, James, 104, 162
Halerer, Michael, 181 (This is probably *Haberer.)
Halle, city of, 55, 105, 110
Hallein, district of, 30, 36
Haltiwanger, Rev. George, 272
Hangleiter, John, 180
Hangleiter, family, 300
Haupt, Mr., 259
Hawk, sloop of war, 76
Hazelius, Dr., 24
Heckel, John, 181
Heidt, family, 299
Heil, Caspar, 180
Heinley, Jacob, 181
Heinley, John, 180
Heisman, Michael, 181
*Helfenstein, Frederick, 117, 181, 204, 205, 300

Helfenstein, Jacob, 203, 205
Helfenstein, Joshua, 203, 205
Helme, Nicholas, 180
Helvenston, John C., 205
Herb, Catherine, 226
Herb, Frederick, 226, 259
Herb, family, 299
Hermsdorf, Capt., 24, 75, 85
Hernberger, John, 112
Hessler, Christian, 112
Hineley, family, 262, 300
History of American Lutheran Church (Hazelius), 24
History of Georgia (Stevens), 24
Holcombe, Rev., 227, 238
Holland, 38, 43
Holzendorf, Wm., 203, 287
Horten, Capt., 118
Hortzog, Martin, 112
Housler, Jacob, 180
Howell, Philip, 196
Huguenots, 21
Hull, Rev. Hope, 237
Huss, John, 150
Hymn of the Exiles, 38

Ihley, family, 299
Indenture Trust, 135
Indians, 63, 92, 107

Jack's Branch, 242
Jackson, Rev. Jonathan, 77, 237
Jasper, Sergeant, 206
Jasper Springs, 206
Jenys, Paul, 62
Jerusalem Church (Ebenezer), 118, 123, 131, 149; inventory of, 190
Jesuits, 29
Jones, Edward, 196
Jones, Thomas, letter of, 111

INDEX

*Kalcher, Ruprecht, 112
Karn, Rev. A. J., 260
Keiffer, Rev. Ephriam, 271
Keiffer, Theobald, 116
Kieffer, Emanuel, 181
Kieffer, Israel, 181
Kieffer, Jacob, 181
King, Mr., 232
Knox, Mr., 183
*Kogler [Koglar], George, 112
Kogler, John, 181
Kraemer, Christopher, 180
Kramer, Christopher, 155
Krauss, Samuel, 154, 180
Krinberger, John Christopher, 181
Kugel, John, 180

Lackner, Frederick, 181
Lackner, Israel, 181
*Lackner, Martin, 112
*Landseller, Veitt, 112
Lavant, Suffragan of, 41
Lee, Rev. Jesse, 240
*Leimberger, Christian, 112
Leimberger, Israel, 180
*Leitner, Joseph, 112
Lembke, Rev. H. H., 127, 131, 133, 135, 138, 145, 146, 148, 293
Lembke, Timotheus, 181
*Lemmenhoffer, Veitt, 112
Leopold, Count of Firmain and Archbishop of Salzburg, 41, 42
Little Creek, 91, 92
Lochner, Veitt, 180
Lockner's Creek, 91, 132
London Merchant, ship, 75, 76
Lowry, Mr., 237
Luther, Martin, 21, 29, 50, 150n
Lutheran Church, 165-182
Lutheran Reformation, 83
Lutheranism, 33

McCay, Charles, 180, 196
McCoy, Colonel, 205
McVean, Rev. John, 227, 243
Mack, Jacob, 180
Mack, Michael, 180
Maitland, Major, 202
Martyn, Benjamin, secretary to Trustees, 115
Massachusetts, colony of, 21
*Maurer, Gabriel, 112
Maurer, Johannes, 180
*Maurer, John, 112
Maurer, John George, 181
Mealy, Rev. S. A., 240, 259
Melancthon, Philipp, 50
Melendez, Pedro, 21
Methodism, centenary of, 77
Methodism, Wesleyan, 82
Methodist Church, 83, 244, 254
Metzger, Jacob, 180, 181
Metzger, John, 181
Metzger, Samuel, 181
Meyer, Jacob, 180
Meyer, Matthias, 181
Michael, John, 131, 180
Michael, Nicholas, 180
Mill Creek, 92, 132
Mingledorff, family, 262
*Moeller [Muller], John Paul, 180
Mohr, Jacob, 181
Moller, Fredrick Wilhelm, 112
Moravian Ministers, 183, 184, 185
Moravians, 75, 78, 79, 80, 82
Morel, John, 196
Muhlenburg, Dr. H. M., 93, 99, 119, 120, 131, 147, 148, 155, 156, 163, 164, 185, 187, 293
Muhlenburg's *Journal*, 182
Muhlenburg's letter to Mr. Davis, 214
Mulberry Trees, 130

INDEX

Muller, Paul, 155
Myers, Rev. Lewis, 256

Negro Slaves, 102, 183
Negroes, 103
Neidlinger, family, 262
Neidlinger, Jacob Gottlieb, 181
Neidlinger, John, 247
Neidlinger, Ulrich, 154, 180
Neidlinger's Sea, 91
Neustadt, Suffragan of, 41
Newton, Sergeant, 206
Nitschman, Bishop David, 75
Nolan, Major, 254
Nuremburg, 37, 38

Oechley [Exley], family, 262
Oechsle, Christopher, 180
Oechsle, John C., 180
Oechsle, John Michael, 181
Oglethorpe, Gen. James Edward, 45, 59, 60, 62, 64, 74, 75, 84, 85, 86, 88, 89, 100, 128
Orphan House, 109, 111
*Ortman, Christopher [Christian], 112
Ott, Carl Sigismund, 112
Ott, John Gottlieb, 181
Ott, Nathaniel, 181
Ott, Sigismund, 181

Paracelsus, Philippus, 42
Passau, Suffragan of, 41
Paulitsch, John Martin, 180
Paulitsch, Phillip, 180
Paulus, John, 155, 180
Paulus, John Adam, 181
Pennsylvania, 80
Pfluger, John, 181
Philip II, of Spain, 21
*Pichler, Thomas, 112

Pilgrims, 22, 24
*Pletter, John, 112
Plymouth Rock, 21
Prince of Wales, ship, 71
Probst, Mr., 222
Provincial Congress, Savannah (1774), delegates to, 196; (1775), 286
Provost [Prevost], General, 202
Prussia, 38
Prussian Dominian, 43
Purisburg, ship, 56
Puritans, 22, 106

Quincy, Rev. Samuel, 61

Rabenhorst, Rev. Christian, 132-135, 148, 183, 184, 188-189, 293
Rahn, family, 262, 299
Rahn, Conrad, 180
Rahn, Jonathan, 199-200
Rahn, Mattheus, 181
Randle, Josiah, 237
Ratisbon, city of, 75
Ratisbon, Suffragan of, 41
*Rauner, Leonard, 112
Reformation, 25, 27
Regensburg, city of, 34
Reidelsperger, Christian, 112
Reiser, Batholomew, 112
Reiser, John Michael, 112
Reiser, Michael, 180
*Reiter, Simon, 112
Remshardt, family, 299
Remshardt, John, 180
Rieser, Balthasar, 180
Rieser, Benjamin, 181
Rieser, Israel, 181
Rentz, John, 180, 181
Republican Cause, 203
*Reuter, Peter, 112
Revolutionary War, 201
Reynolds, Dr., 38
Rhine River, 54

INDEX 317

Ribault, J., 21
Robinson, pastor, 23
Rottenberger, Christopher, 180
Rottenberger, John, 181
*Rottenberger, Stephen, 112
Rotterdam, 54

Saint Matthew's Parish, 64, 131, 162
Saint Rupert, 42
Saint Simon's Island, 84, 118, 286
Salvinger, Mr., 239
Salza, valley of, 42
Salzburg, 28, 38, 42
Salzburg Emigrants' Song, 39, 40
Salzburgers, 25
Savannah, city of, 45, 60, 64, 65, 68, 71, 91
Savannah River, 59, 87, 91, 110
Savoy, Dukes of, 26
Schaitherger, Joseph, 31, 36, 37, 38
*Schartner, Jacob, 112
Scheck, Rev. John D., 266
*Scheraus, John, 181
Scheuber, Justus H., 224
Scheubtrine, family, 262
Schmidt, G. Israel, 181
*Schmidt, Jacob, 181
*Schmidt, John, 112
Schneider, John Gottlieb, 181, 203
Schneider, John G. H., 180
Schnider, John, 203, 287
Schnider, Jonathan, 203
Schofpach [*Schopaker, Ruprecht], 69
Schrempf, Frederick, 181
Schrempf, Solomon, 180
Schubtrein, Joseph, 154, 262, 300

Schubtrein, Joseph, Jr., 181
Schubtrein, Nicholas, 180
Schule, Mathees, 181
*Schwaiger [Schweiger], George, 112
Schwinger, George, 180
Seckau, Suffragan of, 41
Seckinger, Andreas, 181
Seckinger, Andrew, 181
Seckinger, Jonathan, 181
Sherraus, family, 262
*Sherraus, John, 181
Shuele, John, 180
*Sigismund, Frank [Francis], 112
Silk Industry, 129
Sisters' Ferry, 233
Slaves, 102
Snider, John Gottlieb, 151, 273
Snider, family, 299, 300
Spangenburg, Rev., 78
Spaniards, 84, 103; in Georgia, 112
*Speilbiegler, John, 112
Springfield, town of, 67
Standish (Puritan), 23
Steiner, Christian, 154, 180
Steiner, David, 180, 191
Steiner, John, 181
Steiner, Luprecht, 112
*Steiner, Simon, 112
Steinharel, Christian, 116
Stevens, W. B., *History of Georgia*, 24
Stirk, Colonel John, 196, 203, 287
Stirk, Samuel, 203
Stokes, Anthony, 162
Strobel, Rev. P. A., 269-270
Strohaker, Rudolph, 203, 287
Swabia, 43, 50
Swan, a symbol, 150
Symond, ship, 75, 76

Tarringer, Jacob, 180
Teffereck, valley of, 28, 35
Thomas, Capt. John, 75
Tories, 204
Treutlen, John Adam, 154, 180, 196, 203, 287
Triebner, Rev. Christian, 151-156, 184, 191, 199, 208, 209
Trust Indenture, 135
Trustees of the Colony, 45, 55, 74, 101, 129
*Twiffler, Dr. J. Andrew, physician, 61, 62
Tyrol, 26, 35

Uchee Indians, 63, 92
Urlsperger, Rev. Samuel, 93, 100, 104, 105, 106, 126, 132, 133

Vallenses, 25
Vatt, John, 24, 71
*Von Reck, Baron, 24, 61, 62, 65, 75, 103

Waldhauer, Jacob Caspar, 154, 180, 196, 287
Waldhauer, family, 300
Waldhour, family, 262
Walton, George, 196
Wayne, Gen. Anthony, 203, 204, 205, 210, 227
Wayne, Hon. Richard, 227
Weisenbaker, family, 300
Weitman, Daniel, 181
Weriman, Mrs. N., 259
Wertsch, John Caspar, 131, 155, 157, 190, 216
Wesley, Charles, 75, 76, 78, 79

Wesley, John, 75, 76, 77, 78, 79, 82, 83, 236, 237, 295
Westphalia, Peace of, 33; Treaty of, 34
Whitefield, George, 103, 109-111, 295
Winckler, Hans Jurk, 180
Windisch, Matrey, 28
Winslow (Puritan), 23
Wisenbaker, family, 262
Wurtemburg, city of, 43, 132
Wyche, George, 287

Young, Isaac, 196

Zandt, Samuel, 181
Zandt, Solomon, 181
*Zant, Bartholomew, 112
Zeigenhagen, Rev. Frederick M., 93, 143
Zeigler, George, 181
Zeigler, Lucas, 180
Zettler, family, 262
*Zettler, Matthias, 112
*Zimmerman, Ruprecht, 112
Zimmerebner, Ruprecht, 181
Zion Church, 106, 118, 121, 131
Zittrauer, Ernest, 180
Zittrauer, John G. F., 180
Zittrauer, Paulus, 112
Zittrauer, family, 262, 299
Zubli, Rev., 118
*Zubli, Ambrosii, 112
*Zubli, John Jacob, 112
*Zwiffer, J. Andrew, M.D., 61, 62 (The name is listed as Twiffler in Strobel but as Zwiffer in *A List of the Early Settlers of Georgia.*)

www.ingramcontent.com/pod-product-compliance
Lightning Source LLC
Chambersburg PA
CBHW020056020526
44112CB00031B/189